Emergence

Also by Kate Kerr
using the pseudonym Suzanne Mitchell

My Own Woman
Horizon Press 1972

Emergence

An Autobiography

KATE KERR

iUniverse, Inc.
Bloomington

Emergence
An Autobiography

iUniverse books may be ordered through booksellers or by contacting:

iUniverse
1663 Liberty Drive
Bloomington, IN 47403
www.iuniverse.com
1-800-Authors (1-800-288-4677)

ISBN: 978-1-4620-0313-6 (pbk)
ISBN: 978-1-4620-0314-3 (ebk)

Printed in the United States of America

iUniverse rev. date: 3/18/2011

To my children, grandchildren,
and
future generations

Contents

Preface

As we enter the second decade of the twenty-first century, life is very different from what it was when I grew up on a farm near the little town of Toulon, Illinois in the 1920s and 1930s. In most ways life is better; in other ways, the simpler life was easier—less stress in daily living.

I have long wanted to tell the story for future generations of how it was to live during that period. I also wanted to show in this book how a low self-concept develops, how it affects one's life, and how I found a way to overcome it. My hope is that others will benefit from what I have learned.

I grew up on a farm and married soon after graduating from high school. When my son joined the Marines and my daughter was in high school, I started my college education at age thirty-nine. I earned my doctorate in Marriage and Family Therapy one month before I was fifty. After practicing a year, I became a licensed psychologist. I practiced (solo) for over thirty-five years.

In my eighty-plus years of existence, there has been an exponential change in our society's moral standards, our means of communication, the role of women, the practice of medicine, and our country's relationship with the rest of the world. In the United States, we have gone from an agrarian society to a constantly evolving, highly industrialized, and technologically sophisticated society. Technology continues to rapidly march forward. The newest invention is passé by the time it has been in use for a few months.

Now the shrinking size of the world makes each country more dependent on other countries, and, therefore, very vulnerable. No longer can any country isolate itself and hope to survive. Terrorists used to be thought of as fictional characters; not anymore. Our world today is definitely a more stressful place. People are more fearful than they used to be in the early part of the twentieth century.

I grew up in the 1930s with a crank telephone attached to the wall and witnessed the arrival of electricity in our rural area in 1936. In 1955, after I was married with two children, I had my first twelve-inch black and white television. Before World War II, no family had two cars and a long distant phone call was made only in case of emergency. Death during childbirth was not uncommon in the 1930s, even in middle-class families. Many people died of what we now consider "simple" infections. Mass production and use of antibiotics first occurred following WWII.

It is remarkable to think that I am a member of a profession that did not exist when I was born in 1925. At that time psychiatry was in its infancy; counseling psychology became a recognized profession in 1946. Freud was not a household word during the first few decades of the twentieth century.

People with mental disorders were referred to as maniacs or lunatics, then "put away" in an asylum for the rest of their lives. Their families no longer acknowledged them or their existence. There is still a certain amount of stigmatism attached to mental illness; however, it is slowly decreasing. Emotional problems are now openly discussed and recognized. Seeing a therapist is generally thought of as acceptable behavior.

In the 1920s the word "self-esteem" was not yet coined. Divorce was rare. Life expectancy was forty-five in 1900, so there was no time to worry about being happy. The expectation of a good sexual relationship developed during the middle part of the century. No one would have dreamed of going to a Sex Therapist in the 1930s and 1940s—if one had existed.

The fact that I kept a diary or a journal from age fourteen to the present, except for about twenty years, has been a great boon in writing of my life. I also have the letters written in 1918-1919 between my Mom and Dad, while he served in the Marines in France during WWI, and those from my daughter, Suzanne, and my son, Mitchell. I am a pack rat only when it comes to letters from loved ones.

Acknowledgements

After I started writing this book, I joined two writing groups. I want to thank the members of my writing groups for their suggestions and encouragement. I appreciate the help with using the computer that Roberta Burton gave me early on.

Thank you, Bonnie Armstrong, for being available when I was unable to make my computer do what I wanted it to do, and for your encouragement throughout the process. Special thanks for reading the manuscript one final time.

I also want to thank Darrow Fisher, my computer guru, who unceasingly accepted my slow pace on that blessed and cursed machine. Without Darrow I would have had to write my manuscript on my old electric typewriter.

My special thanks to you, Jenny Crowley, for your careful editing of the manuscript including the formatting, inserting the pictures and putting it in book form. Thanks for your reassurance.

I feel indebted to the following persons who, at separate times, were a vital part of my life before I began writing my story:

Dr. Abren: Who guided me in the beginning of my metamorphosis. He led me to the path of self-discovery where I knew I couldn't turn back. I hadn't been able to see my potential; he opened my eyes.

Dr. Quine: Who hung in there with me as I slowly continued down that road to finding myself. He stayed with me as I dropped the pseudo-woman's mask and became who I am today.

Bill Nichols: My professor, supervisor, counselor, and mentor during my doctoral studies. He remains my friend.

Bill Furlong: My accountant and financial advisor since 1976. He is available when I need advice on issues that inevitably arise. He and his wife, Jane, also a CPA, are my good friends.

Brant Copeland: My pastor who listened to and accepted my emotional upheavals during John's illness and death. He has helped me grow in my spiritual life and continues to do so.

My Quest

Oh, bits of hell, frothing furies,
Whirling, bleating, gasping for birth
Piteous primordial mass, unfinished form
Pounding, clawing from the depths
Grating against my sanity; struggling for survival

Titanic temple, force of reason
Create within this chaos, a soul
Soothe the elements now in torment
Whisper softly; quiet, calm

Murmuring memories of life
Promising the prodigal peace of mind

Kate Young
1967

Chapter 1

GROWING UP ON AN ILLINOIS FARM
IN THE 1920S AND 1930S

The day I was born, my Dad and Mother told each other that another girl was great, but disappointment must have hung in the air. I was their fourth child and the fourth girl born within five years. I had joined this farm family of German descent, invited or not. We lived in a small house on top of a muddy hill in Central Illinois, located a mile and a half from the little town of Toulon. It was already an old house when Dad's parents bought it in 1908.

The year was 1925. Calvin Coolidge was President of the United States. Life expectancy was fifty-four years. Average income was $2,239.00 and gas was twelve cents a gallon. World War I had ended a few years earlier and our country was still mostly an agrarian society. We, like most farmers, didn't have much money though it was four years before the Great Depression was to descend upon our country.

Grandpa and Grandma Appenheimer

I never met my Dad's father, Alpheus William Appenheimer, who died of a stroke in 1916. I knew Grandma Appenheimer only until I was six when she died of cancer. Her name was Melissa Olive Witcher Appenheimer; she lived up town near the Baptist Church which we attended. We would stop to see her on Sunday mornings before going

1

to church. She always had a box of animal crackers, a real treat for us, which we shared.

Grandma Appenheimer was a tall, slim woman who was somewhat aloof. I don't think that was so much a personal trait as a cultural one. People didn't show affection outwardly nor did they verbalize it like we do today. I don't remember Mother or Dad hugging me until I was a married woman and hugged them. I like hugging people who I'm close to and am glad our culture has changed in that regard.

I remember seeing the large, dark brown casket in Grandma's living room. Seeing tears in Dad's eyes made me sad; I knew he loved Grandma. That was the only time I saw him cry until many years later when Mother died.

Dad and Mother

Dad was born in Leoti, Kansas, in 1891 and moved with his family to a farm just south of Toulon when he was quite young. He was slim and about five feet nine inches tall; he wore a size eight and half shoe. He was bald at an early age, but still quite good looking, with deep blue eyes and a charming smile. He gained a lot of weight over the years as a result of eating too much and becoming less and less active around the farm.

Dad, Alpheus Ray Appenheimer, was a Marine in WWI. He enlisted on July 6, 1917, and soon after completing his training at Parris Island, South Carolina, he was sent to France in December, 1917. On Christmas Day, his transport ship was torpedoed by a German submarine, but not sunk. He participated in five major campaigns in France during the war. He drove a caisson with a four-line mule team carrying ammunition to the front. He was wounded, spent time in a hospital, was cited for gallantry in action and received two Croix de Guerre, two bronze stars and two silver stars. These medals were awarded for two actions—Belleau Wood and Mont Blanc.

On June 19, 1919, he was honorably discharged. He never talked about his experiences in the war and never showed us his medals. I didn't know he had been so highly decorated until after he died.

He had physical problems dating from that war. He coughed a lot, especially in the mornings, due in part, to having been exposed to mustard gas. Physical difficulties kept him from the more labor-intensive jobs on the farm as he aged. But he was always busy with the work he could do, and with the management of the farm.

Mother, America Swango Appenheimer, was born in 1897, and lived her first eleven years in Kentucky. Her mother, Deborah Taulbee, died in childbirth when Mother was four, and her brother, Alfred, was two. They were taken in by relatives during those years after their Mother's death, and before their father remarried. Those were not good years for Mother; she was a sensitive, independent person who must have felt unloved and unwanted, as she was shuttled from one house to another depending on who volunteered to keep her and her brother.

Mother was about five feet four inches tall and small boned, weighing about a hundred pounds when she married Dad at age nineteen. She was an attractive brunette, with thick, wavy hair and hazel eyes. She, also, gained a lot of weight over the years. Farmers didn't have a great many pleasures; eating was one they could enjoy three times a day. Even though they worked hard and long, most farm people tended to become heavy as they grew older.

Mom didn't have time to focus on herself at all. The only makeup she ever wore was a bit of lipstick, and that was only after we kids were older and encouraged her. She always had one good dress to wear when she went out. "Going out" meant Sundays at church, the occasional function at the Legion Hall or a funeral. When that dress was worn out she would get one more to replace it. She made sure that her girls were well dressed. We had more than one outfit at a time to look our best.

She was not allowed to go to school after the fifth grade. She had to work in the tobacco fields in Kentucky. After they moved to Illinois, she stayed with a family who provided room and board while she went one year to high school. She wasn't able to stay in school because of health problems. From reading the many letters she wrote to Dad during the war I learned how much she wanted an education. She had wanted to become a nurse; however, it wasn't to be.

During the year she attended school, she and Dad began their courtship. Their relationship became serious by the time Dad joined the Marines. They professed their love for each other in the daily letters that flew back and forth between Parris Island, North Carolina and Illinois. On his furlough prior to being sent overseas, Dad convinced Mother to get married, so that he could provide for her.

They were married the day Dad left for France. She rode the train with him as far as Peoria, while he made his return to Camp LeJuene. From Peoria Mother traveled to Kentucky to stay with family. Mom and Dad didn't sleep together before he left because they didn't want to risk her getting pregnant.

Mother was very creative and became an excellent seamstress, which was a great asset with six girls to dress, and a serious shortage of money. We were always well dressed; Mother made almost everything we wore. She raised white rabbits at one time so she could have the fur to use on our clothes or on the doll clothes she made. She took care of the rabbits, skinned them, and laid the pelts to dry until they were ready for her use. When I was in high school, she made me a dress of plain navy fabric, princess style, and put an edging of the white fur around the collar and cuffs. I loved that dress.

Grandpa and Grandma Swango

Mother's father, Benjamin Franklin "BF" Swango, didn't remarry until mother was eleven. He was thirty-two when he married Dolly, who was sixteen. Grandpa was a slim man who chewed tobacco and had spittoons in his living room. I never felt close to him. In fact, we younger kids were always a bit cautious with him. He never joked with us or gave us attention to indicate that he enjoyed us. Bob, who was Grandpa and Grandma Dolly's youngest child, told us how mean Grandpa was to him. That was one reason we didn't feel comfortable around Grandpa.

During my childhood, Grandpa and Grandma Swango lived a couple of miles from us on a small farm. In fact, Grandpa still lived in that neighborhood when he died at the age of ninety four in 1968. Grandpa and Dolly had six children—aunts and uncles to us kids, and half brothers and sisters to Mother. The last two children were born the same year as two of Mother's children. Edna was Dorothy's age, and Bob was Juanita's age.

I have fond memories of Grandma Dolly when I was little. She was quite plump and of good humor. When she visited us, she slept in one of the beds with us kids and she would tell us stories of her life in Kentucky. It seemed the stories always ended on a scary note, such as a mountain lion looking in the window, or a big snake falling out of a tree on her. We thought she told the best stories we'd ever heard; they would scare us to death and we loved it. She had false teeth which didn't fit very well and made sort of a clicking sound when she talked, which added an intriguing quality to her story telling.

The year I was five, 1930, we all went to Grandma and Grandpa Swango's for Christmas dinner. We rode in the hay-filled wagon pulled by a team of horses, Pete and Baldy. Clay complained on the way to Grandma's house that his ears were cold, because he didn't have hair like we girls did. I don't remember much about the day except for the ride in the wagon to Grandma's house. However, one thing I'm sure of is that we had an abundance of good country food.

I remember how old I was, because it was the year Clay, my younger brother who was four years old, got a puppy for Christmas. Silver, a black Border Collie with white feet and a white tip on her tail, rode in the wagon with us. She was named Silver Tip, but we called her Silver. She was neurotic and desperately afraid of storms. She was an outside dog, but when a thunder storm came, she would manage to squeeze past us into the house. She would make a dash upstairs where she hid under a bed until the thunder and lightning ceased.

After Grandma Dolly married Grandpa, they moved from Kentucky to a house a short distance from the one Dad lived in with his family. When my oldest sister, Dorothy, sent us younger siblings copies of Dad's and Mom's letters written during the years (1917 to 1919) Dad was in Europe, she enclosed the following note telling us how our parents met:

"Dad heard that a young girl had moved in next door so he just ambled by to see what he could see. There were boxes and cartons in the yard and just as he was in front of their house, the door flew open and two young women came flying out, leaping over boxes until they were at the last one. They swooped down and carried it into the house, laughing and giggling. One was Mother and the other her beloved stepmother, known as Dolly. Dad learned to love them both."

Dad and that young girl were to raise seven children in a house just half a mile down that country road.

Years later, Grandma Dolly had meningitis which left her mentally unstable. She became unduly frightened of many things, and the last few times she stayed with us, she helped us kids pull the dresser over to block the door so no one could open it. When Mom and Dad found out about it, they couldn't allow her to stay with us anymore.

Grandma was most fearful of Mother, which was sad because their relationship had been such a good one. She finally left Grandpa and moved about forty miles away to Princeton, IL. She supported herself by caring for elderly folks in a house she inherited from her very first client. Psychiatry was not very sophisticated at that time, and it is not known exactly what her mental condition was. She certainly never received any treatment. It seemed a miracle that she was able to take care of herself much less others.

Our House

Dorothy had just turned five when I was born; Betty was three; Juanita fifteen months. Another girl when farmers needed sons to help in the fields. Sixteen months later the only son, Clay, was born. Glenna followed him in seventeen months. Everyone thought there were to be no more babies, because nearly three years went by before Yvonne (Vonnie) was born. Dad was fond of saying, "I have six girls and each of them has a brother." Nine of us lived in that house with no conveniences. If any more had come along I don't know where we would've put them.

Appenheimer Homestead

Our house was very small, with no electricity, plumbing or central heat. It had three bedrooms, a small living room, a kitchen, (the biggest room in the house) and a small room off the kitchen which we called the shed. A closed narrow stairwell with hooks on either side, where we hung some of our outside clothes led to the upstairs. It consisted of two bed rooms—the north room and the south room. The north room was so cold in winter that frost actually formed on the inside of the exterior wall. After the frost thawed in the spring, we had to hang new wallpaper. Clay had that room to himself, since he was the only male child.

We six girls shared the south room, which was not quite so cold. There was a register just above the heating stove in the living room below. Enough heat found its way through that small space to take the worst chill off that room. In the summer we kids slept outside where it might be cooler. We'd take a blanket outside someplace, lie down and go to sleep. One time Betty left her blanket outside and the next night she was surprised to find a large snake curled up where she was expecting to sleep. It didn't seem to worry us much; we certainly didn't let it keep us from sleeping outside. Inside, we girls all slept in two single beds—there were no queen or king beds. It was crowded, but we were kids and didn't think anything of it. That was just the way it was. We shared one chest of drawers and a small rigged-up dressing table with a skirt that Mother made. Since there were no closets upstairs, we had a ten foot rod hung between the chimney abutment and the outer wall. That's where we hung our clothes.

There was a narrow hallway where we kept the "pot", which was one of the fun things about rural living at that time. Every morning someone had to dump the pot, carrying it carefully down the narrow stairs, through the kitchen and to the outhouse. As far as I know, no one ever dropped it or spilled any of the contents. We were very careful.

By the time I was thirteen my two oldest sisters, Dorothy and Betty, were out of high school and gone most of the time, so the crowded situation eased some. We had company often and I really don't know where they slept. We had regular old army cots and two of us could sleep on each cot so I guess cots or the floor was the solution. Regardless of the limited space, anyone who needed a place to stay was welcome to stay with us.

Much of our living was done in the kitchen which had a large, round, oak table. It was big enough to seat up to twelve or fifteen people, and there were that many for dinner quite often. The table was used for many things in addition to eating. We kids often sat around it to read, Mother used it as a place to cut fabric which she would then miraculously make into a dress or skirt or other garment for one of us. That table was also used for food preparation, since there was so little space and so much cooking to do.

The coal range, with the reservoir for heating water, and the warming oven attached above, served for cooking and heating. We had a kitchen cabinet with an enameled pull-out top that was our only counter space besides the table. There was a flour bin and sifter built into the cabinet with a door that could be pulled down when we needed to refill it. The bin held twenty-five pounds of flour which you loaded from the top, then by holding a container under the sifter, and turning the handle, sifted flour was available. The cabinet's lower storage area held our pots and pans. It was too small and not adequate, but that was where the utensils had to go. In the summer we could keep some of the utensils in the shed.

We kept perishable food in an icebox that held a twenty-five pound hunk of ice. Since the icebox was small, in the summer we put the bulky items in the cellar on a floating shelf, which hung from the ceiling at a height that made it convenient to reach. It was cooler there but certainly not cold.

Mother and Dad's room opened off both the kitchen and living room. It was large enough for a bed, dresser and chifforobe. The only picture that I remember in the house hung in their room; it was of the cavalry fighting a bloody battle. It was quite a sobering picture, but I would stand and stare at it sometimes, imagining that one of those warriors was my Dad.

There was a very small room the size of a walk-in closet that was meant to be a bathroom. It even had a tub. But because of the lack of piped-in water, and the need for storage room, the tub was not used for its original purpose. When we were little we bathed in an aluminum tub with water that had been carried from the cistern and heated on the kitchen range. In winter the tub was placed in the living room beside the potbelly stove so we would be somewhat comfortable while bathing. I don't remember at what age we graduated to sponge baths, but we were probably pretty young.

In 1936, when I was eleven, we had a well dug near the mill and water was piped to the house. We had only one faucet; it was located in the shed. Later, we got a sink with a faucet for the kitchen. What an improvement that was, a sink with faucets from which water flowed! We were coming up in the world. We also installed a shower in the cellar. By then there was an electric light hanging from the ceiling in the cellar too. It was wonderful to be able to take a shower anytime you wanted to. Of course, the cellar was dark and damp; not your plush shower stall, but to be able to stand under that flowing water and be refreshed was pure luxury.

A couple of years earlier, when I was nine, the house was wired for electricity. It didn't mean we had lamps in every room or chandeliers hanging from the ceiling. We had a single light bulb hanging down from the center of the kitchen, and more or less the same in each room. Certainly nothing elegant, but magical—just pull the chain and we had light!

The living room was quite small and held Mother's sewing machine, the potbelly wood-burning stove, an old piano and a library table (so-called because it had two shelves on either end). Most of us had at least one year of piano lessons, an indication of Mother's insistence that we have at least a taste of the arts. There must have been some kind of seating in there during the time we were small, but all I remember is Dad's rocker and the chair Mother sat on at the sewing machine. Dad's roll-top desk was in the kitchen. We were banned from even opening it, though I never understood why. He could tell if you touched one paper, or so it seemed to me. Later on the living room was fixed up a bit, though it still held the heating stove, the sewing machine and the library table as long as I can remember. When someone was sick for more than a few days, an army cot was put up in the living room, and it doubled as a sick room. Sometimes there were two cots needed.

A large square mirror hung just inside the living room next to the chimney. I sometimes watched Dad shave in front of that mirror when I was quite small. He used a brush and shaving mug. He would get the brush full of lather, then make a quick motion toward me as if he was going to lather my face. That was typical of the ways he showed his kids attention. He would grab one of us by the arms and tell us to relax, then flap our elbows against our ribs and make a sound like a chicken cackling. Or he would say, "Let me count your ribs," and go slowly from the lower rib up toward our armpits until we started giggling. I liked it when he did that.

The shed was not very big but lots went on out there. In winter it was very cold because the door to the kitchen was kept closed and the shed had two exterior walls. The cistern pump was against one of the outer walls. It would freeze and we had to prime it with hot water. There was a drop leaf table to put things on, the cream separator, and a row of shelves at one end for all kinds of things that would today be put in a pantry. Many of the necessary items one needs with a family of seven kids were crammed onto those few shelves. Cloth curtains were hung to hide some of the clutter, but they were usually agape. In the winter the table would get piled up with crocks, jars, bottles, and whatever found its way onto the table. By spring it was a major job to clean it off. Half of the stuff had to be thrown out. The table emerged with space cleared once more, ready for whatever had no other place to land. No one wanted to spend more time out in the shed than absolutely necessary in the cold of winter, hence the springtime cleaning. The shed also had hooks for heavy winter clothes such as our snow suits, wool hats, heavy scarves, and space on the floor for our rubber boots and overshoes. It was very small and cramped but thank God it was there!

The cream-separator took up one whole corner, and represented an irksome chore. We girls disliked having to wash it each morning. If you have ever tried to wash milk utensils in hard water, you would know it isn't pleasant. Soap didn't work; besides we had only the soap we'd made, and it certainly wasn't friends with hard water. After all the parts were washed, they were put into the bowl (the large container into which the men poured the milk when they brought it up the hill from the barn) until time to milk again. We girls always had to be sure the separator was put back together before the men brought the milk up in the late afternoon. I didn't want Dad to be mad at me, and I sure didn't want him to yell at me.

After saving enough whole milk for our table use and for cooking, they poured the rest into the large bowl. Someone would turn the crank, and soon the skimmed milk would flow from one spout and cream from the other. Imagine pouring that fresh thick cream on your cereal or over a bowl of strawberries fresh from the patch. The skimmed milk went out to the hogs. I have often thought of our drinking that fresh milk without any sterilization whatsoever.

A near tragedy happened in that shed in the middle of the summer the year I was five. We had a kerosene-stove hooked up there during canning season. It sat right under those curtains that were supposed to make the place look a bit nicer by hiding the mess on the shelves.

One day, as Mom was melting paraffin to pour over jams and jellies to seal them, some dripping wax burst into flames. In her attempt to put it out, Mom's dress caught on fire. She was badly burned. She lost her eyebrows and lashes, but not much of her hair. She would have suffered much more severe burns, but she had on only a loose dress and her under pants. She did get the fire out, but spent the next few weeks in bed with third degree burns on her upper arms. Her face was burned but not so badly.

Dr. Packer, the only doctor in Toulon, would come out to the house and dress the burned areas. The only thing he had to put on the raw burns was some kind of salve to keep the gauze from sticking. There were no antibiotics or other miracle drugs, but she did gradually heal. She was left with a large part of her upper arms scarred; no permanent damage was done to her pretty face.

She must have suffered terribly, as she lay in her bed day after day with her arms and face heavily bandaged. The heat of summer in Illinois can be wicked with no air conditioning to bring relief. At five I had five siblings, with the oldest being only ten. Grandma Appenheimer stayed with us until Mother was able to carry on; Grandma must have felt overwhelmed. She certainly wouldn't have had much time to pamper Mother. What inner strength Mother must have had; I'm sure she didn't get much sympathy.

She surely didn't get any from me. My strongest memory is of being up in the mulberry tree with my sister, and feeling bad because we couldn't go to the Sunday School Picnic. I don't remember Grandma's presence during those few weeks. I was a typical five year old—very egocentric.

Dad would sometimes sit on the small front porch when it rained, if there was nothing he needed to do in the barn or machine shed. Occasionally he would ask Mom to pop some corn. She would bring it out to him in the dishpan from which we kids would fill our smaller bowls. To this day, when it is a cloudy, rainy day, I can hear the popcorn popping and inhale that delicious smell. Sometimes, after we kids had gone to bed, we could hear mom popping corn in the heating stove in the living room. That was a comforting sound to me, indicating they were enjoying something together.

Food on the Farm

We raised most of our food, including pop-corn, but we shopped at the Kroger store for what we didn't raise. Dad did most of the shopping until we kids got old enough to drive and were eager to go to town for any reason. But we didn't just drive up town for a pound of sugar or a loaf of bread. There had to be a bigger reason. By the time I was in high school, gas rationing was in effect and no one drove any place unnecessarily.

The Kroger store was not large. There were shelves along the two longer walls and part of the back plus there were barrels of item like potatoes, onions, and apples placed in strategic spots around the store. Other food items were stacked on the counter except for a small clearing on the counter where the clerk put your purchases. The customer read the list to the clerk or handed it to him. The clerk gathered the items and placed them on the counter. We bought such things as sugar, flour, bread (when Mom didn't bake), salt & pepper, mustard. Dad bought bananas when they were so ripe that the price was lowered. Sometimes we got oysters; Dad ate all the oysters because we kids didn't like them, but we liked the soup. We also bought the little, round oyster crackers to put in the soup. When everything was collected and on the counter, the clerk would ring up the items and bag them. You paid in cash.

Choices were limited; there was one kind of white bread, a couple of kinds of cereal, one brand of sugar or flour. There were groceries, period. The store sold toilet paper, but we didn't buy it; that's how we recycled the old Sears and Wards catalogues.

Our parents bought bushels of oranges and grapefruit in the winter, when they were available, because Mother insisted we have one orange or one-half a grapefruit each day when available. The basket of fruit was kept in the folks' room. Woe be to anyone caught trying to take the second orange—they were expensive.

We canned hundreds of quarts of food each summer. We not only canned it, but planted it, hoed and weeded it, picked it and prepared it for either eating or canning. We began with asparagus and rhubarb in early spring and ended in the fall with the last of the tomatoes, pears, and pickles. We canned our own catsup, soups, pickles, tomatoes, tomato juice, beans, carrots, peas, corn, peaches, pears, plums, apple sauce, and anything else that came our way.

If Dad got a bargain on peaches (because they were getting too ripe) he would arrive home with several bushels. We would drop whatever we were doing and begin peeling peaches. There were no excuses for not helping. The kitchen became a production center; we canned many quart jars of peaches which we lined up on the counter, then carried to the cellar.

Around 1939 or 1940, the Locker opened in town. This business was in a building where individual lockers with large freezer drawers were available for lease. We began freezing our food instead of canning it. That made food storage easier, and the food tasted so much better; we had fresh-tasting fruit, vegetables and meat all year. It was many years before home freezers appeared in our farming community.

Of course, being on a farm, we did our own butchering. The men killed the animal, skinned it, and quartered it before bringing it into the house to be processed. After the Locker opened, the meat was delivered to them and they did the processing. We ate parts of the beef or pork fresh, such as liver, brains (sweetbread), tongue, and the heart. We liked these organ meats, but I'm not sure I'd eat them today.

We usually ate red meat at least twice a day, beginning with bacon or ham for breakfast, roast or pork chops for dinner and country-fried steak or chicken for supper. We often had chicken, deep fried in bacon grease. I don't remember having hamburgers and we seldom had fish. It's a wonder we weren't all fat; I think we kids burned off the calories playing outside and doing our chores.

A yucky job was rendering lard. This had to be done at the time of butchering. After the fat was cooked a certain length of time, it was scooped into the lard-press, the crank was turned, the lard flowed into five-gallon crocks that were stored in the cellar. The smell of the hot, fresh fat was unpleasant. It was a greasy, nasty mess, and cleanup was not fun with the hard water and no detergent. The lard press was such a greasy thing we didn't have to worry about it rusting.

It was too bad we didn't have an outbuilding where such onerous tasks could be done. We did have several outbuildings near the house, including a coal/cob house, with a partition down the middle to keep the two separated, the wash house, the hen house, the brooder house, and the outhouse. The coal/cob house and the wash house were very close to our house. The smokehouse was behind them, but I don't remember ever curing any meat.

The wash house was a catchall for whatever we wanted to keep and had no place else to store. When cold weather returned it was a chore to clear enough space for the old washing machine to fit inside the wash-house. We kept it outside during the summer; it was so much more pleasant, and easier to dump the water when finished with the washing.

Laundry day (Monday) was a full day, with clothes for nine people to be laundered, hung out to dry, gathered from the lines, folded and put away. After the clothes were through the wash cycle, we would guide them, piece by piece, through the rollers to get the excess water out, letting them fall into the rinse tub. The rollers were rotated, and the process repeated—taking the clothes from the rinse, through the rollers again, and letting them drop into a basket.

The clothes were hung out on the clothesline that was strung between a big cottonwood tree and a locust tree, then to a walnut tree by the smokehouse. When those lines were full, there were more out in the "back-lot." From the walnut tree the clothesline ran to the back of the hen house, and ended at the knarred old apple tree not far from the orchard. When Juanita and I hung the laundry, I would hand a piece to her, and she would pin it on the metal line with a wooden clothespin. During the winter, those pants, shirts and underwear would be frozen stiff before we could scurry back into the warm house.

The pieces that were to be ironed, were sprinkled, tightly rolled, and put into a laundry basket where they stayed until the next day. In hot weather, we couldn't leave the clothes longer than a day, or they would mildew. We girls were able to do the laundry by the time we were eleven or twelve years old, including most of the ironing. Mother had an ironer at one time that allowed her to sit down while ironing some things; she got quite good at it. I barely remember using the old irons that were heated on the kitchen range, two or three at a time. You disconnected the wooden handle from the iron when it began to cool, then connect the handle to one of the hot irons while putting the cool one back on the cooking stove to re-heat. By the time I was old enough to do much ironing we had an electric iron. Steam irons, which let us stop sprinkling and rolling the garments, were still in the future.

Perpendicular to the wash house was a large, rusty, metal tank where the kerosene for starting the fires was stored. Just pour the kerosene over the cobs, put a few pieces of coal on top, and the fire would be roaring in no time. We kept a tin can full of kerosene on the windowsill in the kitchen by the stove, so it was handy.

Every spring we would get a lot of baby chicks, over one-hundred to raise for eating and for eggs. Inside the brooder house, where they were kept until a certain age, was a large heated tent-like metal cover which lowered within a few inches of the floor. This allowed the chicks to come and go freely. While under that brooder, they were kept as warm as if under their mothers' wings. They were closely watched for the first two or three weeks. If they began to die, it meant they had some disease, and we put medicine tablets in their water. Sometimes we lost a lot of them anyway.

The feeders had to be kept filled until the chicks were old enough to be let out to scrounge for themselves. After they were older, we still had to provide water and a place for shelter during the nights. We put the water in a quart jar, screwed a top on, (which had a diameter larger than the jar), turned it upside down, and the water came out at the rate it was consumed. As far as a shelter at night, I think they just learned to go into the henhouse and roost there.

The brooder house had a slanted roof. In the fall we gathered gunnysacks full of black walnuts and spread them out on that roof to dry. After they dried, the nuts had to be husked before they would be ready to crack. The husks were thick and green when we laid them out on the roof, but turned black before we husked them. Our hands and nails were very black when we finished husking walnuts. To crack open a black walnut, it had to be hit with a heavy hammer. Picking nutmeat out of the shell was another time-consuming job. A quart of black walnuts represented hours of labor: gathering, drying, husking, cracking and picking out the meat. Today we use mostly English walnuts that are not nearly the amount of work the black ones were.

The outbuildings were close to the house, but the farm buildings were scattered over a larger area. These included the barn, pig house, corn crib and the machine shed. We also had the sorghum mill which most farms did not have.

Sorghum Making

Dad was one of the largest producers of sorghum in the state of Illinois, not that his was so big, but the others were quite small. He hired approximately twenty men beginning in September. The sorghum cane, which looks a lot like sugar cane, had to be harvested before the first frost, usually around the end of October.

The men worked in crews—three men to each crew. The first crew cut the cane close to the ground with machetes and loaded it on a hayrack. The second crew pulled the cane to the mill and unloaded it onto a platform attached to the steel rollers. The third crew fed the cane into the large crushing grinder. With two sets of crews, they were able to keep the mill busy. The grinder was turned by a horse walking around in an endless circle. Years later a tractor took over this task and the horses were no longer subjected to such monotonous labor. The crushed cane, called pummies, fell onto a hayrack and were taken out to be deposited in a field north of the mill. We kids liked to climb and play on the pummy hills.

The cane juice drained through pipes from the grinder into a storage tank, until there was enough to begin cooking. The cooking crew commenced cooking mid-afternoon and didn't finish until 3:00 or 4:00 A.M. There were no walls to close in the cooking area; I can still close my eyes and see the steam rolling out from under that tin roof. It lasted from mid-afternoon until long after we kids were asleep. That nostalgic memory is a cozy one for me. It meant things were as they should be; it was sorghum-making time.

The cooking was done in four vats, measuring approximately ten feet by three feet. One man tended each of the first three vats, where the juice began cooking. The men tending that phase, would skim off the "scum," (the foam that rose to the top) and ladle it into a shaft that carried it to a large tank, where it was later carried off and disposed of. As the juice reached a certain thickness, it was directed into the fourth vat, the finishing vat. Dad and his good neighbor, Ernie McRell, tended this last and most important phase, where the consistency and color of the sorghum was determined to be just right. It was important that the reputation of Appenheimer's Sorghum, "The Best Sorghum in the USA" be upheld. When they determined it was ready, the sorghum was drained into a storage tank where it was ready for packaging. It was golden brown, pungent, with the consistency of honey. The flavor was strong, making it unique as good sorghum should be.

Next to the cooking area was the "red building" where the pails were stored and labeled and packaging took place. The sorghum was siphoned into one quart, two quart and gallon pails. Each pail had to be labeled and have the bail, its handle, attached. The labels indicated it was Appenheimer's Sorghum and were attractively done in black and red on a white background.

Men needed work that paid cash, so Dad didn't have trouble getting the help he needed. Many of the men were not known to him personally. When he hired them, he let them know they would not get paid until the first sorghum was sold (so that he would have the money). He knew some of them were pretty tough and was careful when payday came. One year he was bedridden with sciatic nerve problems, and the men came to his bedroom to get paid. When the first one came in, Dad was sitting up with the money on the bed in front of him. The man made some comment about Dad being "an easy roll." Dad, very deftly, reached under his pillow, and pointed a forty-five caliber pistol at the man before he could blink. Dad had been a sharpshooter in the Marines and was no dummy, either. He figured this guy would spread the word that the boss was armed.

He had regular customers for his sorghum—small privately-owned grocery stores in the numerous little towns scattered over the large farming area. He and Ernie McRell would load their cars and take off in the morning, each to cover his specified route, delivering sorghum and collecting the money in cash. In the evening, when they returned home, they put the money on our kitchen table and counted it. It seemed like a lot of money to me as a child, and I wondered how we could be so poor and yet have all that money. I had my first lesson in economics when Dad explained that most of it went to pay expenses.

The men who worked out in the fields brought their lunches, but Mother had to cook three meals a day for six or seven of the others, those who had the more responsible jobs of cooking and packaging of the sorghum. Dinner at noon and supper in the evening were big meals, with beef, pork or chicken, mashed potatoes and gravy, a couple of fresh vegetables from our garden, either hot baking powder biscuits or yeast rolls and always dessert. We never had green salad, Dad called raw vegetables "rabbit food." Dessert was not store-bought cookies or cake. Most often dessert was home-made pie with flakey crust made with the lard that we'd rendered ourselves, and a filling made of fresh fruit—apples, cherries, or peaches. Those pies were delicious! Sometimes we had cake made with ingredients from the farm—eggs from the henhouse and butter we'd churned. The cakes and pies were baked in the oven that was part of the coal range. The oven temperature was regulated by the amount of coal we put in the fire-box. The oven's door had a small, round thermometer imbedded in the front. To see it you had to practically get on your knees.

The third meal was a "box lunch" that we prepared and delivered to the men after supper for their midnight snack. The typical lunch would be cold meat sandwiches, cookies or cake and fruit. The men kept coffee brewing all night at the mill, so we didn't have to worry about that. We kids would gladly take the lunch down to them and hang around for a few minutes. We girls were not allowed around the mill or the barn until after 5:00 P.M. when the tough guys went home. We were free to be around the men whom Dad knew well and trusted, but we were never encouraged to stay long. We knew how to behave, and certainly knew not to use words that even hinted at being curse words.

Glenna and Vonnie, my two younger sisters, tested the limits to that rule. One evening down at the mill they recited the little rhyme, "How the hell we gonna water old Nell if it ain't gonna rain no more?"

Dad overheard them and angrily sent them up to the house with instructions to get their pajamas on and go to bed. As soon as he could, he came to the house, and without a word, proceeded to climb those narrow stairs to our bedroom. Finding the girls fully clothed and playing cards, he spanked them both and ordered them to get in bed.

That was one of the few times we ever knew him to go upstairs. Glenna and Vonnie were shocked and dismayed that he did that time.

Dad and Mother were very strict as to the language we used. Hired men and women were not allowed to curse or use foul language around us. One woman who had just started working for Mother said, "damn" in the middle of the morning and was fired on the spot. She was told to get her things, and someone took her to the bus station.

One incident that stays with me happened when I was seven or eight years old. I was sitting next to Dad at the table when someone said the word "poop". They were scolded and told not to use that word. Dummy that I was, I said, "No, because that word is all pooped out." Dad's arm flew around and hit me in the face, knocking me over backward, chair and all. As if that was not humiliating enough, he made me get back in my chair and finish my meal. That is not a good memory, but one I have never forgotten. It is not that I still hold it against my Dad. I gave that up long ago. But forgiving and forgetting are two different things.

After I was married and had my first child, I said, "mouse turd" in front of Mom. She really scolded me. I don't know what I should have said, maybe "mouse doo-doo."

Making Hay

Sorghum making was the biggest event on our farm; haying was like a practice run. Neighbors threshed hay together; they shared the equipment because it was so expensive and was only used once a year. They either bought a combine together, or one farmer bought it, and the others paid him for the use of it. Another reason for working together was that it took several men to harvest the hay, and by working together, no one had to hire outsiders.

We had to prepare a place for the men to "wash up" before coming in to dinner. We hung a mirror on the locust tree in the yard and rigged up a stand that held a large wash basin and soap. The towels were hung by the mirror on nails in the tree. Buckets of water were sitting on the ground nearby, making everything as convenient as possible.

The seven or eight men ate their noon meal at the home where the harvesting was being done. The host wife was always given a hand by one of the other wives. They prepared a dinner like the ones we had for sorghum makers. The hostess would find out what the men had been given the day before, so as not to repeat it. The women were hopeful that their dinner compared favorably with the one served the day before and the day after. The neighbor women had a chance to catch up on the news of the rural area during the preparation of the meals. Farm women didn't have time to call on each other, or get together purely for socializing. So, they enjoyed the opportunity, even if it was circumscribed by preparing a country meal for hungry men.

Washing all the dishes, pots and pans after a meal like that was not as easy as it would be today. There were no dishwashers, no hot water flowing from a faucet, no detergent to produce sudsy water. We heated water in the dish pan on top of the coal range, and used soap we'd made, which didn't produce suds. We stood by the stove as we washed the dishes, leaving the dish pan on the stove to stay hot. Farming was just hard work for both men and women. It had always been that way; no one thought anything of it. We girls started washing dishes quite young; I started helping (because I wanted to) when I was so little I had to stand on the oven door to reach the dish pan.

The temperature in the kitchen got pretty high with the coal range going full blast all morning. The eight sweaty men sitting around the round, oak table appreciated the large oscillating fan that Dad had set up to blow on them.

Each host farmer had to provide one extra man (or boy) to serve as "water boy" to carry cool water, lemonade, or tea to the sweating workers in the fields. Dad was so protective of us girls—we were not allowed to be the "water boy". But as soon as he was able to ride the pony, Clay, who was just one year younger than I, took that role during haying time. He had a large thermos jug, wrapped in wet burlap to help insulate it (there was no ice), which he carried in front of him astraddle Dan, the pony. It could be very hot in Illinois, and the men handling the dusty hay needed plenty of liquids. The story goes that one of the men asked Clay what he owed him after he drank some of the lemonade, and Clay said, "A nickel's worth of licorice." That story got around and Clay pigged out on licorice for a few days until Dad found out. One can imagine that Clay's lucrative venture stopped in a hurry. Dad didn't like that at all, but the men probably got a kick out of it and Clay thought he'd fared pretty well.

Old Settlers Day

Dan, the pony Clay rode as water boy, was rather large for a pony. He was part of our lives as long as I was on the farm. Some of my sisters thought he was mean, but he and I got along pretty well most of the time. He did have a proclivity towards shying, especially whenever something moved unexpectedly, or whenever he just felt like shying. Most of the time I could stay on his back, but if I fell off he waited for me; it didn't seem too bad.

Dan did almost get the best of me one Old Settler's Day, which was a big day for farm families. Old Settler's day was always held on the first Thursday in August. It was a chance for farm people to socialize and catch up with friends whom they didn't get to see often. That was the part Mother liked—the chance to sit around visiting with the women she knew, and having a day away from the omnipresent work at home. She had the day free, after preparing the picnic dinner and getting all of us dressed and uptown. Of course, we helped when we got older.

Dad especially enjoyed the day; he worked in the American Legion's Bingo Stand wearing his Legion hat. The money raised from the bingo games went to fund the Legion's civic good works. Old Settler's Day took place on Toulon's Main Street, with activities on the courthouse lawn and on the street.

The parade down Main Street took place mid-morning. The year I was eight, I was to ride Dan uptown to join the rest of the kids in the parade. Boys and girls wore all kinds of costumes, riding everything from bicycles to hay racks, pushing doll buggies or pulling wagons with their pets in costume. Every participant in the parade got a dime, so I was eager to be part of it.

The problem was that Dan didn't want to be a part of any parade, and he would not do what I wanted him to as we slowly made our way down the gravel road toward town. He turned into every driveway and every open field that we passed on that mile and half journey. I was more determined than he was, so we finally made it to town, but we were too late for the parade. I was disappointed and tearful as I made my way through the crowd on Main Street. From the Bingo Stand, Dad saw me coming and motioned me over so he could talk to me. He assured me I had done okay, and that I would get my dime, because I was in the parade, even though I was late. As long as I got that dime, I didn't mind missing the parade.

The three churches in town rotated the responsibility of cooking the dinner, served on the court house lawn. Mother helped with the dinner when it was sponsored by the Baptist Church. But even on the years that she helped, we didn't get to eat there. We always took a picnic lunch and ate in the small park a block away from the court house. It was cheaper that way. And we thought eating in the park was fun.

There were always a few rides set up in the downtown area including a Ferris Wheel and a Merry-go-round, but it seemed to me that the Bingo Stand was the center and main attraction. That's because Dad was always there selling bingo cards and talking up the prizes, especially the Indian Blankets that came in many colors and designs. Seeing Dad enjoying himself and socializing with other people made me feel good; I liked seeing that side of him. I didn't see it often.

Dad always gave each of us some money to spend on Old Settler's Day—sometimes as much as a quarter. We held onto it as long as we could. Juanita and I would "hang out" together all day on Old Settlers Day. We'd discuss how we were going to spend our money. Everything cost a nickel, so we could ride on the rides a couple of times and get two or three treats on a quarter. I wanted to ride the rides more than she did, but whatever we decided to do, it was a fun day. Things changed after Juanita started high school and had other friends to run around with.

Fourth of July

The Fourth of July was another of my favorite holidays. As frugal as Dad was, he always bought a few fireworks. We each got our share to set off on our own—the little firecrackers (Lady Fingers), sparklers and things called snakes. You lit them on the sidewalk, and without making any sound, they put forth a foamy, curly substance—resembling a snake. Dad usually had a few rockets and a few secret fireworks. He set off these special noisemakers after dark, bringing forth a lot of oohs and aahs from his children. It didn't take much in the thirties for farm kids to have a wonderful time.

On the Fourth, we always had fried chicken with all the trimmings and home-made ice cream for dessert. I thought the day was great, but Juanita didn't enjoy it at all. She and our dog, Silver, were uncomfortable all day with the bursts of noise and shrieks of surprise—they didn't like *bombs bursting in air.* Juanita paced around and stayed inside of the house almost all day. Silver, who was not allowed in the house, would behave like she did during storms, forcing her way past the screened door and running upstairs to hide under a bed. We knew Silver had trouble with the day, and acted as though we didn't know she was inside.

May Baskets & Other Summer Fun

We had fun on the farm between the holidays. Fun came in simple ways—simple in terms of today's world. We hung May baskets, not only on the first day of May, but any time during the month. We tried to have our shoes handy, so we could put them on quickly, if a "basket" was hung at our house. We went barefoot as soon as the frost was off the ground, but in the month of May, our feet weren't calloused enough to run very far.

We always hung a basket at McRell's house where there were lots of kids our age, and they always reciprocated. The idea was to surprise the recipients. The basket was placed on the porch and before you ran and hid you yelled, "May basket!" The kids at the house, where the basket was hung, had to find each kid who was hiding. A farm provided many hiding places, so the kids who received the basket, had a lot of ground to cover as they searched for their neighbors. After everyone was found, we chatted a bit before the kids who had hung the basket went home.

One evening McRells hung a basket at our house. By the time we got our shoes on, they had disappeared. We started our disorganized search. I ran down by the barn to see if someone was hiding by the slough. I jumped over a low fence and landed right on top of one of the boys crouched down on the other side—found him by default! I don't know who was more surprised, he or I.

The May baskets were originally meant to be little baskets filled with flowers and candy. Ours were made with a piece of construction paper folded into a box shape with a narrow strip pasted on it to resemble a handle. We were satisfied if we picked some violets, usually in bloom in May, and added a couple of dandelions. The basket really wasn't important, except it was the passport to our having fun.

All summer we were allowed to play outside as soon as supper was finished, so we tried to eat as early as possible. We ate at four if we could, and were free to play until the magic hour of eight, which was bedtime for all of us until we were in high school.

Sometimes, during the summer, we would build a dam across the slough—the stream that ran through our pasture, then under a cement bridge at the road, and on through McRell's pasture, on the other side of the road. We usually built the dam on their side of the road, because they didn't have hogs in their pasture, so it was nice and grassy instead being a muddy hog-wallow. We built the dam high enough so we could run across it, but the real reason for the dam was the fun of building it.

We hunted for turtles by feeling along the banks and along the muddy bottom of the slough. We put the turtles we caught in the horse tank to keep them alive. Occasionally we had enough to make turtle soup.

Good Times in Winter

During the long cold winters we were stuck in the house. It was quite restrictive, because there were nine of us in two heated rooms. We kids sat around the kitchen table and played cards or board games or read. The folks managed to buy us a set of the *Encyclopedia Britannica*, though money was scarce. Mother saw to it that we have things which she knew were important for our mental and physical development, and Dad didn't disagree with her.

When it snowed enough for us to use our sleds, we were outdoors a lot. The winter of 1936 we had record breaking amounts of snow. Dad had a dam built across the slough. We could begin our sled ride at the top of the hill up by the school house, slide down the hill across the slough, and travel about fifty yards to the fence by the pig pen. The neighbor kids came from the surrounding farms with their sleds to join in the fun. Everyone was welcome to come in our house to warm their hands when needed, walking through the kitchen and into the living room where the heating stove was. (The kitchen floor was wooden and the living room was linoleum, so it wasn't hard to wipe up the snow tracks.) It not only snowed a lot that year, but also stayed below freezing longer than usual, so we had that wonderful playground for a couple of months. That was a memorable winter. I was eleven years old.

One winter we rigged up our version of a cart, using some big wheels and a few sturdy boards nailed together. A rod between the wheels supported the boards or "seat". We managed to hitch Dan up to it somehow. One of us kids would put on the only pair of skis we owned, and Dan would pull us around the barn lot and across the road into McRell's pasture, where there was a large open space with sloping inclines. Someone would drive Dan, and away we would go, pulling the lucky skier behind. It wasn't exactly Aspen, but we had never even heard of such a place, so it didn't diminish our fun.

Juanita and Me

Dan was good for fun times, but also useful at chore time. We rode him mornings and evenings to take the cows to and from the pasture, where they were kept during the warm part of the year. It was about a mile and a half from the barn to the pasture. Herding the cows back and forth was Juanita's and my job for a few years, although more often than not I went by myself.

Juanita was afraid of many things from the groundhogs to the gophers, but not the tumble bugs. She often talked me into going to get the cows by myself, although she was supposed to accompany me. She would convince me to go alone with the promise of a kiss when I got back. I'm not sure if I was that hungry for a bit of affection, or if I was just in the habit of doing whatever she asked of me. Maybe I found it easier to go alone, but I certainly wanted to stay in her good graces.

There was a spring not far from the road on the way to the pasture. It was fun to stop, crawl over the fence, scoot down an embankment to get a drink of that wonderfully cold, clear water. Sometimes there wasn't time to enjoy that treat, but we enjoyed when we had the time.

The Kelly family's farm was on the way to the pasture. They had an apple orchard close to the fence. Some of those juicy, red apples always fell onto our side and waited for us to ride by and pick them up. They were the best apples I've ever tasted. The road ended just past the orchard, and after making a forty-five degree turn, a dirt lane took us the last half mile to the pasture.

Traversing this quiet country lane presented some fearful moments at times because Kellys kept a bull in one of the pastures bordering the lane. It was the hugest, fiercest, meanest bull ever. He would come right up to the fence, snort, paw the ground, bellow, and scare us to death.

We would rush by that fence as inconspicuously as possible, hoping we would escape his notice, thereby avoiding what we imagined to be sure death. We lived in fear he would jump over the fence, but that never happened.

Also on that narrow dirt lane, that was very dusty most of the time, there were what we called tumble bugs (dung beetles). They were a round beetle, shaped much like a lady bug but a lot larger and solid black. The dung beetles got their name because they laid their eggs in the manure, then with the eggs tucked inside, they rolled the manure into a ball the size of a big marble. With their back legs up on the ball, and their short front legs on the ground, they pushed it backwards until it was the right size. We spent many enchanted moments watching them. Of course, if the bull was in sight, we didn't tarry even for something as fascinating as a tumble bug.

Juanita and I were also delegated to feed the hogs over in the "Gwire" eighty. It was about a quarter of a mile from home, and from time to time Dad would keep his sows with their piglets over there. We were to go over at chore time every afternoon, and throw ears of corn out of a wagon for the hogs to eat. The wagon was a few yards inside the fence where the hogs were. We were scared to death of the sows, and we had every right to be as they can be very mean when they have babies. They were always hungry, and would gather by the gate grunting at each other and rooting, trying to be first in line. We soon learned to leave a few ears of corn outside the gate, which we threw in the opposite direction from the wagon. We'd wait until the hogs all rushed to get to those few ears, then we'd hightail it to the wagon where we were safe. Getting back to the gate was no worry, because we always threw the corn away from the gate and the sows were too busy "hoggin" down the corn to be concerned with us. We never forget to put those ears on the other side of the fence for the next day.

During the winter Juanita and I had to bring the wood for the heating stove to the house from an area by the mill where it was piled. Somehow Juanita convinced me that she should load my arms with all that I could carry; I then took it up the hill, through two gates and into the shed where I stacked it neatly against the wall. Then I returned to get my next load. We repeated that process until the twenty-four-hour supply was in the shed. I didn't complain about that arrangement, I simply agreed to do it the same as I agreed to get the cows alone. I was willing to do whatever it took to keep our relationship flying; it wasn't like she had to twist my arm.

She and I were dressed as twins until I was around eleven; we began to want our individuality by then. Or at least Juanita did, I didn't insist very loudly. Although we did a lot of things together and had a close relationship growing up, she certainly had the upper hand and ruled our private, little world. She simply buffaloed me. We were about the same size and I could have defended myself quite easily. But, somehow, I didn't feel as powerful as she was, and usually succumbed to her demands, or I should say, her requests.

Mother cut our hair alike, a Dutch-bob, until we were old enough to want something different. (Mom cut every one's hair, male and female.) Most people thought we were twins, even Santa whom we saw when shopping with Mother in Peoria or Kewanee.

Juanita was two years ahead of me in school, although she was just fifteen months older than I. That may have been part of the reason that I felt she was superior to me, that I must not challenge her. If she wanted me to ride the pony alone I usually rode the pony alone. I certainly never talked her into riding alone. If she wanted me to carry the firewood up the hill to the house while she stayed at the woodpile waiting to re-load me, that is what I did. Why didn't I insist that she carry the wood and get the cows at least part of the time? What happened to taking turns? Where was my courage? Why didn't I stand up for myself, at least a bit?

Mother the Seamstress

We all had chores to do and were never bored, but Mother was always busy. Along with everything else she had to do, she made all of the clothes for us six girls and some of Clay's shirts. She even made some of our snowsuits and coats. We always looked nice, because she was an excellent seamstress. If we showed her a picture of what we wanted or if we showed her something ready-made, she could duplicate it. As a teen, I hated looking at patterns and fabric. I wished I could just go in a store, try something on and buy it if I liked how it looked on me. But we had very nice clothes and really dressed better than most other kids in high school. Mom would stay up late at night sewing in order to finish something special for a certain day. At Christmas she might have to give more than one of us a half-finished garment because she simply ran out of time. It wasn't that she hadn't tried.

We ordered most clothing which Mother couldn't make out of the Sears' or Ward's catalogues, or the "wish books" as my Dad referred to them. When the new catalogue arrived we all wanted to be first to grab it to see what wondrous things we could wish for. We ordered our shoes, overshoes, socks and underwear from the catalogues. We wore buckle-up overshoes which came nearly to our knees; they kept us dry no matter how much snow we trudged through, how hard it rained, or how much mud we plodded through.

Rain and Mud

Speaking of mud, our country roads were not graveled until I was nine or ten years old. When it rained it was sometimes impossible to get to town, even with chains. After the roads were graveled it was still not easy to get anywhere because our house was up on a hill, and the lane from the road to the hill was fifty or sixty yards long. Often we had to walk, if not from the road, at least up the hill, so boots were a necessity. What fun that was when we began dating!

I dated several boys throughout my high school years, but mostly I went with the one I married at the age of nineteen. When he came to get me, I wasn't ashamed of our living conditions; he also lived on a farm and could understand. I liked some of the other boys, but I think I didn't want them to see where I lived. I wasn't comfortable having guys see our house, with the mud lane, the hogs and the cows so close to the house that was rundown and most often a mess.

One rainy afternoon, I was out rounding up the dumb turkeys and herding them into their shelters, when I became aware of someone approaching. I was barefooted wearing only a thin water-soaked dress that was clinging to my body. My hair was straggling wet. Here came a would-be boyfriend named Bill, with whom I was quite infatuated, and he saw me chasing little turkeys in the knee-high grass. I was mortified and mad at Mom for telling him where I was. What could be worse when you are seventeen?

Animals on the Farm

Turkeys really are stupid and don't know enough to head for shelter when it begins to rain. Some of the little ones actually stand still and drown if left on their own. We also had guineas—a domestic fowl with a featherless head, rounded body, and dark feathers spotted with white. They were nasty when they had young, very protective. My younger sister, Glenna, got flogged once when she got too close to the babies. We didn't have any responsibility for the guineas, because they were self-sufficient and stayed around the farm buildings.

We raised geese from time to time; they also were feisty when they had young. They roamed around the out-buildings near the house. We didn't want to mess with them when their goslings were around, either. Dad liked ducks, and we had a variety of them over the years, including Muscovy Ducks with their large crests and red wattles. They also hung out around the house and outbuildings. But ducks are not mean, or at least the ones we had weren't.

We had many different kinds of chickens including Barred Rock, Rhode Island Red, White Rocks and sometimes Bantam Roosters. Dad liked the little roosters because they were pretty and always challenging each other to a fight. He was the one who was responsible for our having so many different kinds of fowl and domestic animals. He liked to get several different varieties of whatever he liked—including kids.

At one time or another, we had quite an assortment of animals. Dad kept sheep from time to time, especially early on. When the sheep were delivered via boxcar, they were unloaded at the station in town. It made for some excitement when they came bleating down the country road to be herded into the pasture near our house. After a period of time, with an increase in their numbers and when they were fattened up, they were shipped off to market, to be sold at a profit, we hoped.

One of the sheep died way off in the corner of nowhere. Mother had us take scissors and bags and gave us instructions to find the sheep, clip the wool and bring it home. The poor thing had been dead for a while, and the wool was wet and soggy from the weather. But ours was a world in which you wasted nothing, and if we could get wool from that dead sheep, Mom would use it for something. She was out of luck with that one.

We also had goats from time to time. We sometimes had to feed one of the kid's milk from a bottle with a large nipple on it. We also fed small calves from a bottle when one wasn't doing well. We had a couple of stalls built in the back lot near the chicken house where the calves came to be fed. The goats were the cutest, but they were aggressive and would put their heads down and ram you if they felt like it. I still think they are cute; I just don't want one in my back yard.

Pigs are not my idea of a candidate for a pet, but many times a runt had to be nurtured for a while before it could be put back with the others to fight for its share of nourishment. We often had to wrap the runt in old rags and place it in a box near the kitchen range to keep it warm. We fed it frequently, either by spoon or bottle depending on its condition. The runts we nurtured usually lived to join their siblings and grow into dirty, mud-loving hogs.

We helped many a runt survive, but I often wonder how Mother and Dad managed to see that all seven of their children survived those severe Illinois winters, especially since we had no central heat, no insulation, no running water, no antibiotics, and no electricity until I was eleven. The closest they came to losing one of us was in the fall of 1931 when I was six years old and Juanita was seven.

Scarlet Fever and German Measles

Grandma Appenheimer died that fall, and all of us went to her funeral. Two weeks later (the accepted incubation period) Juanita complained of not feeling well; she had a sore throat and had begun to break out with a rash. The next day she was diagnosed with scarlet fever, which was often fatal, especially to young children. Yvonne was six months old, and six more of us were under the age of eleven.

The diagnosis of scarlet fever meant we had to be quarantined. Anyone who came in and out of our house could not leave our property until none of us was contagious. In order for Dad to be allowed to do the grocery shopping and to make other necessary contacts with the public, he had to stay out of the house, so he slept down at the mill. He would come to the window and talk to us through the single-pane glass. He brought our groceries and other necessities to the shed where Mother would get them. I'm not sure where he ate his meals that Mother fixed, but he didn't come into the kitchen.

The old country doctor, Dr. Packer, (who had delivered all seven of us) came to our home immediately and gave all of us a shot, except for Juanita. The shots did not keep us from contracting the disease, but did keep us from having it as seriously as Juanita did. The shots were given in our fannies; when it was Mother's turn, we kids were sent to the other room so she could have some privacy. Being children, we peeked out and saw her lean over the table and get hers. We thought that was funny, getting a peek of her baring her behind.

Juanita became very ill. Our parents were told she should be taken to the hospital. Dr. Packer warned them that she might not make it, either in the hospital or at home. As we each came down with the fever, Mother would not be able to care for the rest us and take the proper care of Juanita, who needed a lot of attention. He warned them that it was not unlikely that they would lose one of us before it was over.

Mother knew how panic stricken Juanita would be if she was isolated from her family. She would have been terrified if she awakened in a strange place with none of her family there. None of us would have been able to visit her because of the quarantine. She would have been one traumatized seven-year old. Together, Mom and Dad decided they could not risk sending her to the hospital.

Juanita went in and out of delirium and wanted one of us beside her all the time. Her fever stayed high, necessitating cold baths as the only means known of keeping it under dangerous levels. The country roads posed problems also. There was likely to be snow, and keeping the country roads open was a challenge. All the farmers living on that road cooperated in keeping it open. There were no snow plows in the thirties, so it was a labor-intensive effort.

Most of us came down with the fever, including the baby, but none of us had it as seriously as Juanita did. The vaccinations had done what they were supposed to do.

When Vonnie, who was six-months old, broke out and began running a fever, the doctor told Mother she shouldn't let her cry too long at a time. She should try to hold her more. How did he think she would get the time to sit and rock the baby? Glenna was three, Clay was four, I was six and Juanita was seven. We younger ones were not much help. But Mother had us organized, and I'm sure Dorothy and Betty were able to help. They were eleven and nine years old, respectively, and used to handling responsibility. I believed I helped by being beside

Juanita when she was awake. She wanted someone right there even when she was out of her head. I missed her as my playmate and knew she was seriously ill. There was much anxiety in the house.

We kids made up games to play. For "store," we made paper money; someone was the clerk, while the sick ones were customers. The kids who were not sick went to those in bed and took their orders, then went to the "store" where we found such things as raisins, rubber bands or a pencil. Remember, we were living in the two rooms which were heated by the potbellied stove in the living room and the wood burning range in the kitchen. We had to have great imaginations, and Mother had to have had tremendous ability to tolerate the physical and emotional stress. It was also difficult for Dad, cut off from us. He had just lost his mother, and now he was isolated from his big family. He would have been such a help for Mother if he could have been in the house. He would have been glad to rock us, especially the baby, Vonnie.

Juanita did fight her way through the valley and began to get better very slowly, and Vonnie survived without being held much. The quarantine was lifted after ten long weeks. Dad was back with us in time to celebrate Thanksgiving with the usual turkey dinner. He was there to put his touch on our holiday table as he always did on Thanksgiving and Christmas. On those two holidays he arranged apples, oranges, grapes and nuts in the center of the table, which seemed very festive to us. Of course, Mother made sure the table was laden with scrumptious food: dressing, gravy, mashed potatoes, biscuits or yeast rolls, fresh churned butter, home- made jams, several kinds of vegetables, and customary desserts. In addition to turkey we might have chicken, rabbit, ham, or maybe a large roast or even goose or duck. We probably had two or three kinds of pies and plenty of home-made ice cream for dessert.

That Thanksgiving Dad and Mom were very grateful for having seven kids who were either well or on the way to being so. If ever we had been moved to say a Blessing it would have been that special day. I am positive Juanita would not have lived had they taken her to the hospital. I know she would not have coped with being in a strange place with none of her family at her bedside to comfort and reassure her. My parents certainly knew best, as so often was the case. No stranger could have known what it would have meant to a seven-year-old like Juanita to have been isolated like that. Mother and Dad knew.

Dad carried Juanita from the cot in the living room, where she had come so close to leaving us, to the kitchen to look at the table before we all sat down. She was not walking yet, but was "with" us and on her way to being able to do things with me and to sleep upstairs with me again. In addition to the nine of us, we often had others join us for a holiday meal: Grandpa Swango, Ernest Swango, (Mom's brother,) Ernest Robinson, (a friend) Aunt Pearl, (Dad's sister) and her husband, Uncle Hank, Aunt Clae, (Mother's sister) and her daughter, Diane. Those relatives were often there as were others who had no better place to be.

After dinner we kids played in the barn and made tunnels with the bales of hay when the weather was bad. If it was freezing weather, we would try to find a place to go skating or play in the snow. It was fun knowing we had the whole day to do nothing but eat and play.

A not uncommon complication following scarlet fever is an inflammation of the mastoid (located behind the ear) and it can cause deafness. In the thirties it was a serious development and one that extended Juanita's illness and caused our parents concern for another few weeks. The good thing was that she didn't have to stay in bed. Dr. Packer prescribed some kind of pink potion for her to drink, which must not have been much more than colored water, because sometimes when she was handed the glass, I would go with her behind the cob-house where she would throw it out. That didn't happen often because Mom watched her most of the time to be sure she drank it. Her ear stank terribly and she would ask me to smell it every day and tell her if it was getting better.

Her mastoid was healing and Christmas was approaching. We were getting back into living without serious illness and the fear accompanying it, when one of us came downstairs complaining of a sore throat. Once more there was an unmistakable rash and fever. It couldn't be scarlet fever, but what about German measles? Even though measles were not as serious as scarlet fever, it was not something to take lightly, especially so soon after having fought off the more serious disease. Once again we took our turn at being in bed for a week or more, until our temperatures were normal for at least twenty-four hours.

The big thing for me was the fact that we had to postpone Christmas. I learned early that life isn't necessarily fair and that one must learn to do things differently when necessary. At least we didn't have to be quarantined which meant Dad didn't have to stay out of the house. The measles seemed like a piece of cake after scarlet fever, even though it took several weeks for it to run its course, and each of us came down with it eventually. When one was sick, she had to stay in bed and was put on a liquid diet—lots of tomato or potato soup, Jell-o and puddings. That was just the way it was. That wasn't the worst part though; we were often given a dose of castor oil which was, no doubt, the worst tasting stuff ever concocted. However, there were some little perks, because when you were sick, Dad gave you a little bit of special attention. He would come in and say things like "Mighty soft" or "Pretty easy". Once in a while he would bring us gum or a bit of licorice candy. For me, it was special just having him pay attention to me, even if it didn't last for very long. Being one of seven children, those moments did not happen often.

My Mashed Thumb

We had a big old eight-passenger Marmon car which was the early version of an SUV. It had the regular two seats of a sedan, and in addition had two individual seats between the front and back seats. We had a gate down by the road which had to be opened and closed every time we came or went. When I was about five years old, we were returning from church, and one of my sisters got out to open the gate. When she got back in, she slammed the heavy door shut on my thumb. I was so stunned that it took a moment before I screamed.

I spent a couple of miserable hours that afternoon whimpering and crying softly. No matter what they did to divert my attention, it didn't work; I continued crying. Mid-afternoon Mother called Dr. Packer who met us at his office located less than a block from his home. He punctured the nail, relieving the pressure. I soon felt comfortable again and got to have a fancy bandage on my thumb. Imagine a doctor coming to his office on a Sunday afternoon for any reason, much less for a kid who had mashed her thumb. It would be a long time before there were walk-in clinics.

The good part was that when the nail began to loosen, Dad changed the bandage for me every day and talked to me about the progress my nail was making. He trimmed off any loose edges until finally the last bit of the original nail was gone.

Poor Drinking Water

A chronic health problem which affected all of us had to do with our supply of drinking water. We had a pump by the house, but it was so shallow that it got worms in it by mid-summer, and we had to carry water for drinking from a spring about a quarter of a mile north of the house. As a result of the less than pure water, we would get boils in the hot weather. None of us seemed to be immune. They were painful and would appear, live their ugly life span and slowly go away without serious consequences. However, one year when Dorothy was in her teens, she had a carbuncle on the under-side of her knee. A carbuncle is larger than a boil and has several heads. When it began sending red streaks up her leg, good old Dr. Packer had to come to our house and lance it. She was in danger of blood poisoning which could be fatal, but by staying in bed, and with the doctor's visits every couple of days, it finally healed. Slowly her leg returned to normal as did Dorothy, but she spent most of that summer on the cot in the living room. With antibiotics and good drinking water, boils and carbuncles are rare today.

Vonnie Tries Kerosene

Speaking of drinking, when Vonnie was old enough to get around on her own, she discovered the can of kerosene which was kept on the kitchen window sill to help start the fire in the kitchen range each morning. Vonnie managed to drink enough of it, before someone saw her, that she became violently ill. Mother called Dr. Packer and followed his directions as to what to do to make her vomit. I can still see Mom running up and down the sidewalk with Vonnie in her arms. I guess she was just releasing some of her own anxiety by running with her. I don't believe the doctor ordered that activity, but something worked and the kerosene was expelled. Vonnie returned to her usual good health and one more crisis was overcome.

My Six Siblings

Vonnie was the youngest of my six siblings. I didn't envy her, even though she was "the Baby" for a long time. Being the middle child of seven had its advantages but also its pitfalls. At least I wasn't the oldest, which would be tough for most of us. Dorothy handled it very well. She was the typical oldest child. She was responsible, with executive type characteristics present even today. She is the family historian, the genealogist, the one we call on if we want to know something about the history of the family. She is dependable, capable, caring and somewhat stoic. She was the one I ran to when I was small, whenever Juanita was getting the best of me. Dot would let me hide behind her. Juanita seemed to lose some of her power when I was standing next to Dorothy.

Betty was less serious than Dorothy. She was fun loving and somewhat mischievous. She liked to play jokes on people and did things with us younger siblings such as forming secret clubs. She, Juanita, Clay and I formed the "MF" (Mouse Finders or Marsh Fires) club. We four had secret meetings up in a field where we could not be seen from the house. We built a small fire, so we could roast marshmallows. Doing something we shouldn't be doing was exciting. I don't know how we got the marshmallows, but I expect Betty got them somehow. The big object of our club, besides getting by with being daring, was to pool our pennies and buy mother a Christmas gift.

Dad gave us a penny for every mouse we caught down at the mill. When I found some folding money stuck to the labeling table in the Red Building, it was a great boost to our treasury It seemed like it was a lot, but I think it was two or three ones. We had to debate whether we should give it to Dad to see if he knew who lost it, but decided as long as it went into our pot for the big gift it was okay to keep it. As Christmas drew near, the decision had to be made as to what to buy for Mother; we decided on a cast iron skillet. I'm not sure we even considered anything frivolous. We must have known she wanted a new skillet.

We wrapped it, and on Christmas Eve we put it outside by the front door. The tag we attached read, "From MF." Our school teacher was named Myra Fritz, and mother decided it must be from her; she called to thank her. When Mrs. Fritz didn't know what she was talking about, Mom kept puzzling over where it had come from. We didn't tell her for years about the MF club; it added to the excitement of having a secret club. And that is the kind of thing Betty liked to do, and still does. She is a fun-loving, impish woman.

As you may have guessed, Juanita was the most influential person in my life, as I bumbled my way through my growing up years. Our being close in age and passing as twins somehow accentuated her precociousness, cleverness and ability to make Mother laugh, juxtaposed as it was against my quiet, non-questioning, submissive behavior. It seemed to me that she was center stage and the stage was too small for more than one.

Clay, who was also near me in age, sixteen months younger, grew up in the same family, but memories of him as a kid are rare. He was a prankster and a storyteller (inherited from Dad) by the time he was in high school. He was the only male with six sisters, but he was the opposite of spoiled. He had to go out in the morning before dawn and help Dad with the chores. He was expected to do a lot of things we girls didn't have to do, merely because we were female. Dad didn't believe in girls helping in the fields or with the livestock, but Clay got initiated into that world quite young. I'm sure he wished he had some brothers instead of so many sisters.

I must have had a lot of interaction with Glenna, who was three years younger than I, but those memories are not retrievable either. She had auburn curly hair and was called "Pretty" when she was little. During her sophomore year in high school, she lived with Dorothy and her husband, Roy, in southern Illinois. During her junior year she lived with Aunt Mae (Mom's sister) and Uncle Frank in Westmont, Illinois, which is a suburb of Chicago. That helps to explain somewhat why there are so few memories of our relationship. She became a generous, caring woman, who is perceptive of the needs of others.

Vonnie was the youngest of seven. She grew up with more material things available to her than we older ones had, but she never got to experience our parents in the early years of their marriage when they were more compatible. She seemed different from my other sisters in some ways, bent on being independent and expressing her individuality. She was a pretty young woman, creative and outgoing. But that was when we were older and I knew her from afar—she lived in Arizona and I lived in Florida.

My Unfortunate Early Adjustments

I have many memories of Juanita who was very powerful in my eyes. I can't remember the first feelings of being inferior to her, but that feeling was there very early in my life. I could not measure up to her, so my unconscious determined that to survive I should be different. Don't talk. Don't compete. Be a blob. Those were not conscious decisions. But it became the way I saw myself before I was old enough to be aware of such things. My ego was protecting itself (me) in the best way it knew how. Early defenses are set in place for us—our unconscious at work when we are too young to know. An inferior self-image was integrated into my personality early; it defined the way I related to my family and to others. After behaving in a self-effacing manner for a long time, it did become who I was and how I saw myself.

I developed a strong sense of inferiority and low self-esteem during those important early years. Juanita was not much older than I, but she was lively, entertaining and cute. And I couldn't stand up to the long-awaited arrival of a son who was born when I was sixteen months old. It had nothing to do with what Clay or Juanita did; it was how I adapted to my situation. I was a few months younger than the precocious one and a few months older than the long-awaited son.

I could have handled it in many different ways, but ended up numbing all emotions so as not to feel anything too much (psychic numbing). In addition, I adopted the most primitive defense of all: denial. *Don't take in what is happening around you if it is too threatening. Don't see reality; see what you need to see.* Psychic numbing and denial— those two most powerful and primitive defenses, would have been all right for the first few years of my life, but I hung onto them into my adult life and became emotionally stunted. That condition defined me throughout my first thirty-nine years. Denial and psychic numbing were my protectors.

I can still see that little girl, who very early in life, unconsciously erected defenses against what she believed to be intolerable. Another way of saying it is that her baby ego figured out the best way to survive. It is common knowledge that none of us is born into the same situation as any of our siblings, nor are we treated the same, because we react differently and that changes the interaction. I know Mother and Dad were not overjoyed when I was born. Three girls was okay, but not the fourth one, and not so soon. Most of us would have been disappointed in that situation. I also know I was aware of it, deep in my soul. Kids know. Again, it was no one's fault and I am comfortable with that. My overriding memory of my childhood is of being inferior and "less than." I just didn't measure up.

Atmosphere at Home

Dad was a kind, loving man who wanted lots of kids. In my younger years, I remember that he loved all of us and would do whatever he thought necessary for our well-being. He had a tender heart, was fond of poetry, a great letter writer, loving toward his Mother and his sister, Aunt Pearl. (I was named for her; she was Katie Pearl, my name is Kathryn Pearl.) He liked to watch the birds and squirrels outside his window, had a bit of the jokester in him and was the greatest story teller ever. When we were small, he liked to rock us and sing funny little ditties to us. I thought he was perfect.

As a pre-teen, I became intensely aware of the lack of affection between Mom and Dad. They respected each other and shared many values, but there was no tenderness or indication of love as far as I could see. I was often aware of Mother's unhappiness, especially when she was humming some hymn; that alerted me to the fact that she was going through a tough time. There was too much tension and not enough light heartedness in that old house. Dad was often grumpy, and seemed to be angry much of the time.

Before he sat down to eat, we would think we had everything on the table that he would need or want. But, invariably, he found something lacking or wrong, and would hit the table with his fist and yell out his complaint. Or he walked heavily through the house, hell bent on his destination. We all knew to get out of his way before he ran over us. He was not to be messed with, and we all knew it; we didn't cross him.

Later in my teen years, he yelled and cursed which he didn't do when I was little. When he was driving with me in the front seat, he'd get angry and yell at me if I came even close to blocking his vision out the passenger window. He would scream and curse which made me want to be invisible. I often felt uptight around him—afraid I would bring down his wrath. He never hit me but once, but being physically abused is no more difficult to overcome than is being emotionally threatened. I could not imagine sitting down and having a conversation with him. I could sit down and listen to him, but not to share my life or to exchange ideas. I certainly wouldn't go to him with a problem.

I experienced Dad's gentle side when I was a child, but as I got older, the atmosphere was more often unpleasant, with not much laughter or pleasantries exchanged among the occupants of that old house. So much of his softness and gentleness seemed to have been buried by the circumstances of life on that farm. The times and cultural influences no doubt had their effect as did the lack of money and the long hard hours he and Mother labored. During the early part of the twentieth century, expectations of marital happiness and sexual satisfaction (for the female) had not reached the American family, certainly not the rural family. The old work ethic was still too strong and the important thing was to work and be frugal. It was much more important to Dad to buy farm land than it was to improve our living conditions. Having a nice home and a better life style were not on his priority list. Mother had no voice in the matter.

When I say I remember a little girl who was not very happy, that is what I am remembering: a home without enough laughter, affection or light-heartedness to counteract the harsh and unpleasant times. I needed to see my parents happy with each other and that was not to be. I can't imagine the difference it would have made in my life if I'd had parents who enjoyed each other and had affection toward each other. Or if they had been available for me to discuss my personal ups and downs as I went through childhood and the teen years. I have tried to picture life as a child with that kind of security.

Many of us who grow up without that secure feeling, grow up unscathed (at least outwardly), but for me it was a sadness which stayed with me for a long time. Again, it was the way I defended myself from infancy that got me in trouble. Instead of expressing my feelings to someone, I pushed them deeper and deeper into my psyche until many years later when, with help, I learned to express them more properly.

We still have the letters which Dad and Mother exchanged during World War I which reveal his sensitive, loving nature. They reveal the sharp wit and intelligence that was part of my Dad. What a shame that life took much of that softness and buried it so deeply that it surfaced only occasionally as he and Mother struggled relentlessly to provide what they deemed important to their seven children. They surely were in love when those letters were written in 1917 and 1918.

I feel certain had they lived at a later time, had they had an education and better living conditions, they would have been happier together. They were both intelligent, were both creative with a willingness to work hard. They were two wonderful people who did the best they could in their world. They raised seven children, all of whom loved them dearly and respected them highly (including me.) They did a lot of things right.

We can't do anything to change our lives until we recognize that our unhappiness is, to a great extent, due to our own behavior, to our own way of coping. And psychic numbing and denial are such primitive defenses that go so deep and so far back that they are not easily overcome without professional help. I could not see myself as others saw me; I held onto the image of that inferior person which was deeply engraved in my psyche. I believed myself to be less than bright, not attractive and without much to offer. I went about my life in a "dulled, bland, contented state"; went through the motions of living with a robot's mind. I lived with that blinded mindset until I was thirty nine years old.

Christmas Candy

There were many fun times, and we celebrated most holidays. Christmas was much anticipated with preparations beginning right after Thanksgiving, when Mother started making candy, and we kids began making out our wish lists. Mom made a lot of different kinds of candy but the candy bars and chocolate creams were the ones for which she was noted. I never heard of anyone else who made those the way she did. I might say "we did" because we girls helped as soon as we were tall enough to reach the work area.

The creams were made of fondant which we molded into little balls. We added different flavorings including peppermint, almond and wintergreen. After the candies became firm, we dipped them in dark chocolate which had a small amount of paraffin added.

The bars were made of divinity; they were rolled into bars about three inches long, dipped in chocolate and also stored until Christmas. The trick was to keep the two legged critters out of them until Christmas.

We also made peanut brittle, fudge, caramels, toffee and all kinds of cookies. We made popcorn balls with sorghum which were delicious. We made them at other times too, not just for the holiday season.

Later, when we were all married, each of us brought her own homemade goodies and we had big trays of sweets. When we were little Mother and Dad put out no more than was thought to be good for us to eat, but when we siblings were the parents, the loaded trays were sitting around all day and we had to attempt to control our appetites for sweets.

Our One-Room Schoolhouse

Six of us received the first eight years of our education in the Maxfield School, a one-room schoolhouse just down a hill and up a hill from our house. Vonnie went to town for her seventh and eighth grades after consolidation, when the one-room schoolhouses became extinct. There was no kindergarten to prepare one for first grade, so most kids didn't start until they were six. Without any school district rules, parents decided when their child started to school, usually at age six. Juanita started just before her fifth birthday in the spring, completing first grade and beginning second grade when she was five.

I was not able to start school at age five. My parents asked the teacher to come to our house to see if she could understand me, and much to my chagrin, I didn't pass her assessment. My problem was not so much speaking clearly as it was that I just couldn't say many words. I was so disappointed; Juanita was beginning second grade, and I couldn't even get into first.

I stood in the corner of our yard, watching across the way and seeing the kids playing during recess. I was so envious. My parents had consulted a doctor about my inability to talk and were told there was nothing wrong physically. Of course, a psychological cause was not even thought of in the 1920s.

Juanita was a quick learner and read to us younger kids before I was even able to talk. Since we passed as twins, it was more hurtful for me that she was able to do so many things that I was not able to do. I didn't understand why I couldn't keep up with her. And now I was two years behind Juanita in school instead of one. Knowing she was in the second grade, while I couldn't even begin first grade due to some flaw that wasn't my fault, didn't seem right to my five-year-old mind.

When I finally entered first grade, I was more than ready, although I still was limited in my ability to say many words and to pronounce them clearly. I couldn't pronounce my Rs until I was in second grade.

The school building was located so near our home that if you ran down a hill, cut through the barn lot, jumped over the slough, ran up a hill, crawled over a fence, you were AT SCHOOL. What a joy to be with the other kids and do all the fun things that I had only observed for the last two agonizing years. We had a fifteen minute recess mid-morning and mid-afternoon when we played all kinds of fun games such as Red Rover, Red Rover, May I Come Over?, Mother, May I?, and Andy Over. We also played our version of baseball.

In addition to the two recesses, we had an hour at noon for lunch, during which we Appenheimer kids ran home, got something to eat, and were back in time to play for a while, unless, of course, Mother had something for us to do, which was not unusual.

One of the chores we might be asked to do was to catch two or three chickens and cut their heads off so we could have fried chicken for supper that night. This wasn't too difficult since we had our dog, Silver. We let her know which chicken we wanted and she ran it down and held it with her front paws until we caught up with her. We carried the poor thing to the slaughtering block by its legs.

We put the victim's head under its wings and whirled it around a few times, so it would be dizzy and more docile. After we decided it was dizzy, and while holding it by the legs with its wings held so it couldn't flap around, we put its head on an old stump which we kept out back for that purpose. Holding the corn knife with its long, sharp blade in hand, we would decapitate that chicken with one fell swoop—if it cooperated and if our arm was steady that day. Otherwise, we might have to swing the blade more than once. Sometimes that first blow merely hacked off the beak or went the other way and cut into the crop, but we got better at that task as we had more practice. Pity the unfortunate creatures on whom we learned.

Once the head was separated from the body and the body quit twitching, we thrust it into a bucket of scalding hot water for just a moment—that made plucking its feathers much easier. The heavy, musty smell that rose from that water when the newly dead chicken was stuck in it, was just part of the process, there were worse smells on the farm. Our assigned chore done, we hurried back to school without worrying about the few blood splatters we might have here and there that attested to our time having been well spent. All of that was doable in an hour, along with a quick lunch.

The schoolhouse was one big room except for about ten feet across the front of the building. That front part was sectioned into three small rooms of equal size. One was the boy's cloak room, one the girl's cloak room, the third served as the entry-way and washroom. After each recess we came in, washed our hands, combed our hair and if we so desired we got a drink. There was a water bucket with a dipper which you used to fill your tin cup. The cups hung in a row above the table that held the bucket. Each cup had a name over it. *I wonder now if those cups were ever washed!* There was a small mirror on the wall over the towel rack. The towel was a continuous loop which fit over a roller and you pulled it down hoping to find a clean, dry place.

We all liked to be asked to fill the water pail at the pump because you could dilly dally and enjoy the outdoors for a few minutes. Except the older kids had told me not to stand on the wooden platform because the boogie man who lived in the well would reach up and grab me. They also told me there was another fearful creature that lived under the telephone poles and that was why some of the poles emitted a humming sound when you walked by. It was a long time before I knew for sure that it was safe to stand on the wooden frame of the well or to walk by the telephone poles whether they were humming or not.

In the back of the large room of our school was the round coal furnace. We were always comfortably warm during those cold Illinois winters. The furnace had a flat top which was insulated so the kids who were lucky enough to get to bring their lunches could use it as a warming tray for their hot foods.

The desks had seats attached; they were arranged in four rows according to size. There were three or four desks in each of the rows. Each desk had its small ink-well in the right hand corner. The top of the desk lifted up revealing storage space for books and such.

There were tall windows along the east and west sides which looked out over the rich farmland. Under the windows on the east side was a low utility table where we kept things like paper, scissors, jars of paste, crayons and other equipment used by elementary school kids in the 1920s and 1930s. George Washington's portrait hung on one wall, and a large map of the United States on another. There were three large blackboards, two in front and one on the west side. We all liked to be asked to take the erasers out to pound the chalk dust out of them. Another chance to enjoy being outside.

The teacher's desk was in front, facing the rows of desks. The red recitation bench was in front of the rows of desks facing the teacher. Each class took its turn sitting on the bench and reciting for the different subjects. For reading class we read out loud and discussed what we had read; for arithmetic we handed in what we'd been assigned and probably did some problems on the board. So it went for each subject that included history, geography, spelling, reading, English, and arithmetic. The curriculum did not include science, art, music, drama or physical education, but we got our exercise during recess and the lunch hour. We did have some time on Friday afternoon during which we colored pictures and did what might have been called art in those days.

All eight grades weren't usually represented in any one year, and this fact helped the teacher have time to teach those of us present. The children of six families attended, and only two of those had more than three kids; one family had one child. The McRells had seven boys and one girl as opposed to our six girls and one boy. Our two families made up a high percentage of the student body.

I was the only one in my class until third grade when Charles McRell was demoted from the fourth grade. Mrs. Fritz told him in the middle of the day in front of all of us, and he had to move over into an empty seat right behind me. He started crying, and continued until he threw up, with some of it landing on my back. Mrs. Fritz told me I could go home. I flew home only to find that mom was out in the garden, so I changed my dress and went back to school. I'm sure the teacher was amazed to see me, and I don't know how good I smelled, but I took my seat as if nothing had happened. Charles and I were the only ones in that class through eighth grade.

Some of our courses were quite superficial compared to today. I know my knowledge of history was not very inclusive, even after the four years of high school. It was all so simple back then. Most families didn't even have radios; we got ours when I was in fourth or fifth grade, and our social and intellectual stimulus was minimal. But the quality of education was of no concern, because that was the norm throughout our farming community, and no one knew the difference. After all, most of the boys were going to be farmers, and the girls would marry one of the farmers, so why worry? Of course, many went on to college and professional careers, but some did not, especially the girls.

Lake Calhoun

While I was in the elementary grades, and the depression still had its grip on the economy, we managed to join the Lake Calhoun Association, which was the only such recreational facility around. It cost something like twenty dollars, but that was more than Dad had to spend on such a luxury. Mom promoted the idea, knowing we would benefit from a family membership. Determined to get the money together, we each put in any money we had, which might be fifty cents or less, and Mother put in some she had hoarded away. The man who worked for Dad put in what he could (we would take their kids when we went.) With what she had collected Mother went to Dad who put in the balance, and we got our membership.

Lake Calhoun was where the action was—that's where families, young kids and teenagers went for recreation. We had swimming lessons during the week. Mother drove us over for those lessons and she drove us to Kewanee (about fifteen miles) for dance lessons. We each had at least one year of piano lessons. She was the one who made sure that we got experiences in sports and the arts which she thought were important for us.

Lake Calhoun wasn't much of a lake, but was the only one around. We were used to the muddy creek, so we didn't mind. A wooden walkway led out to the platform with a diving board. Once we were good swimmers, we were allowed to swim out to the second raft where there was a high diving board. After Mom could rely on us to watch out for each other, she'd take her blanket up on a hill, under a shade tree and away from the noise. She could read and doze while we were swimming. She must have loved that time, resting in the peaceful, quiet outdoors away from the continual demands.

There were two separate dressing areas with showers, one for men and one for women. A small refreshment stand where ice cream, soft drinks and candy were sold sat between the two areas. We knew better than to ask for money to spend for a treat. Our treat was just getting to go; we didn't feel deprived.

Labor Day was a minor holiday, but important because it meant school was starting the next day. I don't recall celebrating it in any way until we joined Lake Calhoun. Most of the members went to the lake on Labor Day because a fish fry was held on that day. People brought their own picnic dinners except meat. The hot fried fish was free with no limit on how much each family could eat. Sometimes friends who were not members would join us, and often brought large cans of pork'n beans that we never had, because we didn't buy canned beans. I thought they were much better than the ones we canned, and was so glad when I saw that can of beans appear on the table.

The Baptist Church

In the summer, we always went to the lake on Sunday afternoons, but on Sunday mornings we attended the Baptist Church, where we were members from the time we were born until we either married or left home. Mother had to get up at 4:00 A.M. to get shoes polished, and dresses pressed, so everyone looked presentable. By the time each of us was ten or eleven we took care of our own clothes and helped Mom with the younger ones. We filled up one whole pew—stair-steps of tow-headed little ones with shiny faces and subdued demeanor (hopefully). When Dorothy was eleven, there were seven of us. We knew better than to misbehave—not that we were threatened or scared of what would happen. We just knew we better be good during that hour.

Of course, we weren't such angels all of the time. Sometimes we would get the giggles over some ridiculous thing, maybe just the fact that we were not supposed to giggle. But all Mother had to do was give us "that look" and we straightened up.

We attended Sunday school before church. As a small child our classes were held in the basement with Miss Hines and Mrs. Claybough. We learned some of the stories of the Bible, memorized a few Bible verses, the Lord's Prayer, and put our pennies in the little tin cup that was passed around as we sang Jesus Loves Me.

During the high school years our Sunday school classes were held upstairs. For a long time Mr. Griffith, the County School Superintendent, was our teacher. He was a staid, rigid person, about as dynamic as a spent firecracker. Classes were very boring to me. I don't think I learned anything, partly because of the presentation, but mostly because I wasn't interested. I went for the social aspect and because that is what we did on Sunday morning. Often in church or class, I would think about what I was going to wear at the next school event or on my next date, or I'd think about what I was going to do that afternoon. I didn't absorb much about the contents of the Bible, or the significance of Christianity and what it might mean in my life. When I was in high school I received a nice Bible for having the best attendance at the youth meetings on Sunday nights. I won because of the challenge, not that I necessarily wanted the Bible.

When I was still in high school, it seemed to me that sin meant one thing: sex before marriage. Not too much emphasis was placed on what we could do for society at large, loving each other, taking care of the less fortunate, or just what love can accomplish when we practice it in our daily lives.

During those years I never thought about what it does for one's soul simply by having one hour a week during which you get outside your own private world, worship the Lord, sing hymns full of praise and contemplate the wonders of His universe. But our regular attendance at church was not entirely wasted on me either. I was prepared for later in life when I would need to fall back on a belief in something more powerful than myself. I am grateful for that foundation and in awe of Mother, who so fervently wanted her children to have the advantage of a religious background, and rose before dawn in order to get her brood there in their Sunday best. She never had a day off. How tempting it must have been to take a Sunday morning off once in a while and just rest. But I doubt the thought ever entered Mother's mind. On Sundays we went to church and Sunday school, period.

High School 1939-1943

I wasn't a scholar of religion, and I certainly wasn't a scholar when I entered Toulon Township High School in the fall of 1939. Although the United States had not declared war yet, the whole world, even in farming communities like ours, was in turmoil. The world's focus during my four years of high school was on World War II. It affected everyone, including teens in high school. Friends and relatives were being drafted, or had enlisted. The social mood was somber. Even so, my high school years were good.

My freshman year I managed to become one of the majorettes for the newly formed marching band. Juanita was a junior and at first showed an interest in being a majorette. My parents said they could afford to pay for only one of us and, of course, she was older so should get to if she wanted. Luckily for me, she decided she didn't really want to, so I was in. The ten or so would-be twirlers took a few lessons in Peoria, and then it was just practice, practice, practice.

Midway through that first football season I was asked to be the lead majorette, which I was for the rest of my four years. When I was a senior, I won first in the state for schools the size of ours and was eligible to go to the nationals, which were held in Minnesota that year. I didn't get to go, but I was confident in my ability and proud of the medals I had won. More importantly, I simply loved doing it. I enjoy band music and marches to this day and still feel deep within my bones, the exhilaration of those long marches with the band behind me and being able to strut my stuff. So you see there was *that part* of me that was able to let go and do what I liked to do. It just wasn't enough to allow my psyche to let go of those strong defenses which continued to paint my self-image with dark colors.

I got to go to all the football and basketball games and Mother went to most of them with me. One time when it had been raining, we had a small crisis. I had polished my white boots which were part of my costume, and Mother carried them as we headed to the car. At the end of the sidewalk she fell and the boots went into the mud. She was not hurt and was so apologetic. Right away she said she would help clean up the boots and I could just go on. I told her I could clean the boots while she changed and got cleaned up. In a jiffy we set out again. She was a wonderful mother, and I knew she really hated to miss a game.

The football and basketball games were fun, but the proms were always special, especially for us girls. I wore Juanita's prom dresses both my junior and senior years. I really didn't like one of them—a black taffeta skirt with a white satin top—but I wouldn't complain. If I had just said I didn't want to wear it, I'm sure I could have had one of my own. But I think I wanted so to please my parents, I was also aware of our lack of money. Anyway, I wore her hand-me-downs both years and felt badly about it. My inability to speak up about such things, because of my low self-esteem, negatively influenced me then and for years to come. Only I could change being the one who was "less than" and the time was coming, but still a long way off.

Working for Zella and Roy Dutton

Throughout my high school years I worked for a farm family on week-ends during the school year and all week through the summers. Zella and Roy Dutton had two little girls, who were three and five when I began helping them. Zella had migraine headaches on an average of once a week. On those days she stayed in bed all day with the blinds drawn, and I had the responsibility of getting dinner for Roy, their hired man and the two girls. They didn't have electricity or running water. Everything was made from scratch, and vegetables were grown in the garden. But they had a generator which kept a refrigerator running, so we could keep things cold.

I really enjoyed living with them. I didn't work any harder than I did at home, but I felt appreciated and special in many ways. Roy and Zella got along so well, and it was plain to me that they enjoyed being with each other. The atmosphere was filled with love and kindness, such a pleasant experience for me. The girls and I were included in the conversation during meals. And I actually got paid $2.50 a week, money I could spend on clothes at the end of the summer.

One day Zella came stumbling in from the garden, talking in gasps and trying to tell me she had seen a big snake out by the gate. She wanted me to get Roy, so he could kill it. I figured I could kill the snake with a hoe that was right there in the garage. She was close to collapsing, and I assured her I could kill the dragon. I went out and made short work of chopping that snake into two pieces. They never got over telling that story. I'm not at all sure I could do that today even if I wanted to.

Roy and Zella had to go to a funeral one day, and I was to get dinner ready for the hired man and the girls. All went well until we were finished eating and the girls ran outside. The man got up and started coming around the table saying he just wanted a kiss. I don't remember what I said to him, but I know my body language must've told him how scared I was. As he came on around the table, I got my chance and ran outside where the girls were. He went back to the fields. When Roy and Zella came home, I told them about it. Roy fired the man when he came in that afternoon. He never doubted my word nor hesitated to make sure it didn't happen again.

I felt so much a part of their family after I'd been there a while. I felt I was special, which surely was a new experience and one I seemed to hunger for. A few years after I was no longer with them, Zella went to an allergy clinic somewhere in the west and found out her headaches were a result of an allergy to wheat. She cut wheat from her diet and was free of those debilitating migraines.

Rosie the Riveter 1943-1944

High school had been fun for me; I didn't demand too much of myself, as far as grades. My major concern was dating and having a good time. I had come from that one-room school house with an average attendance of 12 students to the High School with about three hundred students, small but big in comparison. I liked it. I was popular and well-liked, but I held tenaciously to my sense of inferiority. I went through those four years without being able to shake the negative self-image I carried with me. Even though I received As and Bs without too much work, I continued to believe I was not too bright. That doesn't make sense, but primary defenses can hide reality from their victim who can't see the world as others do.

My husband-to-be, Dean Young, and I graduated in 1943. World War II was raging. The United States had been one hundred percent involved since December, 1941. As did most able-bodied male high school graduates, Dean went immediately into the service. He joined the Navy and received his basic training at Great Lakes Naval Training Center near Chicago. I went to Ypsilanti, Michigan where I became one of many women referred to collectively as "Rosie the Riveter." I worked as a riveter on the wing of the B24 bombers in the largest factory under one roof in the country, River Rouge. Before the war it had been a Ford manufacturing plant.

Where did I get the idea of going to Ypsilanti and working in a factory? An eighteen year old who had never been out of the state of

Illinois? Mother heard these jobs being advertised over the radio and suggested I might be able to get work there. I would make more money than as a secretary in the little town of Toulon, IL. So she contacted them, and I was hired as a riveter, as was, I suppose anyone who applied. They needed able-bodied workers—including riveters.

Juanita had gone to the University. But I didn't dare attempt such a thing as to take a college course. Why did Juanita and I choose such different paths at that important juncture in our lives? I had always thought she knew best.

Juanita and I were raised as twins and brought up under the same roof with the same parents, but we were not treated the same. The difference in the way we were treated was not overt, but was more subtle and certainly not done consciously. And that difference was in expectations. My behavior had given the message: don't expect too much.

I was eighteen years old, but I couldn't rely on my own attributes, couldn't see the world as it actually was but as it appeared to my heavily defended self. I should have been able to see that I was attractive, bright, capable and worthy. Instead, I felt I was not very smart, not very attractive, and certainly not worthy. I hesitated to make decisions, and often would ask Juanita for her opinion, instead of figuring out what I liked or thought.

With that self-image, I soon had my tool-box in hand and was on a bus headed to Detroit. I was so green and naive I think the Lord looked after me those first few weeks. As soon as I got off the bus, I asked a cab driver to take me to a good hotel where I could stay for one night. He dropped me off at a small hotel. The next morning, with my suitcase, my tool kit and all the courage I could muster, I went out onto the streets of the city to find a policeman for directions to the factory called River Rouge in Ypsilanti. Talk about some meek soul coming in out of the countryside! The policeman gave me directions to the bus station, and the bus driver told all of us where to get off to report for orientation.

We were shuttled several places and had to wait in long lines to complete the paperwork for becoming honest-to-goodness employees. But at the end of the day, we each had a badge, a dark one-piece uniform, a scarf to tie up our hair, and instructions of where to report the next day.

It took all day to go through the process of being quizzed, informed and oriented. During that process I met a woman who lived in Ann Arbor. She told me there was a vacant room in the house where she lived, so I rode with her later that afternoon and took the room. It was upstairs, very small and about the size of a closet. An army cot served as a bed, an orange crate was set on end for a lamp stand and there was a rack for a closet. There was no window.

After a restless night, I readied myself for the day and went down to catch my ride. What a shock awaited me at the bottom of the stairs. A man was laying with one of the girls on the couch and another man with another girl on the floor—in a house where only single women lived. I was aghast. So began my learning the ways of the world. I could not deny that those girls were sleeping with men to whom they weren't married.

The first week on the job I met a woman at the portable lunch wagon which came around at meal time. Pauline was also eighteen and just out of high school. After the first day, we started eating our sandwiches together and got acquainted. She sympathized when I told her of the awful place where I was staying, and told me she wanted to move out of her father's house, but he didn't want her living alone in the city. We decided to get a room together, and our next day off we rented a room in Ann Arbor where we lived together for the next year. We had a bed, a desk, a couch and a closet. We shared the bathroom down the hall with several other roomers. It was anything but luxurious. But she and I got along very well and didn't mind our meager quarters.

Pauline's father was a Methodist minister who lived about twenty miles from Ann Arbor. She had an older sister, Eva, who spent a lot of time with us and was in love with a married man, Ed. He sometimes came to our place to get her. I learned to like Eva a lot and Ed was nice, but I had difficulty accepting their relationship; things like that were just not supposed to be. One night Pauline and I came home, and Eva was there, obviously in great anguish. Ed's wife had been waiting for them when they left the house to get into his car. I think that led to Ed's divorce, because he and Eva were married later and lived together until he died. He was quite a bit shorter than Eva and nearly twenty years older. I couldn't understand it all with my frozen little mind. It would have been impossible for me to believe that later in my life I was going to be an actor in a similar episode.

Pauline had married her high school sweetheart, Dick Amo, immediately upon graduating. A couple of weeks later, he was shipped to Juneau, Alaska, where he remained for the duration of the war. After graduating from basic training at Great Lakes, Dean was sent to Miami to train as a Rear Gunner in a fighter plane. Pauline and I wrote "our men" every day and received letters from them nearly every day.

We worked swing shift, two weeks on each of three shifts. We managed to stay on the same shift, so we could ride together, and so we would be sleeping at the same time since we had only one room. We worked six days a week. We learned to adjust to sleeping different hours every two weeks. The most difficult shift for us was the midnight to eight A.M. It took some time to get adjusted to sleeping during the day. We had to eat all of our meals out, which was new to both of us; we found a couple of family-run cafes that were reasonable. Neither of us was sophisticated enough to object to greasy, boring food.

We usually went to at least one movie on our day off; sometimes we went to two in one day. All the good old war movies which made us cry were our favorites. "To The Shores of Tripoli," "The Best Days of Our Lives," "Guadalcanal Diary" and "Bataan" are some that I recall. Most movies were about the war—everything was about the war, and everyone was involved in it, one way or the other.

Many things were rationed, including gas. You received gas coupons allowing you an amount of gas depending on your work. Farmers got an unlimited amount for their tractors and other needs. Few farmers abused that right. When I was a student in high school, we couldn't have many dates to go out of town to a movie, and people didn't take vacations which required driving. No tires were being manufactured; rubber was for war vehicles, planes, and other equipment. Coffee, sugar, meat, detergent and many other items were rationed. Nylon was non-existent on the home front; all went for parachutes and other needs of the soldiers. Once in a while some detergent would arrive at Kroger's and each of us would get our one box. No appliances were being manufactured, no refrigerators, stoves, mixers, furniture, nor even the smaller utensils if made of metal or rubber. Even gum and chocolate were scarce; those items as well as cigarettes were being sent overseas to the fighting men.

I don't remember any one ever complaining. Everyone had someone in combat, preparing to go into combat, or someone who had been killed in combat. I had four brothers-in-law and three uncles in the war as well as nearly every male I knew under forty. With all of our men gone and in danger, how could we complain of not having coffee or a new pair of nylons?

Pauline and I didn't have a car so the shortage of gas didn't impact us. Most things we needed were close enough to walk to including the theaters. I didn't even miss having a car; I had never had one so didn't know the difference. I was making what I considered a lot of money, certainly a lot more than the two and a half dollars a week I received working six days for the Duttons.

Everyone at the factory was expected to buy U.S. Savings Bonds, and I was glad to be one of them. But I still had enough discretionary money to buy my siblings and my parents a nice gift for Christmas. I had fun picking out a sweater for each of my sisters and felt great being able to send such nice presents. I spent Christmas (my first ever away from home) with Pauline's parents. Eva was there and a couple whom I didn't know. I was quite homesick and just glad when the day was over.

My work as a riveter was a challenge, but at eighteen it didn't seem too difficult to me. I had a partner who was called the "bucker." The riveter drives the rivet in place with a riveting gun, and the bucker is on the other side of the metal you are riveting, holding a flat piece of iron with a handle, bucking each rivet as you go along the seam to be closed. If he failed to be in place, the rivet and the gun went through the material, which then had to be mended. As you can imagine, that slowed the team up a lot and was to be avoided.

My bucker, Charlie, was a man in his thirties who liked to goof off; he joked a lot and often told me I went too fast. Some days Charlie was slower than other days. When he missed the mark two times in one four-hour period, I became upset and was near tears. We had just been told we needed to increase production. His causing us to mess up twice was too much.

Our supervisor, who was a soft-spoken kind man, saw I was upset and told me to take a break. As soon as I returned he asked me if I was okay.

"I'm usually fine, I became anxious because we had to repair twice this morning, and now we can't make our quota."

"If you don't make your quota one day, it's okay. Your team has a good record." With that he left, and I went back to the job of fixing the hole so Charlie and I could get back to work.

Riveting was physically demanding work; there were times when I had to lie on my back and hold the gun above my head which was difficult, but I had a sense of pride in doing what I saw as my part in the war effort. The newsreel at one of the movies showed a B-24 dropping bombs during a major battle and Pauline and I talked about it later—we might have helped build that plane. But I was beginning to have some physical problems related to hernia surgery I'd had two years earlier. After consulting a doctor, I decided to leave the riveting job and return home where I could find work in an office. I'd proven to myself I could go out on my own and survive. I'd fulfilled my need to do something meaningful for the war effort. I soon found myself back on a bus, but this time I was not so anxious.

Pauline stayed in Ann Arbor until the end of the war. We continued our friendship until she died suddenly in her early thirties, of a brain tumor, leaving three small children. I was sorry to lose such a good friend.

I got a job as secretary for a lawyer in Toulon which I kept for only a few months. Dean was still in Miami; all I could think about was joining him and getting married. By June I had a one-way bus ticket to Miami, had quit my job, said my goodbyes and off I went—hell bent on getting married.

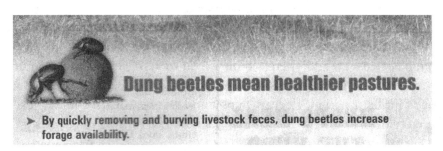

Dung beetles mean healthier pastures.

➤ By quickly removing and burying livestock feces, dung beetles increase forage availability.

1977 Kate visiting the abandoned one-room schoolhouse

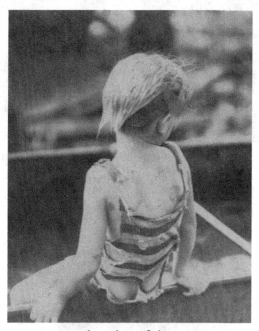

Kate sitting on the edge of the swimming pool
(horse tank) in her swimsuit in 1930

1927 Clay, Kate, Juanita, Betty and Dorothy

Clay and Silver

Juanita and Kate (back row),
Glenna and Vonnie with Silver

Kate and Juanita in barn window

Kate in 7th grade at schoolhouse.

Kate and her Japanese parasol.

Kate at parade in Peoria.

Kate's dress sewn by Mom with rabbit fur collar

Mom and Dad as young newlyweds

Mom and Dad on their 25th Anniversary

1977 Old barn standing alone other buildings gone

Grinding sorghum cane with pummies falling on haystack

Sorghum Mill with red building on left

Chapter 2

A Vanilla Marriage

One year after getting out of high school and soon after returning home from my defense job in Michigan, I bid goodbye to my parents and my younger siblings, boarded a bus, and set out for Miami to marry my high school boyfriend, Dean Young. He was 5' 7" tall and I was 5' 5" tall. Dean was a good basketball player because of his quickness on the court. During his elementary years, he had been an acrobat, and I thought he was cute. We were married in the chapel of a Methodist Church in Miami on July 31, 1944.

We both turned nineteen that month; the minister may have had qualms about marrying us, but marrying young was not unusual in the forties, when the average age for females was twenty and for males twenty three. But looking back, I realize that I didn't know diddlysquat about life in general or the responsibilities involved in being married. I certainly didn't begin to know who I was or what undeveloped characteristics lay dormant within me. However, I thought I was in love, and it was exciting to go to Miami. Besides, we had necked a lot, and I wanted to have sex. And we dared not have sex, rather I dared not, until we were married, because there was too great a risk of getting pregnant. That was the worst possible thing for a young, unmarried woman in the first half of the twentieth century. What a pitiful motivation for getting married.

My Dad had given me twenty dollars when he took me to catch the bus to Miami. As he handed it to me, he said, "This is for dinner the day you get married." Twenty dollars paid for a nice dinner in 1944. It's significant that I don't have memories of those first few weeks as Dean's wife.

I rented a room not far from a bus line and got a job making shell jewelry. The room was a second-floor room, skimpily furnished and rather dreary, but there were not too many rentals available. The job required little brain power. I stuck different shells on a small piece of plastic and let them dry. I got paid by the piece, and I didn't earn much, but that wasn't a priority; at least I had a job. Dean had no way of notifying me when he had a night's leave, but he usually joined me a couple of times a week.

As often as possible, I took the jitney over to the big USO Center in Miami Beach. If Dean got off duty unexpectedly, he knew I would be on that beach on my days off. The few hotels on the beach in the early forties were some distance apart and were occupied by the military services. I could hardly believe I was sunning on the beautiful beaches of Miami, while those unfortunate people back in Illinois were digging out from a big snow storm. I got a lot of attention from the crowds of sailors, but I couldn't acknowledge that I actually had a very nice figure and was cute. I was a nineteen-year-old married woman and not supposed to notice other men. It was safer for me to ignore the sailors' attention.

Miami was a relatively small city with many outdoor cafes and fruit vendors—already a touristy atmosphere. However, for an Illinois farm girl it was an exciting, bustling city. I rode the bus everywhere I went. The unfamiliar smell of the exhaust that choked me, the clanging of the doors shutting, and the racing of the bus's motor pulling away from the curb is still a vivid memory.

Dean's training as rear gunner took place near Miami at the Opa-locka Naval Air Base. In preparation for being sent to the European front, he was transferred to Norfolk, Virginia. Tragically, Dean's pilot was killed during night training at the Norfolk base. That meant that Dean had to go back to Miami and train again with another pilot. He had told me that men were killed during the training, especially during the night flying, but it didn't seem real until his pilot was killed. I was glad that Dean didn't have to go overseas, but sad that it was because of a young man's death.

Moving Around With the Navy 1944-1945

When Dean left for Norfolk to be deployed, I went back home. So, when he called me with the news that he was returning to Opa-locka for additional training, I happily headed back to Miami. Women traveling alone during wartime had to be ingenious in order to get a seat on a bus. Service men had priority, and most often there were no seats left for civilians, except for wives accompanying their husbands. After a few times of being left at the station, I learned to "adopt a husband" long enough to board the bus with him. Traveling was exciting for me; if there were inconveniences, they didn't ruffle my feathers for long.

This second time in Miami, I got a job typing and filing in the Adjutant General's office. I enjoyed the job a lot, but didn't get to keep it for as long as I had hoped. Dean's new flight crew was soon shipped to Detroit, then immediately transferred to Memphis. An officer's wife hired me to take care of her one-year-old baby girl. I took her to the zoo and to the park, where I pushed her in her stroller or watched her as she ran and played. People would tell me what a cute baby I had; I would smile and say, "Thank you."

I found a room through a Baptist Church whose members rented rooms to service men's wives. That was a fun experience; they invited me to eat with them a couple of times a week, which was great. They had a little dog named Skeeter, and I can still hear that southern lady say, "Skeetah, you ah-a-may-us."

Dean got leave less frequently than he had in Miami. When he did get the evening off, we'd eat at some nearby diner and then we'd have sex. We never had a lot of time together since he had to get up early the next morning to return to the base.

After just a couple of months in Memphis, Dean received orders to report to a base near Long Beach, California. He got a furlough before reporting for duty in Long Beach. We traveled by bus to Illinois to tell our families the exciting news that I was pregnant. We enjoyed those few days with our families. Sharing the excitement of the pregnancy and of going to the West Coast was wonderful. We weren't mature enough to be concerned about making any preparations for becoming parents. We never talked about the possibility of Dean's going overseas, and my being by myself and pregnant. We were still just kids having an adventure.

To California by Train

We decided to go by train from Chicago to Los Angeles rather than by bus. We thought it would be more comfortable. But we soon found out that conditions on a bus might have been better. As we traveled across the Southwestern states, the summer's heat became terribly unpleasant. We had to leave the windows open (no air-conditioning on the train), and the hot air, filled with black smoke from the coal-driven steam engines, blew in through the windows and occupied the space with us. We became more and more speckled with soot as we slowly, steadily made our way westward. I spent many wretched hours back in the caboose hanging over the railing throwing up. But after two full days we arrived in Los Angeles looking like a couple of blackened waifs. It took forty-eight hours to go from Chicago to Los Angeles in 1945.

I was unable to find any kind of work in Long Beach. I rented a room in a high rise on the beach at the base of Long Beach's famous Rainbow Pier. I could look out on the ocean and go to sleep listening to the peaceful rhythm of the surf as it came ashore. Since I could not find a job, I could guiltlessly enjoy endless hours sunning and reading on the sandy beach.

Dean was on the base most of the time and, again, I never knew when he might get a night off, so I was essentially on my own. Enjoying the luxurious surroundings and my leisurely life, I really didn't mind. My pregnancy was coming along without any problems, except that one afternoon while the two of us were standing in line at a movie theatre, I fainted. When I came to, we went on in and enjoyed the movie. That never happened again.

I was under the care of a navy doctor who had given me a book for counting calories, and told me if I wanted the Navy to deliver my baby I could not gain more than nineteen pounds. He warned me that I would be disqualified for their care if I went over that magic number. I learned all I could about calories and still use that knowledge today to keep my weight under control. But it surely was difficult to gain such a small amount while pregnant. I ate a lot of vegetables, especially after I moved back with my folks.

World War II Is Over

We were in Long Beach when the war ended. Victory in Europe occurred on May 8, 1945. The first of two atom bombs was dropped on Hiroshima, Japan, on August 6, 1945. The second atom bomb was dropped on Nagasaki three days later. The Japanese surrendered on August 15, 1945. The war was over; celebrating began.

I went out by myself and walked around amid the cacophony of blowing horns, people singing, fireworks exploding, people making any kind of noise they could. Dean didn't get off, and I didn't want to stay out in the crazed mass by myself. Near my hotel, the celebrating was less boisterous. I was able to join in all the discussions and conjecturing about the dropping of the atom bombs which had heralded the war's end. I stayed on the boardwalk where I could safely enjoy the celebratory atmosphere. All over the country people were wildly celebrating.

Because I was pregnant, I was sort of a misfit as the evening faded into night. Some of the sailors were getting pretty brazen, grabbing any woman available and smooching her. People didn't seem to know how to express the tremendous emotions that were brought forth by the end of the long costly war. Most of the mass of celebrants on the streets were strangers to the area and to the hundreds of other individuals milling about, laughing, crying, singing, shouting—anything that released some of the exuberance everyone was experiencing.

I felt vulnerable being in that crowd by myself, so I left and went on up to my room while the celebrating continued into the wee hours. But I had a lot to think about—what was I going to do and would Dean still have to go overseas? *The War Is Over* kept racing through my head. Maybe it would sink in during the next few days. I was eager for Dean to come home so I could find out what he knew about his status in the Navy.

Most of my teen years had been dominated by the war. Now it was over, and those who survived would be coming home soon. It was almost more than one could take in; the war was really over. No more dread of a loved one being killed in action or severely wounded. No more slaughter of innocent civilians. On the more frivolous but meaningful side, Americans would once again be manufacturing cars, tractors, lawn mowers, refrigerators, and cooking utensils—even such expendables as nylon hose, toys, chocolate, and detergents. It would be some time before the world would get back to a semblance of normality, but we knew now that we would be moving in that direction.

WWII had ended and the Cold War was to begin before the decade was over. Also, before the forties ended, we would see the birth of the United Nations. Franklin Delano Roosevelt had died April 12, 1945, and Harry S. Truman was now president.

Men would be joyously reuniting with wives and lovers, mothers and fathers, brothers and sisters. Dads would be coming home to see their sons and daughters, some for the first time. For us it meant Dean might not have to go overseas and might even be discharged before our baby was born. He had not been told anything for sure about what he could expect—there was a lot of scuttlebutt; nothing was for certain. We decided I should return to Illinois as soon as I could get a ticket, knowing he might still be sent overseas. At least I had matured enough to know that I shouldn't be alone in California with a baby due.

Back To Illinois

With the assistance of a chaplain, I was able to get a lower berth back to Illinois, only because I was visibly pregnant. No hanging over the caboose this time. There were few passengers who were not in uniform. The train was divided into compartments of four seats which were made into berths at night. The other three occupants of my compartment were all male officers who were very solicitous of me. I joined them in a card game, everyone having agreed ahead of time that the "low man buys the others' dinners." I guess I didn't think of losing, because I surely couldn't afford what was bound to be four expensive dinners. Of course, I lost. One of the gentlemen said, "We said low MAN." Very graciously they relieved me of that financial burden. I must have looked pitiful or so young and innocent that they felt protective of me. What a different trip that was from the one Dean and I had made just a few months before. And what a difference in the lifestyle I was facing by heading back to Illinois.

I was soon living with my folks and three younger siblings—Clay, Glenna, and Vonnie. I was able to watch my diet much easier on the farm. I ate a lot of fresh vegetables and fruit and managed to keep my weight-gain below nineteen pounds. I even helped make the Christmas candy without eating any, and I refused the yeast rolls, pies, and all the other good foods abundant during the Holidays. I had a lot of will power even then.

Clay's Accident Late 1945

Clay had been deferred from the service his first year out of high school, because he was needed on the farm. But he enlisted in the Marine Corps in late November 1945. Before reporting for basic training, he was given the standard two weeks off. He stayed busy getting things done around the farm to help Dad prepare for his absence. Since it was already mid-December, they decided that before Clay left, he should help an older neighbor pick the last of his corn, otherwise it might not get picked. The neighbor welcomed the help, and Clay began picking the next day. A light snow had fallen during the night, and it turned quite cold.

Mid-morning of the second day, as Clay was going up and down the rows of corn, Mr. Miller, the neighbor, drove up to see how he was doing. Clay jumped off the tractor and walked over to talk with him. As the man got back into his car, Clay started back around the picker to get on the tractor. But, as fate would have it, he slipped on a patch of ice and fell right in front of the metal claws which were intended to pull the ears of corn off the stalk and carry them up into the wagon. One of those claws got just enough of Clay's pant leg to pull it and his leg into the grasping machinery. He frantically screamed, hoping Mr. Miller was still within hearing distance.

Mr. Miller did hear and came running. When he got close enough, he saw Clay's leg was being chewed up, and the only reason he was not being pulled further into the metal monster was because Clay still had enough strength to brace himself against the machine. But Clay was losing a lot of blood and growing weaker. Mr. Miller panicked and couldn't think of what to do, so Clay yelled out instructions: turn off the tractor; unscrew that top bolt; unscrew the ones below; lift that lever and… The claws began to loosen. Mr. Miller was finally able to lift the machine enough to free Clay's mangled leg.

My brother rode in the back seat of Mr. Miller's car into town where Dad was working for the Rationing Board. As they entered the city limits, they spotted Dad at a gas station where he was getting gas, because Clay had a date that night. After lifting Clay from the neighbor's car to Dad's, they took off for the Kewanee Hospital, fifteen miles away. Clay never lost consciousness.

An orthopedic surgeon was called in from Peoria; he and the Kewanee general surgeon, whom my folks had dealt with before, began to work to try to save the leg which was severely injured. They labored together into the night doing all they could to set the shattered bones. By the time Dad arrived home in the wee hours of the next morning, he had been told that Clay might have a limp, but they had saved his leg. Mother stayed at the hospital with Clay.

A few days later, Dad didn't come home from his evening hospital visit. I was in the seventh month of my pregnancy, still living with the folks. I couldn't get to sleep, not knowing what was going on with Clay. I had finally dozed off when I heard Dad's car come up the hill. I was waiting for him when he came into the kitchen looking like he didn't know where he was. He walked right past me into the living room and sat down without saying a word. It was obvious that Clay had taken a turn for the worse.

I followed Dad into the living room and waited for him to speak to me. When he didn't, I asked, "What happened, Dad?"

He continued his glassy-eyed stare at nothing. "They took Clay's leg off."

After a long silence, Dad said, "They think he'll be all right. They have a new medicine to fight infections. It was used on the wounded in the war. It is called pen-i-cillin."

According to Dad, a foul odor from under the sheets had alerted the nurses that gas gangrene had begun its deadly work; the decision to amputate was made quickly.

During that dark night, the amputation was done below the knee, saving the joint.

There was no doubt that Clay's life was threatened. He very well may have died but for the miracle drug, which had just recently been released to the general public. It was the first any of us had heard of penicillin. It was, indeed, a miracle drug to fight infections. I don't know why they hadn't started Clay on penicillin as soon as he was admitted, but perhaps at that early date, they didn't think to use it as a prophylactic tool. We certainly had no idea how the family of antibiotics was going to change the field of medicine.

Recovery was slow, but Clay made steady progress and by Christmas Day he was well enough to sit in a lounge chair with his stump elevated. After we had our usual Christmas dinner, we put some of each dish in a container; all of us got into two cars and drove to the hospital. There was just enough snow on the ground to make driving difficult and hazardous. There was one big hill, which presented a challenge between us and the paved road. We knew if we could make it up that hill, we could make it onto the paved roadway. And slowly the two cars inched their way up and over the hill.

We entered Clay's hospital and found him sitting up with nothing covering his bandaged stump to hide it. We were so glad he was alive; it softened the hurt of seeing him for the first time with one and a half legs. Dorothy and Roy's two boys, who were two and four, looked and looked where Clay's leg was missing. Then they looked at Clay and back at the stump. Finally, one of them asked quietly, "Where is your leg, Uncle Clay?"

Clay continued to improve and was soon back on the farm learning how to climb the stairs and maneuver around the farm buildings on his crutches. Dad wanted him to get back into the routine of helping with the chores as soon as he could. Ironically, Dad's brother, Will, had lost a leg at the same age as Clay and had given up on life after that. Dad was doing what he could to see that Clay didn't just give up also. I don't believe Clay was even tempted to indulge in such behavior. He was soon helping with the early morning chores on his crutches, which he didn't use very long before deciding he could get around better without them. He became adept at hopping from the barn to the machine shed and from the house to the hog house. I never saw him lose his balance or fall as he hopped from one workspace to another. It would be several months before his stump was healed sufficiently for Clay to be fitted for a prosthesis.

The week after Clay came home I had to go to Kewanee to see my doctor for my eight-month checkup. Clay went with me so that he could go to the hospital and say hello to the nurses who had taken care of him. He talked me into letting him drive most of the way to Kewanee. We did wait until the folks couldn't see us before he moved into the driver's seat. He was determined to begin doing the things he had done before. I took back the driver's seat when we got to the city limits. Clay went with me again two weeks later, when I went for what I hoped would be my last checkup before the baby arrived.

The due date was approaching, and my wish was granted—Dean was unexpectedly discharged and came home shortly before our baby was due. We moved in with his folks who lived in town, as there was no housing available in Toulon at that time; with the housing shortage, living with our parents was about the only option we had. It was much more comfortable at his folks' home where we had our own bedroom downstairs. The bedroom had plenty of room for the baby's things, too. Dean got a job with the county working for the Highway Department. It was hard physical labor, but it was a temporary job until the next fall, when he planned to go to school.

Mitchell B. Young Is Born 1946

Dean hadn't been home but two weeks when Mitchell Blair Young was born on February 14, 1946, during a blizzard that raged all day long. His birth heralded what was to become known as the Baby Boomer Generation. We were very happy to have a healthy boy, but because of complications, I wasn't able to really enjoy him for a few weeks.

The doctor who delivered him was in his eighties and had returned to practice during wartime to help out with the serious shortage of doctors. He was a small man, who seemed to have left his good personality at home that day. It became quite clear to us before it was all over that he shouldn't have been allowed to deliver babies, but, again, we didn't have a lot of choices. His name was Dr. Coffin.

After I had been in labor several hours, Dr. Coffin left the hospital for some reason and got caught in the storm, making it impossible for him to return when he planned to. The baby was not going to be born without some help, and we had to wait for the doctor's return which wasn't until around six that evening. He used forceps to turn the baby's head, cutting him on either side near his eyes. We were told that because of the complications and delay during the birthing process, there was no way of knowing, until he was a few months old, if Mitchell had suffered any brain damage.

The first day after delivery, I was expected to sit up and walk, but I could not. In the 1940s women were confined to a hospital for two weeks after giving birth. Dr. Coffin treated me as if he thought I was just exaggerating when I told him I hurt too much to sit up. My breasts became so swollen that I could no longer nurse the baby. I stopped eating. Still the doctor insisted there was nothing wrong, and at the end of the second week, he gave orders to get me up and walk me down the hall. With the nurse by my side, I tried to stand and nearly passed out. The pain was unbearable.

After mother visited me that afternoon, she went immediately to the doctor's office. "What is causing my daughter to have so much pain?" She asked as soon as she had introduced herself.

"Your daughter has been slow in getting back on her feet. She refuses to get out of bed. I have ordered the nurses to get her up and assist her with walking."

Mother was as angry as Mother knew how to get. "My daughter is not eating. She is running a fever. She nearly passed out trying to sit up. If you don't do something immediately I will call in another doctor." Mother was a quiet woman who didn't like confrontations. However, she would do whatever it took when it came to the well-being of one of her children.

The next morning I was wheeled into the operating room, given ether, and examined. It was discovered I had a severe internal infection. I was immediately started on high doses of penicillin, the same antibiotic which had saved Clay's life just two months earlier.

If Mother hadn't insisted something be done, the infection might have killed me. My husband had been visiting me regularly. He never asked the doctor or the nurses any questions regarding my prolonged recovery. I could have lain there and died, and he would never have thought that he needed to talk to the doctor. My complaints to Dr. Coffin didn't seem to carry much weight. He couldn't get beyond his opinion that I was just a big baby who wouldn't try to move if it was the least uncomfortable.

My body responded rapidly to the antibiotic. My breasts returned to normal within a few days, and I began to eat everything they brought me. I was soon walking and asking for my baby again. I couldn't nurse him because of the infection, but I could sit up and hold him, which I hadn't done for more than a week.

Finally, after three weeks, we brought our baby boy home. He cried a lot and never seemed satisfied after he had taken the allotted few ounces of milk that the doctor had instructed me to give him. Ignorant as I was, I took him to the same Dr. Coffin who had delivered him. The younger doctors had begun returning to practice in Kewanee, but I just stuck with the one I had. He kept telling me Mitch had colic, probably because I was giving him too much milk. So he cut the amount back a couple of ounces.

When Mitchell was a month old, he began to lose weight. I talked to Mother, who called the pediatrician in Peoria whom she knew to be good. He had us come to his office that day. One look at Mitch and he said, "You're starving your baby." As soon as we got home I filled that bottle up to the top and let him drink until he could drink no more. How badly I felt to think of all those times when he was crying to the top of his lungs until he was exhausted, and it was because he was hungry. What joy I felt to let him eat until he fell peacefully into a deep sleep.

This act of starvation would not happen today. Parents don't let their babies cry much, but in 1946 we thought picking them up every time they cried would spoil them. At least that is what Mother believed, and I depended on her knowledge when it came to what to do when something was wrong with Mitchell. It was to be some years before I began to think through things for myself and to use my common sense. It takes a certain amount of self-confidence to rely on one's own good judgment.

We moved to my parents' home soon after the baby and I returned from the hospital. Yes, back to that old farmhouse with its pot-bellied stove for heat and coal range for cooking. Dean's mother had complained to my mother that our presence in her house had disrupted her life and left her no time to relax. Mother told me about their conversation.

When I told Dean, he agreed to move back to the farm. Although the house was rickety and crowded, we knew we were welcome. We never discussed it further. I didn't allow my negative feelings toward his mother to come to the surface except briefly. I thought it was crummy of her to have talked to Mom rather than to me, but I pushed those negative feelings back down and went on as if it had never happened.

I felt relieved to be back where I knew I was loved and not resented, even though Dean and I had to share the south room with Glenna and Vonnie who were in high school, or perhaps I should say, they had to share it with us. They slept in one bed and Dean and I in the other with Mitch in his crib at the foot of ours. Privacy was hard to come by, presenting a challenge to a young couple.

We stayed with Mom and Dad for a year while Dean attended classes at the University of Illinois's satellite campus in Kewanee. He was one of the thousands of veterans who took advantage of the GI Bill. This program enabled many veterans to get a college education, who otherwise would have found it nearly impossible to do so.

We Move To Champaign-Urbana 1947

Dean had been planning on going to Western Illinois University where his sister went to school, but it was basically a teacher's college, not where one would study accounting which was his intention. I wrote the University of Illinois and asked for a catalogue and an application form. I also found out about the satellite campus in Kewanee. Dean would never have requested this information. He would have gone to Western Illinois rather than moving toward something unfamiliar. He lacked initiative or the ability to think of alternatives; he would have clung to the familiar. But he readily switched to the University of Illinois after I did the paperwork.

By the time he finished his first year in Kewanee, I had begun earning money by selling Stanley Products on the party plan. In August 1947, when Mitchell was eighteen-months-old, we finally got a place of our own in Champagne, Illinois, where Dean continued his studies at the University's main campus.

We moved into a twenty-seven foot trailer, purchased with money Dad loaned us. It was conveniently parked on campus on the back part of a sorority house's lot just one block from the University library. In exchange for having our trailer parked on their property, Dean tended their furnace. The trailer had a tiny bedroom with a bed and a few built-in drawers, a very small kitchen, and a minuscule living room where Mitchell slept on the couch. We three had to go to the basement of the sorority house to shower and to use the bathroom. Certainly not ideal considering those cold mid-western winters, but it was livable, especially for a student's family. After all, I had grown up using an outhouse.

I earned our living during the three years we were in Champagne. Dean didn't work at all while he was in school. He didn't help me with the care of Mitchell, the cooking, or the running of the household. He tended the sorority's furnace, attended classes, and studied. He even went to the football games; I simply didn't have time to go with him. Again I accepted his behavior; to me that was just the way life was supposed to be. I accepted everything, but I hated that Mitch had no place to play and no other children around. He was two in February, 1948 and needed to be with other children.

By the summer semester, Mitchell had been accepted at the University Research Pre-School, staffed by graduate students in the field of Early Childhood Development. It was difficult to get accepted because of the number of applicants, but our living conditions helped our cause. It was a big relief for me knowing that Mitch was around other kids his age and was in good hands.

I paid off the loan for the trailer in a little over a year. During the second year, we became eligible for Federal Housing offered to veterans and their families. Juanita and Haydn (they were married a few months after Dean and I were) had been living in the housing project while Haydn worked toward a degree in Geology. The little three-room house seemed wonderful after being in that trailer for a year. There were two bedrooms and a living area, which served as living room, kitchen and dining room. The kitchen had a hot plate for cooking and a small portable oven which could be lifted off when not in use. A pot-bellied coal-burning stove for heat and a table with four chairs fit comfortably in the living room area. And a BIG plus was our own bathroom. But the best thing about Federal Housing was that the place was crawling with little kids.

It was really nice that Juanita and Haydn lived in Champagne at the same time we did. Haydn had gone to the same high school as we and had also grown up on a farm, so the four of us were old friends. We got together frequently to eat, play cards, or just socialize. Juanita kept

Mitchell when I had a Stanley party in the afternoon, but I took him with me most other places. Betty and her husband, Larry, had moved to Tuscola, Illinois, about thirty miles south of Champagne. We visited them when possible and, sometimes, the three families got together. Larry was a radio announcer for the local station in Tuscola.

I Earn Our Living 1947-1950

When we moved to Champagne, I switched from Stanley Products to a plastics company that offered more of a variety of products from curtains and dishes to picture frames and women's electric razors. It was a small operation run by a couple out of their home in Peoria, about one hundred miles from Champagne. They had not intended to go outside of the Peoria area, but I liked their products, so they reluctantly let me open up the Champagne area with the agreement that I would drive to Peoria to attend meetings at least once a month. I did quite well and began hiring other women.

I soon had six to eight women working under my supervision. For the rest of my three years in Champagne, I had some responsibilities with them, but the most time consuming part of the job was the hiring and training. Once the women started, they called on me primarily as the go-between for them and my boss. The good part was that I got a small percentage of their sales. But I will immodestly say that none of them sold as much as I did.

The business plan was to get someone to host a party in her home in exchange for free merchandise. (In the 1940s the majority of women were homemakers; few worked outside the home.) The parties were held in either the afternoon or the evening. I showed my merchandise and explained all of the reasons why they should buy at least one of each item. While the hostess was serving dessert and coffee, I talked to her guests about having a party in their homes. I offered them more than most dealers were willing to give, but that allowed me to book more parties than the others. I also offered a bonus if they had at least a certain number of guests attend the party, so most of my parties were well attended.

The parties were often twenty or thirty miles from my home. Sometimes I had to drive country roads that had only one lane of pavement, so when you met a car, each car had to get one set of tires off the pavement. You drove very slowly if the road was muddy.

The worst part of the job was the bad weather in the winters. If it started to snow, I made sure the hostess was going ahead with the party, and if she was, I would bravely go forth, praying it would not snow so much that I would get stuck somewhere.

Many nights I didn't return home until after midnight, depending on how far I had to drive and how slow the hostess was in doing her part. Dean was always sound asleep, never worrying about my safe return. I sometimes worried about what would happen if I got stuck or for any reason could not return home. But Dean evidently didn't have the same worry.

I did get stuck one time, right in front of a farmhouse that stood about fifty yards off the road. I was trying to turn around on one of the one-lane cement slab roads and got both back wheels off the cement road. I spun my wheels uselessly. I had to get help to get all four wheels back on the cement slab. The fifty yards between me and the house was a muddy lot. I blinked my lights several times, hoping they would miraculously come running to my rescue. That didn't happen, so I gathered up my courage, took off my heels and hose, and slowly made my way through the mud toward the light in the farmhouse window. A dog was barking inside. I could see a figure peering out at me, but I couldn't tell if it was a man or a woman.

I held my breath and prayerfully knocked on the door. *What if these were not kind people, what if it was some weirdo living in the country alone? What if...* But my prayers were answered; a kindly man came to the door. He said he would be glad to get his tractor and pull me back onto the slab.

I arrived a little late at the party, somewhat shaken, mud half-way to my knees and just glad to be there. They welcomed me warmly and were happy to wait while I washed the mud off, put my shoes back on, and set up my wares. The next morning I told Dean how frightened I'd been when I got stuck, but he reacted in his usual unconcerned manner. I hadn't expected a much different reaction from him.

One other incident which scared me, also involved those infamous one-way slabs and muddy shoulders. Leaving town one evening, I became aware that a car seemed to be following me. It stayed behind me as I left the city limits and drove into the thinly populated farming community. I was becoming suspicious that whoever was in the car was up to no good. In fact, I was becoming quite frightened. Several miles out of town, the car passed me; I could see more than one man in the car. Then what I feared most happened—they were slowing down, forcing me to slow down behind them.

I was afraid to attempt to go around them and was almost paralyzed with fear, when to my relief I saw a lighted farmhouse not too far down the road. I trusted the men in the suspicious car would not come to a complete stop in front of the farmhouse. Sure enough, they drove past the driveway. I pulled in, drove as close as I could get to the gate, jumped out of the car, and ran to the door.

An elderly couple responded to my frantic knock, and I told them what had happened. They let me call my hostess to tell her I would be a bit late. After a few minutes of gathering my courage, I set out again to my destination which was not too far away.

A couple of other times I was frightened. One involved the heavy snow that I always dreaded. The weather was becoming worse as I drove out of town, and soon became blizzard conditions. As I neared the Chanute Air Force Base entry gate, halfway to my destination, I noticed that my lights were beginning to dim and that the car was losing power. The alternator had stopped working. Stranded, the car rolled to a halt at the light controlling the traffic in and out of the base. Snow was being driven across the pavement making for very low visibility; I felt lucky to be under the bright lights. I got out of the car to get my flashlight which was in the back, when a car came out of the base and pulled over in front of my car. A soldier got out of the car and came over to see what was wrong. He helped me put my boxes in his car and drove me to the hostess' house. I appreciated his willingness to help me in such threatening weather.

The hostess gave me the phone number for a mechanic. I had him tow my car and install a new alternator. By the time I was ready to leave the party, the car was repaired, and I had survived another crisis. No matter what the weather conditions were, nor how far I had to travel, Dean never offered to go with me. It didn't worry him at all; he never showed any concern for my safety. I never complained.

Each week I ordered the new products and delivered what I'd sold the previous week. And, of course, I collected the money and deposited it. All three years we lived in Champagne, this was my job, and I did very well financially. I earned more money than Dean did the first couple of years he worked for Caterpillar with his accounting degree. But I refused to let it enter my head that I was smart, or that if I could be successful in that work, I could pass a college course, or be successful at whatever I chose to do. That idea was dead before it was born.

The fall that Dean began his senior year, I realized I was going to have another baby just about the time he would be graduating. Even though we had not planned it, the timing was actually very good. Until I was eight months pregnant I was able to continue working, lifting the big boxes, hoisting them into the car, driving to the hostess's house, carrying the boxes up to some hostess's home or apartment (often up a flight of stairs), unpacking, making the presentation, repacking and driving home. The doctor said it would be okay to continue work since I was used to it.

The Old Farmhouse Burns Down 1949

That fall we received a phone call that the old farm house had burned to the ground. When we arrived in Toulon the next weekend, we stopped to look at the ruins. Standing there on those old cellar steps, looking at the ruins, brought back many memories of what used to be my home: the screen door into the kitchen covered with flies in the summer; the old coal-burning kitchen range; Dad's desk which was off limits to us kids; the crowded south room where we girls slept; Mom's sewing machine in the living room, and the all-purpose shed where the cream-separator was kept. All of those things destroyed in a few hours.

The night of the fire, Mother had been babysitting for her two grandsons, Dorothy and Roy's boys, who lived temporarily in the schoolhouse near our home. The boys were in bed, and Mother was doing her hand-sewing, enjoying the quiet. As she peacefully let her mind wander, she heard something outside and thought it must be some small animals scrapping. But the far-off rumble became louder, and she decided she'd better investigate. As she stood up, she saw that the night was lit up. Hurrying to the window, she gasped, "Good Lord, my house is on fire!" The flames and heavy smoke were boiling into the black night. She knew Dad would be sleeping, having fallen asleep an hour ago. She raced down the gravel road, over the cattle guard, and up the hill to the front gate.

As soon as she entered the yard, her worst fears were assuaged when Dad met her with a dazed look on his face.

"Are you okay?" She anxiously asked.

He looked at her for a moment before he could answer. "Yes, I'm all right."

He had awakened when a piece of burning material fell on his back. He had only enough time to escape through the ground floor window. Mother found him pacing back-and-forth.

When the volunteer firemen arrived, Mom and Dad were standing dazed and unbelieving, as the house continued to die. It was an old wooden house, and it burned like kindling wood. They had lived in this old farmhouse all of their married life and had raised seven children inside its walls. Everything they had accumulated during those busy years was gone, except for the bedside table and a drawer full of snapshots that Dad had taken out the window as he escaped the inferno. But Dad and Mom were safe. They had recently purchased a larger home at the edge of town and were preparing to move. But now they would have to buy everything—even small things such as scissors, pots and pans and linens. The consensus was that the fire had started in some rewiring that had been done in the attic a week earlier.

Back To Illinois with Our Baby Girl, Suzanne 1950

Suzanne Young was born June 7, 1950, ten days before her dad graduated with a degree in accounting, but with no job prospects. The moment she was born, they held her up where I could see her, and said, "There's your girl!" I had told them how much I wanted a girl. Having a boy and a girl seemed like the perfect family to me at the time. Now, I realize that two boys or two girls would have had its advantages, too.

Suzanne was a beautiful baby. She entered the world with much less stress than her brother had experienced. She would never get to see the infamous "old house" where her Mother spent the first nineteen years of her life.

After Suzanne's six week checkup, we moved back to Toulon to live with my folks once more. There were four of us now—Mitchell, four and a half, Suzanne six weeks. Our moving in must have been a tremendous change for my parents, but I knew they didn't mind our being there. Dad not only enjoyed having the baby in the house, but he also enjoyed Mitchell and genuinely liked having us around. Mother enjoyed the children also in her quiet, reserved way. She and I always got along well. Glenna and Vonnie were out of high school and gone. The folks' new house had three nice sized bedrooms upstairs, so we had our own room this time. We didn't expect to live with them long, just until Dean was settled in a job, hopefully in a few weeks.

Suzanne's neck had begun to break out by the time she was a week old. It gradually became a serious problem. I took her to several doctors who just gave me an ointment or a lotion to put on it and dismissed us. After about five months, she learned how to scratch; her neck became infected and was a raw, bloody mess. Mother accompanied me to take Suzanne to the pediatrician in Peoria (The one we had taken Mitchell to when he was a baby and wasn't getting enough to eat.) It didn't take that good doctor long to diagnose the problem as an allergy to cow's milk. The solution of switching Suzanne to goat's milk was miraculous. Her neck began to improve immediately and she was cured within a month.

Our Move to Joliet, Illinois

I also had developed allergies but thought it was bronchitis. When the doctors asked if I had allergies, I always answered, "No." It was a new phenomenon to recognize allergies. I had not heard of an allergist, nor did I realize that it was a specialty. But when the pediatrician finished with Suzanne, he turned and asked what was wrong with me. Not only was I coughing a lot, but also had lost some weight and didn't look well. That afternoon he sent me to an allergist, who wanted to put me in the hospital for tests. I agreed to consider it and told him that I would get back to him.

Dean had been trying to sell insurance that summer and was getting nowhere. He looked even younger than his chronological age of twenty-five. He had no aptitude for selling anything to anyone; he was not assertive enough to be convincing as a salesman. I had become uneasy about having no income and continuing to live with my parents. I typed up several applications for Dean and sent them to companies we thought might hire him. (He had agreed for me to do this for him.) It wasn't long before he was called for an interview with Caterpillar Tractor Company in Peoria. Dean was hired to work in their new plant in Joliet, about a two hour drive from Toulon, forty miles southeast of Chicago. I don't know how long Dean would have sputtered along, spinning his wheels in the insurance field, before he would have taken the initiative to find a job with a salary. He began his new job with Caterpillar late in August, 1950. Unable to find a home so we could join him, he commuted from Toulon to Joliet, leaving Sunday evening and returning Friday evening.

After four months, I went to Joliet with him one Sunday night and found a house the next day. It was not a great house, but I knew I could find something more desirable once I lived in Joliet. I told myself he was too busy with his work to find a house for us. I imagine my folks were more perceptive, but if they questioned Dean's desire to have us join him, they said nothing to me.

My allergies were worsening, causing episodes of spasmodic coughing, which was rapidly wearing me down. When the doctor in Peoria heard that I was moving to Joliet, he referred me to an allergist in that city. After the allergist tested me for many kinds of allergens, he started giving me shots twice a week for a time, reducing it to once a week, and letting me give them to myself at home. That regime continued for nearly five years with the eventual tapering of the injections the last year. I have never had that type of allergic reaction again. Today allergies are so common, they don't usually get out of hand like mine did in the early 1950s.

The duplex I had rented for us abutted the infamous Joliet Penitentiary property. Their corn field was the only barrier between the prison and our home. This duplex, our new home, was a cold, barren uninviting place with no carpeting, no drapes—really nothing to make it comfy. At least the four of us were living under one roof–no more living off of my parents. The neighborhood was called Lidice, named for a city in Czechoslovakia, which had been destroyed during the war. Primarily Czechs lived in our neighborhood, but because it was the dead of winter when we moved into the duplex, we didn't venture outside very much and didn't meet any of them.

By spring I found a more desirable house to rent in a neighborhood full of kids the same ages as our children. It was a three bedroom house and even had a dining room. We settled into that comfortable old house, and I went back to work in order to save money for a down payment on a home of our own. I was realistic and knew we would never own a house if I waited for us to save the down payment out of Dean's salary.

Our new house, that we purchased two years later, was built not far from where we lived, but it was in a brand new development. It was a typical "beginner's" house with three bedrooms, a living room, a kitchen and one bath. But it had a full-sized basement which we fixed up as a place to entertain. Not elegant, but it was nice, with comfortable furniture and a ping pong table. I also had a corner of the space for my sewing, where I could leave an in-progress project without worrying about the mess.

Life in the Fifties

We lived in Joliet the decade of the fifties. We were the typical family consisting of a man, a woman, a boy, a girl and a dog. Dean worked five days a week, eight hours a day; I ran the household, and the kids went to school. We had good friends, nice neighbors and went to church on Sunday. Mitchell was in Boy Scouts and participated in the youth group at church. He had a paper route and friends that we knew and liked. Suzanne was a Brownie Scouts, went to the "Y", took dancing and acrobat lessons, and played with her friends whom we also knew.

I did the laundry on Mondays, ironed on Tuesdays, and cleaned on Fridays. The washing machine was in the basement, and I hung the clothes out to dry on the permanent clothesline in our back yard. I ironed at least six white shirts each week, prepared three meals a day, and took the kids where they needed to go. I planned the meals two weeks in advance, making my grocery list accordingly, so there was little running back to the store until the next pay day. Dean was in a carpool; with only one car, I had to plan around the days that he drove. He earned the living, did most of the yard work, and took care of the car. We ate out only on special occasions. We led an average middle-class life in the good old USA.

During the decade of the fifties, the Soviet Union launched Sputnik (1957). Because of the Cold War, the political tension was high. The

Russians had beaten us in the race to put a satellite in orbit. Rosa Parks refused to move to the back of the bus, desegregation caused strife in the South. Howdy Doody held forth in black and white on a twelve-inch TV screen. Milk in glass bottles was delivered to the back door of your home. Diner's Club issued the first credit card. The median family income was $3,900.00. A new car cost $1,500.00, and gas was eighteen cents a gallon.

Life didn't change a great deal for the ordinary American family during those ten years. We continued living our secure lives as we were accustomed to doing. Our family attended the Methodist Church, where Mitch was in the youth group, and I taught Sunday school. After listening to the sermons, we never had discussions, never commented on the music or the minister's message. We never stayed around after the service to get acquainted with the other parishioners. I had no curiosity about what went on during the week within the church. However, as with my own religious background and upbringing, my children's experiences in church gave them a foundation in religion which they have relied on through some of their most difficult times.

Every other weekend, we drove our Ford to visit our folks. Three of my siblings were living in the area, so we got to see a lot of family. Mitch and Suzanne loved it because they got to play with their cousins and see their two sets of grandparents, who lived a half mile apart. The fried chicken dinners and home-made ice cream were part of the attraction, too.

We didn't have a savings account; we never had $20 leftover by the time it was payday again. But we didn't have any debts either, except for the house and the car. The often-maligned and over-used credit card, with its seductive way of leading one to financial disaster, hadn't yet become a necessary part of life. The conservative, mid-western life in a small town surrounded by people similar to us made us content with our place in the world. I certainly did nothing to disrupt that peace.

The first junior college in the country was in Joliet, but it never entered my mind to take a course or to investigate that possibility. I didn't step out of those stultifying boundaries that I had wrapped around myself. Partly it was my own lack of initiative and curiosity, but much of it was the culture at that time. Women were still operating from the precept that men made the living, and women stayed home to take care of the household, the kids, and the husbands. It took Betty Friedan and the 1960s to put a crack in that long-standing structure. If you were smarter than your husband, you better not acknowledge it, especially to yourself. Don't rock the boat—that message was never written nor voiced, it was just the way it was and always had been. It was not questioned any more than we would question why we spoke English instead of Greek.

An Early Morning Phone Call

My peaceful life was suddenly disrupted on a Monday in the middle of July, 1957. The phone rang about 3:00 AM that morning. I stumbled to the kitchen and apprehensively answered, wondering what terrible thing had happened to cause anyone to be calling. We didn't make long distance calls without a very good reason, especially at 3:00 AM. Dorothy, my sister, was calling to tell me that Mother had died suddenly of a massive heart attack. After I asked a couple of questions, I told Dorothy that I'd call back later. I was so stunned. Mom had never had any heart trouble that we knew of. Her death was totally unexpected.

Pulling myself together, we prepared to go. We packed the car and were pretty much ready to leave before we wakened the children. Mitchell was eleven and Suzanne was seven. In their sleepy stupors, they were not too inquisitive. They slept most of the way to "Grandma's house," while their father drove and their mother lost herself in a confusion of unanswered questions, memories, and disbelief. Dean dropped us off and went right back to Joliet; he returned for the funeral two days later. It never dawned on me that he might have stayed for my sake. Perhaps that is understandable since we weren't connected enough for him to be of much comfort or support. It surely didn't cross my mind that, perhaps the opportunity to have a couple of days without his family around was too much of a temptation for him to resist.

Mother had kept Glenna's boys the Sunday evening that she died. Glenna and Phil had returned to pick them up about 9:30 PM. Mom was sewing on a dress for one of her little granddaughters when they came in. They chatted a bit, and after they left, Mother had gone upstairs and taken a bath. As she was drying herself she was overcome with pain and had fallen on the bed waking Dad. Mother was sixty years old.

Dad called Dorothy, who lived close by; she made the necessary calls to our family. Most of us kids arrived later that same day, all in shock and in dread of entering that house with Mother not there. Mom's presence had filled the house; how would life be without her, especially for Dad? He didn't even know where his clothes were kept. Now when we came to Grandma's house, there will be no grandma—no smell of good things cooking—no one sitting up late at night for good conversation—no one sewing pretty dresses and decorating dolls—no one...

At Dad's request, we seven siblings stayed in town several days after the funeral. We did the things he asked us to do; we were company for him and for each other. He was going to be so lost when we all left.

I was thirty-two that summer; it took me years to realize the magnitude of my loss. We had visited my folks the weekend before Mom died. As usual she and I had stayed up talking after the others had gone to bed; she so loved to sit in the kitchen with her hand-sewing and talk. We never ran out of interesting things to discuss and if some of the others were with us, which was good too.

What a shame she couldn't have received the education she so wanted early in her life. I know it would have pleased her that I had been granted the opportunity which she had been denied. Sometimes I believed that I accomplished what I did for both of us.

Suzanne's Illness

Mother died in July and in August, Sue awakened me a couple of nights saying her stomach hurt. During the day she seemed to be all right, so I didn't worry until the day before school started. Suzanne came in from playing, lay down on the couch, and went to sleep. That was so unusual that I took her temperature and looked her over for any obvious signs of illness. I was dismayed to find her legs and body covered with tiny little hemorrhages. The doctor had me bring her in right away and she was immediately admitted to the hospital. He told us it might be something quite controllable, but the symptoms also warned of leukemia or meningitis, two life-threatening diseases. It was a couple of days before all tests indicated it was neither of those dreaded ailments. It was a disease that I had never heard of called purpura. This disease causes a drop in platelets, thus the internal bleeding. Purpura is sometimes caused from having taken sulfur, which Suzanne had been given for an infection a few weeks prior to the onset of her symptoms.

For nearly three weeks Suzanne was in the hospital; she continued hemorrhaging for several days. Sometimes when I arrived for my twice-a-day visits, she would be as white as her sheets. She was a perfect little seven-year-old patient, never cried once, no matter what took place. The nurses and doctors praised her and made her feel special; they kept her supplied with cold drinks, balloons, and attention. I took her radio to her; even at seven, she had favorite songs, like "Wake up Little Suzie." That song was very popular that summer. I'm sure it was uplifting for the nurses and doctors that Suzanne was one little patient who was going to get well.

During that first week when the doctors weren't sure what was wrong with Suzanne, I called my family in Toulon and asked if anyone could come up and stay with me a few days. I needed support. Dean was working nights at the time and usually went to see Suzanne during the day, but not always. He was not comforting to me, but my family was, and they responded to my plea. Dorothy came and stayed a couple of days which helped me a lot. If Mother had been living, I know she would have come and stayed with me. I missed her terribly, especially at this time. It's an obvious indication of how little I could rely on the children's father for emotional understanding. Running back-and-forth to the hospital, worrying about Suzanne, and grieving over the recent loss of my mother, I didn't think much about Dean's lack of support.

Life Gets Back To Normal

Suzanne came home from the hospital on a beautiful fall day, wearing a new pink dress and white sweater which I had purchased for the occasion. What a joyful day that was; I felt so grateful that she was healthy again. School had started a day after Sue entered the hospital, so she was eager to join her second grade classmates. Happily, off she went to school the next week with her best friend, Barbara Orsini, who was also in the second grade. Life was good again.

Barbara was happy to have her playmate back. She lived across the street with her dad, who was a city fireman, and her mother who was, of course, a housewife. Barbara and Suzanne were the same size, but Barbara had very dark hair and Sue was a true blond. They often wore their hair in ponytails and looked cute together as they pedaled their bikes, roller skated, or just ran back-and-forth tending to their important play business.

Mitchell didn't have one best friend; he had several friends with whom he was pals. He was his own person even them. Often, he preferred doing his thing rather than being committed to programs like Little League or Boy Scouts, both of which he tried for a year, before letting us know he didn't want to do that anymore. He had a "secret place" at a nearby park that included a vine on which he could swing out over a ravine and pretend he was Tarzan. One day he came running in with blood streaming down his face soaking into his shirt. I had him get in the shower so that I could see where the injury was. It was not a serious wound and was the result of his falling off his Tarzan vine. Being a head wound, it bled a lot, but wasn't serious.

We were friends with the Orsinis, but the couples we saw the most were Walt and Lois Bender and Bob and Mary Glass. Walt and Bob worked at Caterpillar; Walt was Dean's supervisor. Both Mary and Lois were housewives. Frequently we went to each other's homes, sometimes invited and sometimes just to drop in for a cup of coffee or to chat. On weekend evenings, we got together to play cards or to listen to music and talk. We often enjoyed a cookout with our families. Many weekends the three families went together to a lake club, where we had memberships, and we swam, sunned, and enjoyed picnics. There weren't a lot of amenities: a club house with showers and a snack shack. However, the water was clear, a great improvement over Lake Calhoun.

The large group of friends to which we belonged, most from Caterpillar, had parties frequently. The Glasses, the Benders, and Dean and I usually went together. Dean and Lois flirted a lot, and when I objected he convinced me it meant nothing, that she didn't mean anything to him. As you would guess, I needed to believe him, so I did. But that didn't hinder us from being with them often. Until...

On Memorial Day in 1960 our families had a cookout at Benders. Dean had more to drink than usual and actually became quite drunk. He lost all inhibitions; he and Lois were far too flirtatious for even my high tolerance level. I left the party early and told him he could come with me, or he could stay there. He got in the car; we never said a word as I drove home. He stumbled into the house and fell asleep on the couch where he spent the night. The next morning I told him we were not going to socialize with the Benders anymore. He knew that I meant it. It was becoming too uncomfortable for me and more difficult for him to convince me it meant nothing to him. After all, it had been going on for several years. I was not stupid, just firmly defended and slow to accept reality.

A Life-Changing Decision

Our lives continued as if nothing had happened; we never talked about it; we just quit seeing Lois and Walt. But about three weeks later, on June 26, 1960, one day after my thirty-fifth birthday, Dean found me alone and said, "I have something to tell you that will surprise you."

I couldn't imagine what it would be. "What is it?"

"I've decided to quit Caterpillar, and we'll move to Fort Lauderdale."

"Are you kidding? Move to Fort Lauderdale? When did you decide to do that?"

"I've been thinking about it and just decided to do it. We'll call Bob and Phyllis this afternoon and see if we can go down for a visit next month." Phyllis and Bob Claxton had become our good friends when both men were attending the university in the forties. We had visited back-and-forth a couple of times during the intervening years. Just two years earlier we'd visited them in Fort Lauderdale.

What a huge decision for Dean to have made by himself, with no discussion, no consideration of the ramifications for us and our children, no thought of how moving so far from our large, extended families would impact all of us. It was out of character for him to make such a significant decision completely on his own and just announce it to me. This same man could never decide where to go on a Sunday drive without consulting me. Now he had decided to uproot his family, leave a good steady job to go to Florida without any planning, no idea of housing, available work, or schools for the children—just pick up and go. And we had no savings except for the small equity in the house.

I never gave a moment's thought as to what possibly could have provoked his decision. Anyone who knew us well must have known, but I just marveled at his uncharacteristic decisiveness. We did not discuss how or why he had decided to do such a thing. We never discussed anything though, so that was not unusual.

I was no more adult about the decision than he—I began thinking how exciting it was going to be. We're going to move to Florida, eat coconuts and mangos, smell the oleanders and swim in the ocean. We had really liked Fort Lauderdale when we visited Bob and Phyllis. At that time we had fantasized about how nice it would be to live there. Ft Lauderdale seemed like an ideal place to live compared to where we had lived all of our lives—the land-locked area of central Illinois. That's how mature my thinking was. Or, perhaps, I should say "lack of thinking." I never even let myself question why he suddenly wanted to leave Illinois, nor did I connect it at all with my cutting us off from the Benders. He must have thought about it, and if he wanted to move, it was okay with me. Not a care in the world or a lick of sense. We simply put our house on the market, said our goodbyes, took Mitch and Suzanne, who were ready to enter the ninth and fifth grades respectively, and off we went on an adventure. From the little city of Joliet, amidst the farming communities of the conservative Midwest and in proximity to both of our extended families, we moved to the tourist city of Fort Lauderdale, Florida, nicknamed "Fort Liquordale." It was a wide-open beach city, where we were totally out of our element.

Life in Fort Lauderdale

Cars had no air-conditioning, and we made the trip in late August. It wasn't much fun. Having left our house in Joliet in the hands of a realtor, we arrived in Fort Lauderdale August 30, 1960. We left most of the furniture to be shipped after the house sold. The Claxtons had located an apartment for us where we lived until we rented a house. We lived in the rented house, which was on a canal, nearly a year before we bought a home not too far away. Our new house which cost $7,500 was situated on a large corner lot, but not on a canal. However, with the many windows in the house, we welcomed the omnipresent ocean breeze. I put sheer curtains on the windows which extended across the kitchen and front room. My favorite memory of that house is of those white curtains fluttering endlessly. The house was never terribly hot even when the temperature was in the nineties. We settled into the last home the four of us would ever share.

Dean considered different ways to make a living, but decided to start an accounting practice for small businesses, doing their monthly accounting and their year-end tax work. It took him awhile to get his business established, but he eventually did; in time he did quite well. He got his first account early in November, and slowly built from there. At first, I did much of the actual accounting work (with his supervision) at a desk in our bedroom He spent most of his time soliciting clients and delivering the accounts as we finished them. It would be more than a year before he had enough income to meet our monthly expenses. It was not in the realm of imagination that I might get a job. I was fulfilling the woman's role dictated by our culture in the early nineteen sixties.

I found myself in a social milieu to which I didn't belong, nor did I know how to handle the ways in which it affected my children. Drugs were rampant in South Florida and alcohol was much more a part of social life. Very few people had deep roots or extended family in the area. The party atmosphere was created by the many tourists, and the instability caused by the rapid growth of that area by people like us moving south (many doing so to escape a troublesome situation). The area didn't offer much in common with our conservative backgrounds. Most of the transplants had left families behind and had no long history of the land as we had back in Illinois. I was absolutely ignorant of how these factors would influence my children and my ability to guide them. I saw it as a fun place for kids to live.

Only much later did I realize what a tremendously difficult time this was for Suzanne and Mitchell. To make it worse, it never dawned on me that the move would create any difficulties for them. The adjustment for all of us was exacerbated by the cultural upheaval that began in the sixties. Much of the decade was dominated by the Viet Nam War. It was a period of profound change led by the sexual and social revolutions. Civil rights and anti-war movements added to the social unrest. It became the age of the Hippies.

In the conservative area of Illinois where we had lived, we'd not yet been affected by the cultural upheavals. That changed suddenly when we moved to South Florida. I didn't know anything about a cultural revolution; I just knew my world was changing too rapidly.

But life went on for us anyway. Mitchell joined the football team at the big Stranahan High School, probably more because of his Dad's prodding than out of any desire of his own. He hung in there his first year, but walked out on it at the beginning of his sophomore year, even though we tried to talk him out of giving up. It was Dean's pushing him, and not his love of the game, that had caused him to be on the team in the first place. Mitchell deserved a lot of credit. It was not his desire to play football, and he had enough courage to act accordingly and quit the team in the face of his father's disapproval.

Suzanne's life changed a lot, also. She stopped taking her dancing and acrobat lessons and no longer went to the "Y". She made friends with girls her age on our street, but it was not the same. I never got to know their mothers as I had before, and I lost some of the sense of security, in regard to whom she was with and what she was doing. Other mothers didn't seem to have the same concerns that I had regarding what their children were doing. Sue had to grow up too fast in South Florida, and I was lost as far as helping her. The loss of the proximity to extended families created a profound vacuum.

All of us missed our families—the loving grandparents, all those aunts, uncles and cousins whom we saw so often when living near them up North. Holidays were never the same without our families. Of course, Suzanne and Mitchell would have changed over time anyway, but it happened so suddenly when they were quite young. That move to Ft. Lauderdale and what it meant for my son and daughter, is one of the things I regret the most in my life. It came about, to a great extent, because of their father's need to get out of Illinois as well as my lack of maturity and good judgment.

In time the kids began to find a niche for themselves. Mitch went scuba diving and water skiing with his new friends. He worked some at the A&P supermarket earning his spending money and money to date. He never had a serious relationship with a girl during those four years. Sue also liked to water ski and to go to the beach with her friends. Dean and I socialized the most with Phyllis and Bob, and we played a lot of canasta which was the rage at that time.

We attended a small non-denominational church, but not as regularly as we had in Joliet. Mitch never felt at home in the youth activities. Though he attended the church activities for a couple of months, he just wasn't comfortable with them. Most of the time, he and Sue went to church with us, until Mitch joined the Marines, and

Sue started high school. She didn't always go with us after that, but did go to church activities quite often with some of her girlfriends. After Dean's practice grew and he became busier he often didn't go to church with me. I didn't mind going by myself and continued going most every Sunday. I attended church faithfully, but I didn't hang around after the service to get to know anyone; I never attended any of the activities of the church, nor did I even think of joining any of the women's circles or councils.

We joined a so-called yacht club, which was more for socializing and swimming than it was for anything to do with yachts. We met several couples there who became good friends. The kids went with us sometimes, but preferred going to the beach.

We had many cook outs and picnics on the beach; we never tired of the ocean those first few years. We lived within ten minutes of a beach which compared favorably to the best in the world, and we fully enjoyed it. The beaches were not crowded nor built up like they are today; there were miles of public beaches.

It also took years before I began to get bored with the constantly pleasant temperatures, without the high humidity that is a problem in North Florida. If it was hot, there was always a breeze, so it was seldom miserable. Most people that we knew didn't have central air-conditioning and neither did we.

We had quite a bit of company the first few years we lived in Ft. Lauderdale and enjoyed having them visit us. The kids loved to introduce their 'northern' friends to water skiing, swimming in the Atlantic, fishing in New River, and feeding the alligator that lived under our dock. At first we all thought it was great to have an alligator hanging out in front of our house. He was a big one, probably five or six feet long. We even let the kids go out in a little plastic boat, no bigger than a bathtub and paddle about in the canal, the gator's back yard. Soon we found out how dangerous that critter could be. No more feeding the "cute alligator" and no more paddling around in a little yellow tub.

We had a large mango tree in our back yard; we had to cut it down because Sue was allergic to the leaves. We discovered her allergy in a very painful way for her. All of us worked together to trim the lower limbs, which hung so low it was difficult to walk under them. After working with us for a while, Suzanne began to break out and ended up being quite sick. She was covered with a rash resembling poison ivy, especially on her face and neck, since she had stood under the limbs looking up as she trimmed. We gave up growing mangos in our back yard.

Mitchell's Scuba Diving Scare

One Saturday Mitchell and two of his friends set out to spend the day enjoying their favorite sport—scuba diving. They went about a mile off shore and spent a couple of hours diving before a storm threatened and the wind began to strengthen; they knew enough to get back to shore. However, when they tried to start the motor, it refused to turn over; after many tries they gave up. They sat in the boat hoping someone would come close enough to see them. All the time the waves were getting bigger and rougher. The sun was mercilessly hot; the boat was rocking enough to frighten them. After a couple of hours, Mitchell told the others he was going to swim to shore and send help. Of course, this was the wrong thing to do, but he was seventeen and invincible. He put on his flippers, took a deep breath and dove in. With the first big wave his friends lost sight of him. He was on his own.

Back at the house when it was an hour later than we had expected him and he was not home, Dean and I were anxious and admitted our anxiety to each other. A half hour later our phone rang. "Is this Mitchell Young's mother?"

"Yes."

"This is the Coast Guard. May I speak to your husband?"

"What are you calling about?"

"Please, Mrs. Young, I want to speak to your husband."

I yelled for Dean, "It's the Coast Guard!" He dropped what he was doing and grabbed the phone.

"This is the Coast Guard. Your son, Mitchell Young, has been reported missing. We have a helicopter and two boats out searching for him. Stay off the phone and close by. We will call you as soon as we know anything."

Dean hung up the phone and with a stone-face he repeated the message to me. We didn't say much to each other. I went outside and paced from the front patio, to the back door, and through the house, praying silently. We would look at each other and try to say something positive, such as how strong Mitchell was, and he would make it. Then I would resume the pacing and praying.

How much time elapsed I have no idea; it seemed an eternity. My mind raced. *Why don't they call and give us an encouraging word? How far out was he? Where are the other boys?* Then Dean or I would say some inane thing again and go back to our silence. I visualized Mitchell coming closer and closer to shore, getting tired, but not exhausted, and I would send him messages to keep swimming, not to panic, not to give up. I concentrated totally on that message getting through to him. I guess that's praying.

During this time, one boy's father, who had a good-sized boat with a radio, went out to see if he could spot the boys. He knew that they should've been home, and he was worried. He knew where they usually went diving, and within a short time, found the two boys still sitting safely in their boat. He was told that Mitchell had headed for shore, that they had lost track of him with the first big wave. The boy's father immediately got in touch with the Coast Guard and reported the situation.

Mitchell was a strong young man and a pretty good swimmer, especially with a pair of flippers attached to his feet. But with the huge waves, the rough wind, and a mile or more to swim, he began to wonder about his decision. He thought about the possibility of sharks, but they had never concerned him much when he was diving, and they weren't going to worry him now. He just kept stroking and kicking, imagining himself sitting in front of the television later that night with a bowl of popcorn and a cold drink. When a wave lifted him high enough, he would catch a glimpse of the beach, which was reassuring. He just kept stroking and kicking.

Mitchell knew it was taking much longer than it should have, and knew we would be worried. He had no idea the other boys' father had come out in his big boat, or that the Coast Guard had been alerted and were scanning the coast line for signs of him.

When our phone rang my heart nearly stopped. I let Dean answer; I knew they wouldn't tell me anything.

"Hello, Dad, I thought you might…

Dean and I sat down, sharing that moment of profound relief, our eyes filled with tears. We were exhausted. Our grateful family sat together that evening going over the details of the afternoon's events. Mitchell told us that he never doubted he would make it to shore. Such is the optimism of youth. Sue had missed out on most of the drama, as she was spending the afternoon with one of her friends. She got the whole story and some of it more than once, as we marveled at our good fortune. Mitchell had a new flat-top hair cut which didn't leave much protection on the top of his head. A thick yellowish crust formed where his scalp was badly sunburned. That was the only visible sign of what could have been a tragedy.

Changes in the Air 1964

Not too long after that frightening crisis, and when we had all more or less adjusted to being Floridians, many things began to change. Mitchell graduated from Stranahan High School. He was very glad to be out of school and carried through with his plans to join the Marine Corps. He was to report to Parris Island, South Carolina in about six weeks. In the meantime, he made a trip to Illinois and spent time with the family. After his return home, he continued his work at the A& P Supermarket until it was time to report for his basic training.

Suzanne finished eighth grade that June. She had one more year in Junior High since it included ninth grade. She was glad to be out of school for a few months. She went to camp for one week and volunteered at Easter Seal part-time until school started again.

I had begun to lose weight earlier that year, which was very unusual; I had always found it difficult to keep from gaining. I was struggling with many feelings which were new to me and didn't know exactly what was going on. One morning when Dean leaned over my shoulder to explain some accounting theory to me, his face was close to mine, and I could hear his breathing. I wanted to pull away from him. I also had recently realized that no longer did I hug him spontaneously as I used to do. *What was going on? My secure, comfortable, closed-off life had a crack in it. How could I have let that happened?*

Knowing he was now earning enough to pay someone to help him, I decided to quit working as Dean's unpaid bookkeeper. Without my knowing just what it was that bugged me, those new feelings of discomfort around my husband had become difficult to tolerate. *Had*

I reached a point in my life that I just might be receptive to new thoughts and ideas?

Inner Turmoil I Don't Understand

I didn't know what I wanted to do with all the time I had after I no longer worked long hours on the accounts. *Why was I feeling so discontented?* I had not wanted Mitchell to go into the Marines with us at war in Viet Nam, and I sensed that Sue was not very happy with her life. I was feeling at odds with myself and couldn't understand why. I had a good husband, my kids were healthy; we were a normal happy family. *Why in the world couldn't I just enjoy all I had? Why wasn't I satisfied?* These were new feelings for me, and I didn't seem to be able to ignore them and go on with my wonderful life.

Our family doctor was concerned with my weight loss and with my complaints of many minor ailments. During one of my frequent visits to the family doctor, he looked closely at me and asked, "Are you happy at home?" Unexpectedly, I began to cry. When he suggested that I see someone and discuss what I was experiencing, I agreed to do so. I was glad to try anything. My first appointment with Dr. Abren, a psychologist, was a short time later. I had no idea what I was getting into, what a long, lonely journey I was embarking on. Initially, I thought, "I'll go six weeks; that should do it." I was starting down that "road less traveled" which Scott Peck wrote about a few years later. I'm not sure anyone would take that first step if they knew what was ahead. I realized later in my therapy that I couldn't have done it if I'd been surrounded by my family. Their influence was too powerful. It was right that I begin that painful journey alone.

A Silent Message 1964

My discontent was exacerbated because I was struggling with what to do since I wasn't tied to that unpaid desk job. Sitting home all day watching TV and reading novels, clerking at Sears, or selling party-plan products were all things that I knew I didn't want to do. *But what could I do? Be someone else's bookkeeper? Maybe I could work for a small office and just do typing; I liked to type and was good at it. But another desk job wasn't appealing.* These thoughts had been bothering me for some time, and now that I was free, I felt I had to do something constructive. The psychologist couldn't help me make that decision, he hardly knew me.

A couple of weeks later, while I continued to struggle with my dilemma, I awakened from a fitful sleep. I went out to the living room; I didn't turn on a light, but sat on edge of the daybed and propped my elbows on the window sill. Looking out the open window, listening to the soft rain falling, I thought about how the rain washed the leaves on the hibiscus hedge and how each leaf dripped rain water. I thought only of the rain as it fell on the hedge and washed the leaves. I was focusing intently without letting anything else interfere and put myself into a hypnotic plane without intending to. It allowed my mind to be sharply receptive. Then it happened. The answer to my dilemma came to me silently. It was not a voice; it was not a vision; it was knowledge that penetrated my consciousness. Go To School. The date was June 21, 1964, four days before my thirty-ninth birthday. It was a profound experience—an epiphany. The problem of what to do had been solved for me; I went to bed and slept soundly.

My First College Course 1964

Such an unlikely thing as going to school had never entered my closed mind. I had always felt I wasn't smart enough to go to college. But I accepted that message without reservation. I asked Dean if it was all right with him if I went out to the Junior college to take some courses, and he told me it was okay if I could get out there and back. I didn't know how, but I knew I could find a way. I could use our car when he was working at home, and I would find rides.

The next day I went out to the college, picked up a catalog and an application form, went home, filled out the application form and returned it. I pored over the catalog for hours, and decided what I would take if I was accepted. I could hardly wait to get that acceptance, so I could register. By the end of June, I took the placement tests, and registered the middle of August for English, Spanish, Zoology and Psychology.

On August 24, 1964 at the age of thirty-nine I attended my first college courses. Just two months after my dilemma of what to do with my life had been solved for me, my focus in life was changed. I never had doubts about what had come to me silently that night as I watched it rain.

A week before my classes started, Mitchell left for Parris Island to begin his rigorous boot camp. Eager to go, he had become bored with life at home. But he told me before he left, "I am glad to go, but nervous." None of us realized what a life-changing experience he was embarking upon.

A Family, But Separate Lives

That fall we were each absorbed in our individual lives. The marriage coasted along in its usual emptiness, with no big hills or valleys. Mitchell adjusted to Camp LeJuene and was doing well; Suzanne had begun dating Mike Powell. They had a group of friends with whom they socialized. My studies and my therapy kept me occupied. Gradually, I accepted that the kind of therapy I was experiencing was going to take a lot longer than six weeks, even though I was going twice a week. I had become attached to Dr. Abren and was glad to go more often; a week between sessions seemed hard for me to deal with. Dean had hired a woman to take over my role in the practice, so he, too, was making an adjustment.

My handwriting was a problem the first couple of years of school, because I was so tense and anxious that my hand shook. That bothered me a great deal. Because my writing was barely legible, I was embarrassed to hand in anything I had to write in class. I talked to some of the teachers and offered to read it to them if they couldn't decipher it. I'd lost more weight and was down to one-hundred-ten pounds from my normal one-twenty-five. Though I felt more unattractive than usual and knew I was too thin, I simply couldn't swallow much food.

Mitchell finished his boot camp and met Sue, Dean and me in Illinois for Christmas with our families. He looked great and was full of tales of his experiences. We were all glad to be back with the big family. However, I missed seeing Dr. Abren.

Sue graduated from Junior High that summer and worked part time in a day school. She also helped me with cooking and often baked something special. Mike, her boyfriend, ate with us occasionally, as did her girlfriends. Although she was only fifteen, when Sue had company, she sometimes cooked the meal.

I wrote in my journal at the time, "Sue is a delight, if she just liked school." And, "She is such a doll around the house." It would be years before I fully understood just how absent I was in her life, when she needed a real grown-up mother. Mitchell still needed a strong parent also, but he was not living in the house anymore and was free of the unspoken heaviness pervading our home.

Mitchell in Viet Nam 1966

Much to my dismay, Mitchell volunteered for Viet Nam and left the states in September. He spent a few months in Okinawa where he and forty-three other Marines received special training in demolition. Specifically, they learned how to go into the caves where the Viet Cong lived or had their headquarters, blow them up with explosives, and take prisoner any of those who survived. This was an especially dangerous assignment, sometimes taking place during, or immediately after, an engagement with the enemy.

He left Okinawa in January 1966, arriving in Viet Nam on the sixteenth. In February he was in Operation Double Eagle, which was a bloody, hard-fought battle. We heard about it on the evening news and saw pictures of the battle. Watching the young men fighting for their lives, it was very disturbing and frightening knowing that Mitchell was one of them. Later that same month, he was sent out on a ten day patrol; no one ever volunteered. If they ran out of rations, which they often did, they ate what they could find, which was never very appetizing. There were casualties on patrol.

The next month, he was in Operation Utah in which he was one of ten engineers (that is what the men carrying the explosives were called) with a company of infantry. Seven of the ten came back alive. He wrote, "It was real bad, real hairy; I am ready to come home."

In April he wrote that he had malaria and was to be sent to the Philippines. In the next letter, he said it was not malaria; he was in Da Nang for more tests. Within the next few days, we had a letter that he would be in the hospital there for five weeks. We never did get a diagnosis and didn't know for sure what his ailment was.

A couple of months later he wrote, "I will be spending the next sixty days out in the field. I am tired of it all, tired of being filthy."

Next we heard, "I had a narrow escape, our tank ran over a mine and was blown up. I was standing on the outside of the tank and was blown into the air. Twenty of us were pinned in by VC, and we were low on ammo, but more of our tanks came and the VC left."

Knowing Mitchell was in such danger was difficult enough, but there was no support from our community. The American people didn't want to be fighting over there; the men who were gullible enough to have volunteered were looked down upon. So our burden was heavier than if those we knew, our friends and neighbors were supportive and recognized that our son was risking his life every day. Members of our families sent messages of concern which helped.

I Continue Therapy and School

No matter what my kids were doing, my therapy continued, very tearfully and painfully. Many of the tears were tears which should have been shed years ago, but I had been too well-defended against recognizing painful feelings, much less expressing them. All of those old familiar defenses were gone, had been peeled away. I was being forced to see my life, past and present, as it really was—without the defenses, which had allowed me to live in an unreal pseudo-perfect world. I was experiencing the pain and sadness which I had denied for so many years.

With my emerging insights, I was realizing that I had options—I didn't have to continue in the status quo unless I decided I wanted to. Even though I felt anxious, and often sad, I knew intuitively I was moving in the right direction. Therapy was opening my eyes to the unhealthy ways I had always acted and reacted to life. I began see how some of my behavior was not serving me well, especially in personal relationships. I could see that I might not be inferior, that I might even be a pretty neat person.

Concurrent to continuing therapy, I was entering my sophomore year at the Junior college and learning much from the books I was studying, from the professors, and from the students around me. There were times when I stood on the walkway after a class, lost in thought of how the world was opening up to me. I was reading books and plays that I'd never even heard of. Chaucer's "Canterbury Tales" and Aristophanes's "The Birds" had been around for centuries, and I'd not read either of them. Such literature jolted my thinking. I was enraptured.

Young students walked around me without a clue as to the impact their education could have on them. I was finally growing up and realizing that I was barely one step ahead of my kids. I was growing up with my son and daughter and that wasn't supposed to happen.

I began to think in terms of actually getting a degree, and without thinking about the many possibilities, I decided I would get it in English and teach in a high school. I liked both grammar and literature, and thought I might be able to make it more exciting to students than many teachers did.

But toward the end of my sophomore year, one of my English teachers suggested I get a Master's degree, so I could teach at a junior college. She added that I would not have to take all the education courses and could focus on English courses. That was something I would never have thought possible, but I liked her, and decided that if she thought I was capable of teaching in a junior college it must not be too farfetched. Accordingly, I altered my plans.

That same semester, one of my history teachers asked me to come to his office after class. He said he'd heard about me and had a proposition for me. If I agreed, he would assign specific books for me to read, and we would meet every two weeks to discuss them. There were two other students who were going to do this, and we would all contribute to the discussion. My first thought was that he must think highly of me, and he must think I'm smart. I quickly accepted his offer, although it meant much more reading and more time spent on that course than if I just took his class.

Toward the end of that semester, he told me that if he wasn't married he would like to date me. I left his office with my feet barely touching the floor. I found him very attractive, he was a retired naval officer, was a spiffy dresser, and good looking. His comments were another great boost to my hungry ego, and one more step toward breaking down that negative self-image I was still lugging around. But it was a slow process. I had carried that view of myself for forty years; I couldn't toss it aside easily, but it definitely was starting to have cracks in it.

Another Crisis for Mitchell 1966

In the early fall of 1966, Mitchell wrote of another close call. "I had been on patrol and was suddenly blown about forty feet and knocked unconscious momentarily. I came to and was a bit disoriented, but could hear my buddies yelling at me. I started to run, and they yelled, 'Get your rifle! Get you rifle!' (It is drilled into a Marine to never, never leave your rifle behind.) In my dazed state, I had left mine on the ground. I ran back, picked it up and made a mad dash toward those friendly voices. The VC were shooting at me; I could hear the bullets whizzing by my head. I kept telling myself that if I got shot in the back to just keep going till I got over that hill in front of me. The guys kept yelling, and I kept running and dived over the crest of the hill, landing in a patch of prickly thorns. Thorns can feel good sometimes when compared to a bullet. The guys told me, 'It looked like you had an invisible shield and just couldn't be hit. Those bullets were flying so close to you on both sides and over your head.'"

What torture it was to read his letters and to know he was still facing those dangers. Even at that moment, someone might be shooting at him, trying to kill him.

I Wrestle With My Marriage

My marriage was more and more unbearable for me. There was never any affection between Dean and me, never had been. Sex, yes, but no affection. I am actually quite an affectionate woman and began to realize that my husband never had been toward me. He never touched me except when we had sex. Realizing that I initiated sex much more often than he, and that he often seemed easily distracted (I can't say love-making because that would be misleading) and with the help of my therapist, I began to accept such uncomfortable bits of reality. Dean and I were spending less and less time together. He was continuing to build a good accounting practice. I was totally engrossed in school, and enjoyed the stimulating discussions I had with some of my professors. My greatest personal concern was for Mitchell in Viet Nam and for Suzanne who was going through her teen-age years in an unhappy, unhealthy atmosphere. As I faced reality more and more, I began to feel great remorse that I had been such a failure at the one job I had always thought I would be so good at: Motherhood. It had been my sole purpose in life for twenty years, and I hadn't even known I was not prepared for it.

I had been talking a lot with Dr. Abren about how miserable I was around my husband. I wished I was not married to him; I even expressed a wish that he was an uncle or a cousin. But I found it nearly impossible to seriously consider divorce. I didn't know anyone who was divorced at the time; there were no divorces in either of our extended families. During those therapy sessions, we worked a lot on my view of the marriage—why I had married Dean and why I was still married to him. I knew I could not continue living with him much longer, because I was emotionally divorced already. Life in our house would not improve as long as I continued living such a false existence. Finally, I found the courage, after much inner turmoil, to broach the idea of divorce to Dean. "I have been thinking a lot about divorce. I think we need to talk about it."

Without hesitation he said, "I'm quite prepared for it. I've been expecting you to say something about divorce for months."

I almost screamed. I thought, *What would it take to get an emotional reaction from you? Here I've been struggling with how to bring this up to you, and you say you've been waiting for me to do so.* When I tried to talk with Dean about some of the logistics, he balked.

"I can't afford two separate households right now. I don't know when I can; I'll have to think about it," he said. And that was the end of that.

Here I had been going through hell to reach the point where I could say the "d" word to him, and he just shrugged it off, saying it would be okay with him. I had been wrestling with how not to hurt him, how to explain that I had struggled to arrive at such an unimaginable decision. He just said that he was "prepared for it." When I told Dr. Abren, he said, "What did you expect?"

That was a powerful experience for me, one which helped me later in my professional life. We can't live too long in an unhealthy, miserable marriage and do anyone any good—kids, spouse or self. So often we continue in a destructive relationship, thinking we don't want to hurt the other one, while the other one may also be miserable, but not capable of being honest about it. I am certain my two children would have been better off if their parents had divorced years earlier. I remembered how I suffered knowing my parents were not happy together. However, I also know that my immaturity and low self-esteem had to improve before I could even acknowledge that we were living in a vacuum.

Mitchell Home Safely 1966

Good news broke into the dismal mind-set in which I'd been functioning. In early October, Mitchell wrote that he would be leaving Viet Nam before the end of the month. I was glad to disengage from thoughts of unhappiness and divorce to focus on his coming home. He had made it safely this far, please, dear God, don't let anything happen to him now. Don't make him go on anymore of those dreadful patrols.

Mid- month he wrote that he would be leaving Viet Nam around the 21st. They were to spend a couple of days in Okinawa before heading for the states. He would call us as soon as he could. At 4:00 AM on October 24, 1966, the phone rang. Sue answered and yelled, "It's Mitchell!" He was in California and expected to be home in a couple of days. I was so excited, I couldn't go back to sleep. I started thinking which of his favorite foods to prepare and began moving some of my stuff out of his room, so he'd feel he still had a place in our home. I made a lot of phone calls to spread the good news. Mitchell was coming home.

Two days later, the three of us drove to Miami to meet his plane which landed on time. It seemed he was never going to come into view in that narrow doorway. A thousand people must have piled off of that plane, but finally there he was. Lord, but he looked good to my eyes! He wouldn't have to go out on any more deadly patrols, get blown off of tanks, or carry his rifle with him every minute.

After Sue and I hugged him, his Dad reached out and shook his hand. I thought it was too bad he couldn't hug him. We walked through the airport making small talk. *How do you start a conversation with your son who had been fighting for his life only a few days ago?*

He was home safely, so soon after knowing that he was in grave danger; it was hard to take it in. I can only imagine how it must have been for him. After some of the things he told us that week, before he had to report to the base, we knew we were very, very fortunate that he was alive with all limbs intact. When he left Viet Nam, there were just fourteen of the original forty-four demolition engineers alive. It took years before Mitchell recovered to pick up his life and move forward, and he still had nearly two years to fulfill his obligation to the Corps.

Mitchell spent much of his time during those two weeks at home sitting on the floor in his room with the door shut. He was putting together his sound equipment which he'd sent home from overseas. Later he also spent his time listening to music. I couldn't comprehend what a difficult time he was having adjusting to suddenly being home. Just one week before, he had been the hunted and the hunter in a war that he realized most Americans didn't believe in. I didn't know what to do for him, and perhaps there was nothing I could have done at that time. To add to his difficult adjustment, I felt I must tell him that his Dad and I were thinking seriously of getting a divorce. I knew his Dad wouldn't speak to him about it.

So, when Mitchell asked me to go for a ride in his brand new TR4 sports car I knew it was time to talk with him.

He was totally unprepared for the news. He would never have had a clue from his parents' interaction. We weren't relating much differently from what he was used to. We had never fought, never even raised our voices to each other, rarely if ever showed any affection for each other, so things weren't any different from what they had always been as far as Mitchell could tell. The timing couldn't have been worse, telling him his family was disintegrating when he so desperately needed a safe haven, a sense of stability. But it could be kept from him no longer; it was best that I tell him rather than to attempt to hide it from him. I believed I needed to be honest with him in regards to what was going on in his own family. He didn't say much when I told him; I didn't know if he was just not surprised or if he simply could think of nothing to say because it caught him off guard.

Sue, her Dad and I drove to Illinois for Christmas. Mitchell was getting a leave and would meet us there. Just a year ago, he had been in Okinawa headed for Viet Nam. He was slim and trim having lost nearly fifty pounds. Some of his close relatives, who had seen him just before he reported to Parris Island, didn't even recognize him. Several members of my family were visiting at Dad's house, when one of Mitchell's cousins walked across the room, extended his hand to Mitchell and said, "I don't believe I've met you." A couple of his aunts didn't recognize him either. He was a different young man from the one whom they had seen last year—different on the outside, also within.

Christmas with Our Families in Illinois 1966

No one in my family had an inkling that I was thinking of divorce; I didn't think they would understand the turmoil of my life these past two years. It is hard to explain to anyone the trauma of the kind of therapy I was undergoing, or how difficult it had been having Mitchell fighting in a war that most people didn't support, or what an emotional battle I had fought to come to the place where I could think of divorcing my husband. Dr. Abren was the only person who knew what it had taken for me to come as far as I had, and I was depending on him to help me keep moving in the right direction.

I had been seeing him for two and a half years, much of the time twice a week, and felt sort of naked in the sense that I wasn't who I used to be, but still didn't have a very good image of who I was becoming. I certainly wasn't there yet. I'd given up my old dysfunctional defenses and had just begun to build more healthy ones, so I felt quite vulnerable.

The visit turned out to be very good for me. I was reminded that I was lucky to have a big family who loved me. And even though they had no way of knowing me as I saw myself, I knew the love was there and that was good

When we returned to Florida, I began my junior year at Florida Atlantic in Boca Raton, a forty minute drive from Fort Lauderdale. I liked the small campus. There were even a couple of other students over thirty, so I wasn't quite so alone in that sense. And it was comforting knowing I would be a student there for the next two years, when I would, hopefully, earn my Bachelor's degree. While I was engrossed in my classes, Suzanne and Mitchell were dealing with their own life situations.

Update on Mitchell and Suzanne

When Suzanne was dismissed from school for a week because her bangs were too long, I went to the school, where I stood on the walkway when the students were moving from one class to the next.

I stopped a few girls with bangs as long as Sue's and took down their names. Then I went to the principal's office and gave him the list. "My daughter is coming back to school tomorrow to stay until the girls on that list have also been dismissed for a week."

He looked over the names of the nine girls I had listed. He looked at me with pursed lips, his eyes not quite focusing on me, and said, "Goodbye, Mrs. Young." That was the end of foolishness about long bangs.

Mitchell had to finish his four years at in the Marine Corps which was not easy for him. He was finding it difficult to stay on the base, doing what seemed like trivial things after fighting in the jungles of Viet Nam. Even though I worried about him, I didn't know how to help him.

Dr. Abren 1967

I was tired of having no fun and being so unhappy myself. I even felt discouraged with school sometimes and would think, *"I just can't do this; I can't go on like this,"* but that thought was always short-lived. I knew my studies kept me afloat, although it wasn't easy having no discretionary money for clothes, travel, or buying gifts. In some ways it was okay; I still liked most of my classes and could almost say I enjoyed studying. I was still an eager student. I got strokes from some of the professors who showed a special interest in my work. I liked school and knew I would not give up. Dr. Abren was always there reassuring me, acknowledging that it was a difficult journey, but worth it. So I probably got more strokes than either of my kids, but something was surely missing.

At times I felt as though I was attempting to swim across a swollen river, and was out in the middle, finding it impossible to go back, but still fighting hard to get to the other side. I wasn't sure what I would find when I got across, but was certain it would be better than what I was leaving. As badly as I felt about neglecting my kids during this time, I knew I couldn't make it across that river if I tried to pull them along. I felt pretty sure that once I had my feet on solid ground, I would be able to offer a hand to both Suzanne and Mitchell.

During the past several months I had come to the realization that I might have to change therapists, which would be extremely difficult for me. Dr. Abren was my primary support, the one person who knew where I was in my tumultuous journey of personal growth. And I had fallen in love with him which is fairly common. It had reached the point where I felt as though I survived for my next appointment with him, eager to see him rather than being eager to get on with the therapy. He had begun to give indications that my feelings were reciprocated. After one of our sessions, he said, "Would you like to go to lunch with me?"

Although I was surprised, I was also eager to extend our time together. "Yes, I would like to." I grabbed my purse, he opened the door for me, and after locking it, we walked to the elevator without saying much. I was self-conscious in the role of companion and couldn't think of what to talk about. We walked a short distance to a cafeteria across the street. I still had little appetite and being with him I had even less. "I'm not very hungry," I explained as I neared the cash register with only a muffin on my tray.

"Is that all you're going to eat?"

"I don't eat very much for lunch," I said. As thin as I was, I felt embarrassed to not eat more. Dr. Abren had some kind of a sandwich and a small salad. I ate as slowly as possible so I wouldn't finish too much before he did.

We sat in a booth facing each other. We were closer in the booth than in his office, and I was aware of his dark brown eyes and of how good he smelled. We held eye contact more than one would in a more casual relationship. I wanted to reach out for his hand, but restrained myself. "Do you eat here often?" I asked.

"I eat here when I'm at my office at lunch time."

"You're not in your office every day?"

He chuckled. "I have an office closer to my home where I work two days a week."

"Do you take clients to lunch often?"

"Are you hoping you are the only one I take to lunch?"

"Yes. I want to be special to you." I admitted.

"Can't you tell you're special by now?"

We talked about mundane things such as the weather and the advantages of living in the South. He held the door for me when we left the restaurant. I was aware that we had never touched each other. I wanted to throw my arms around his neck and hug him, but didn't. "Thank you for lunch," I said

"Maybe we can do it again soon," he responded.

"I hope so."

On the way home I reflected on what his taking me to lunch meant. I finally had to admit to myself that he had feelings for me beyond being my therapist. My positive feelings for him were powerful and should have been treated for what they were: transference—the playing out of emotions that belong to earlier experiences, especially childhood.

But our sessions became more and more focused on my wanting to be with him sexually. He was letting me know that he also wanted our relationship to change to one of lovers. I just had difficulty acknowledging it. He even asked me what I'd feel if we had an affair. I told him I wouldn't feel guilty because I was already divorced in God's eyes. Of course, he was married, but I pushed that aside and refused to think of it.

Finally, as I was leaving him after a difficult session, I told him I wanted so much to put my arms around him, and he whispered, "Why don't you try?" I left with turmoil piled on turmoil. Until then I had been able to doubt that he was in any way encouraging me, but I knew by what he said and the way he said it that day that he wanted ours to be more than a patient-therapist relationship also.

I could hardly wait for my next appointment during which we, again, dealt more than was appropriate with my feelings toward him. As I was leaving, I moved toward him, and we put our arms around each other. He didn't try to kiss me; we simply stood there embracing for what seemed like a fleeting moment. His hands were on my back pressing me close to him. I tried to make it last forever. Finally, I forced myself to drop my arms, turned, opened the door and slowly walked toward the elevator.

I drove home feeling less than elated. I felt I had stepped over a boundary that was there to protect me. It was up to me to protect myself, and I knew intuitively that I didn't have the strength to have an affair with him, knowing it could only end with heartbreak for me. And I had the strength to act accordingly. I just didn't know how I would make it without seeing him, but decided during that fretful night, that for my own survival, I had to stop seeing him.

I drove to my classes in Boca Raton the next morning but couldn't stop crying. I felt so alone and lost. I left class early and drove home to call him. I was shaking when I dialed his number. "Hello." Hearing his voice made me take a deep breath.

"Dr. Abren, this is Kate." I forced the next words from my throat. "I can't come to see you anymore."

"Is this because of what happened yesterday?"

After a long silence I was able to say, "I don't know, I just know I can't see you anymore."

"My God, Katie. (He had never called me by my first name before, and a diminutive form made it even more intimate). Now listen to me. I want you to call a friend of mine, Dr. Quine. He is a psychologist with whom I used to work at the University of Miami. Call him and get an appointment right away. I will call him later today to talk with him. He is a good therapist who will help you, and he is right there in Fort Lauderdale."

"All right, Dr. Abren. And I want you to know that I love you, and I hope I will find a man whom I can love as much as I love you today."

"I think the fact that you have loved me is an indication that you will find a man whom you can love and who will love you in return."

After a long silence he said, "What else can I say, Katie, except good luck to you and I will miss you. Goodbye."

"Goodbye, Dr. Abren. I will miss you so much."

For several reasons, that was one of the most difficult things I've ever done. As I said earlier, I was extremely vulnerable, having shed my life-long defenses and not having new ones in place yet. I was heading into a divorce which was quite traumatic for me. I was geographically distant from my extended family and had not shared with them the difficulties of the past years. I had more or less lost touch with most of my friends since I was so submerged in school and therapy. I felt painfully alone.

A couple of days later I met Dr. Quine and started trying to put myself back together. It took a couple of months for me to get comfortable with him. During that time I missed Dr. Abren so much, and desperately wanted to go back and see him, but knew for my own good that I must not. Looking back I have realized how very strong I was, which has helped me know I can overcome a lot. I have realized I was stronger than my therapist—he was the one who should have held the line.

That painful experience not only made me acknowledge my own inner strength, but also helped me understand transference more than one could ever learn from a textbook. The whole relationship should have been dealt with more professionally. Dr. Quine assured me it wouldn't happen in his office.

Life at Home 1967

Life kept dragging on at home. Sue and I made an agreement that she would fix dinner on Monday nights; I would fix it Tuesday and Thursday nights. She was seventeen, quite capable in the kitchen, and didn't seem to mind cooking. Three nights a week Sue, Dean and I ate together; the other nights we were each on his own. This helped me, because I was more relaxed and would eat more if I didn't have to eat with Dean. I was still trying to get my weight up to normal.

Mitchell called to let us know that he was coming home for an emergency eight day leave. A buddy was going to drive him down and would immediately return to the base. Mitchell wanted me to get him an appointment with my medical doctor and with Dr. Quine.

The phone rang an hour or so after Mitchell's call. "Hello. This is Sgt. Peale calling from Camp LeJuene. Is this Mrs. Young, Mitchell's Mother?"

"Yes," I said with a rush of anxiety.

"I know Mitchell called to tell you that he is on his way home for an emergency leave. I wanted you to know why he's been given an eight-day leave. Yesterday, when the officer told Mitchell's platoon their weekend leave was cancelled because some recruit's rifle had not passed muster, Mitchell lost it and grabbed the officer by his neck. He let go of him and started to leave the room as abruptly as he'd moved toward him. The officer in charge wants you to know that Mitchell is not in trouble with the Corps. We are aware that Mitchell is having a rough time since returning from Viet Nam; he has proven himself to be a good Marine. We are hoping the eight days will help him."

While he was home, Mitchell told me that he couldn't survive if he couldn't get off the base on the weekends. He also told me how close he came to going AWOL at times. Inner strength prevented him from doing so.

Mitchell saw Dr. Quine several times during those eight days; I'm not sure how much help it was to him, but it did get him through that crisis. I knew it was difficult for Mitchell to cope with the divorce in addition to the problems he brought with him from Viet Nam. At least I didn't try to deny that he was having a hard time as I might have earlier.

After Mitchell returned to the base, I once more faced the

unpleasantness of the pending divorce. I wanted to separate, but Dean said we couldn't afford it. I was sleeping, studying, and living in what had been Mitchell's room. It was uncomfortable being around Dean, even though, with our new sleeping and eating arrangements, I didn't see him very much.

One day I noticed that Dean had gotten a manicure; I was turned off. It was something that he had never done before; I wondered "why now?" Perhaps he was trying to be more attractive to other women. He had come home mid-morning a few days earlier and confronted me in my room; without raising his voice, he gave me an ultimatum, "Either we have sex or I am going to get it somewhere else."

"I don't care what you do. You're on your own." *Why did he say such a thing to me? Did he think it would make me jealous?*

Dean looked at me as if he hadn't expected that response. "How should I go about finding someone?"

"I guess you're going to have to figure that out for yourself."

Even knowing him as well as I did, I couldn't believe he would ask me such a thing. Lord! The good part was that I truly didn't care. I needed desperately to be out of there, but I simply couldn't quit school and go to work. I'd have my degree in a little more than a year—if I could last that long.

Mitchell wrote regularly. In some letters he sounded as if he were doing better, while in others, I could tell, he was barely hanging on. Suzanne was working four nights a week that summer of 1967 at Pizza Hut and continued dating her boyfriend, Mike. He was three years older than she and a nice young man. Mike was always respectful of us. He had graduated from high school and was working for his Dad in his printing business.

Sue seemed to be happier when school was on a break. She had a bridal shower for one of her friends. She did all the preparations and even paid for the cake. I was very impressed and proud of her. She was doing quite well, considering the atmosphere in our home. We three lived under one roof but as separate beings. She was an innocent member of our dysfunctional family. Her parents were in a silent struggle; she must have wondered how much longer the two adults in the house would continue their charade.

Moving Ahead

Dean came again to the house in the middle of the day. He entered my space and stood with an uncomfortable look on his face. After a couple of deep breaths, he blurted out, "I've seen a lawyer." I sat there with my mouth open until he added, "I thought I should tell you."

That's a dumb thing to say. Of course, you had to tell me. Did you think you could divorce me without me knowing it? "When did you do that?" I asked.

Twisting his left foot back-and-forth, he said, "This morning." He couldn't look at me, but turned around and walked into the kitchen.

It was difficult to believe that Dean had filed for divorce after repeatedly telling me we couldn't afford to separate. He must have wanted to be the one who filed the petition. It made no difference to me who filed. At least now we could move ahead. I hoped we could come to an agreement without involving attorneys. I had been working on budgets, trying to convince him that we could afford to separate and divorce. And now he'd hired a lawyer. Why hadn't I gone ahead and taken that step? Making such a move myself, with his saying there wasn't enough money, wasn't part of my modus operandi.

At least he had done something, had taken that first move toward divorce. I had been wrestling with the idea for a couple of years, even longer than that counting the time I was unhappy and wanting not to be married to him. I had felt emotionally divorced for so long that it was not a negative feeling for me, but one of relief—we had finally begun the process. I hired a lawyer to represent me.

Now that we had agreed that we were getting divorced, I felt free to ask him a question I had been wondering about. Later that same day, I found him sitting in the living room reading the Time Magazine and asked, "When did you stop loving me?"

He looked up with a blank expression, "It doesn't matter now," he said dismissively.

Not to be put off, I said, "Just tell me when it was that you knew you didn't love me anymore."

Pulling on his ear and looking uneasy, he said, "What the hell difference does it make now?"

"It makes a difference to me, I want to know. When did you stop loving me?"

After another short hesitation, he simply said, "I never did love you."

I inhaled deeply, turned and walked back to my room. *Well, I don't have to feel guilty for divorcing him; he must have been wanting out and just too weak to say so. Never had loved me? Why did he marry me? Why did he stay in such an empty marriage for twenty-four years? Would he have stayed married to someone he didn't love forever? Never loved me? How could I not have known? Have I been the stupid one! How could I have lived twenty-four years with a man and not have known that he didn't love me?*

Those questions would be answered in the near future as I began to put the pieces together. It was enlightening, and I was glad I had pushed for the answer. It helped me a great deal to figure out my own part in having married him, creating a marriage that should never have been. I was present and participated all of the time, so could hardly blame him.

Dean would not move out of the house until our settlement was agreed upon on the advice of his attorney. With two lawyers working on it, we seemed to be unable to agree on anything. In my opinion, they were creating discord rather than giving us assistance. There was no savings, no custody problem or retirement to fuss about, so what was the big problem? I knew he didn't want to pay me alimony. I wasn't asking for much, just four hundred dollars a month until I had my degree. But the uncertainty and haggling over it was taking its toll on my ability to cope. I felt desperate to have it finalized.

Sunday afternoon I drove to Florida Atlantic University to use the library. While there, I drafted an arrangement which I thought he might accept, and which I could live with, although it was far from being fair in my opinion. I had put him through four years of college, raised two kids, kept house for him for twenty-four years and worked for him to get his practice off the ground. He was now earning a very good living. It seemed to me he would feel obligated to at least help me until I earned my bachelor's degree. It was only eighteen months, for Pete's sake!

My physical and emotional health were going to collapse with much more of the high level of stress this agonizing process was creating within me. I had to do something. The agreement I wrote that day was based on what he had been wanting. I lowered the alimony to two hundred a month, feeling certain I could borrow two hundred to get me through school. That evening I showed him what I had written. He immediately said it was all right as far as he was concerned, that he would check with his lawyer.

"Why do we need lawyers? We should tell them this is what we want, and they can draw up the legal papers and get a hearing arranged." After some hesitation, he agreed.

It moved smoothly after that; a court date was set. Dean rented a furnished apartment, took some of the kitchen equipment, some of the linens, his personal belongings, some of the family pictures, and moved out of the house on December 4th, 1967, an overcast, sunless day.

Who can put into words the emotions one feels at such a time? For me it was, first of all a feeling of relief, mixed with regrets, sadness, disbelief, and anxiety about my future and about how the kids were dealing with the divorce. Even though I knew it was very difficult for them, I also knew it was for the best for all of us. They deserved to live in a more pleasant atmosphere, and there was no way that was going to happen as long as their Dad and I were together. Maybe I could offer them something better in the future, but this divorce had to happen before that could materialize.

Soon after her dad left, Suzanne had her wisdom teeth pulled. One of them got infected, giving her a bad couple of days and nights during which she stayed in bed. When I was commiserating with her on the second day she said, "It's the worst pain I've ever had." After a moment's hesitation she added tearfully, "physical pain, that is."

I knew what she meant but still wasn't able to take the opening and help her talk to me about her feelings. I was dealing with such strong feelings myself. I continued feeling guilty that I was unable to be there emotionally for her and her brother. But I was striving to get to the place where I would be able to give them what a mother should be able to give, and what they deserved and needed.

Dean came to the house for Christmas; we opened presents and had a big dinner, but it was awkward for all of us. There was no overt animosity between us, there never had been. But it certainly wasn't a joyous time for any of us.

I Change Directions 1968

Early in 1968, my path took another turn. Dr. Quine asked me, "Have you ever thought about going into social work? You would be good at it. However, it would mean two years of schooling beyond the bachelor's."

I was still planning on getting my master's in English, which would only take one year. "In two years I'll be forty-five years old," I snapped back at him.

"In two years you will be forty-five years old anyway," he said. I thought, *Dr. Quine, you are always encouraging me, expecting so much of me. You think I'm capable of doing whatever I choose to do.* Some of his confidence was seeping into my own consciousness and even being integrated. I was beginning to let go of my long-term negative perceptions of who I was and what I could do. Social work had never entered my mind, but the more I thought about it, the more I liked the idea. It was one more sudden turn I made on my bumpy road to maturity. Without Dr. Quine's suggestion, I would have been an English teacher. Immediately I began looking into social work schools. I really liked the idea of being in the helping professions.

Divorce is Final

Our divorce hearing was just a month later on February 5, 1968. The judge and both lawyers discussed the case for several minutes. Then the judge perused the papers before him, looking over at Dean, then at me. In my ignorance of law, I became concerned that he was hesitating in proceeding. Finally, after what seemed hours to me, he asked my lawyer, "Does your client know she is getting a raw deal as this is written?"

"Yes," I quickly interrupted, "And I accept it." He had no way of knowing the anxiety he created in my mind by raising any question which might delay the finality of the divorce. I would manage financially somehow. *Just let this be over with so I can get on with my new life,* I thought.

The judge asked each lawyer a couple more questions, studied the material on his desk and looked quizzically at me for an uncomfortable moment. "Divorce granted," he said, as he gathered up the papers in front of him and dismissed us.

It was over and I was no longer married. After taking some deep breaths, I rose and followed my attorney out of the courthouse. Thanking him, I turned toward my car, and said to myself, *"You're free. You're on your own."*

1953 Mitchell and Suzanne

1959 Dean, Mitchell, Suzanne and Kate Young

1956 Mom, Clay, Dad, Dorothy, Betty,
Juanita, Kate, Glenna and Vonnie

1957 The Family—the year that Mother died

1964 Mitchell graduates high school

1964 Kate's first day of college in Ft. Lauderdale

1964 Suzanne and Mitchell at Marine Boot Camp graduation

1966 Mitchell in Viet Nam

1967 Mitchell and Dad soon after Mitchell returns from Viet Nam

1967 Mitchell after Viet Nam

1968 Suzanne graduates from high school

1950 Parent's uptown home in Toulon, IL

1945 Kate

Chapter 3

WHAT DO I WANT TO BE WHEN I GROW UP?

I had felt divorced emotionally for some time so the finality of the court hearing in 1968 didn't have too great an impact on me. It did clear the way for me to move on; I put the house on the market one morning and drove to Boca for my classes that afternoon. When I returned home in the evening, there was a SOLD sign in the front yard. At first I thought they had put the wrong sign up, but I found out it had sold while I was at class. I was prepared for it to take two or three months. I would have to get my ducks in a row immediately, but it was nice not to have it drag on.

I didn't want much of the furniture which would only remind me of a life I was escaping. I took some lamps, the linens, the kitchen equipment and personal belongings and moved into a two bedroom apartment. Sue and I did the best we could to make it seem like home. She spent some of her time with her Dad. I was glad to be making a new beginning in a place of my own.

I had difficulty establishing credit which, in 1968, was a real problem for women. Even Sears, where I had worked, would not consider extending credit to me. Finally, I got a card at a gas station. It was important to get my credit established now that I was on my own.

A couple of months earlier I had sent in my application to Barry College in Miami where I wanted to study for my Master's in Social Work. The second week in my new quarters, I was notified I had been accepted. What a big relief that was, now I could relax, knowing for sure what I would be doing after I finished at Florida Atlantic.

Later, I was awarded an HEW grant for $3,300 for each of the two years that I would be at Barry. No strings were attached. What a windfall! That was a lot of money, and meant it would be easier for me to navigate the next part of my journey. Sue and I went out to dinner that night to celebrate.

The Truth Is Out

About a month later, I was feeling pretty good when I walked into Dr. Quine's office for my appointment. I surprised him and myself by sitting in a different chair from the one I'd always used. Before I could say anything, he asked me, "Did you talk with Dean?" I told him I hadn't.

"Well, I received this unusual phone call from your ex-husband. His name is Dean, isn't it?"

"Yes." I answered, wondering why Dean would call Dr. Quine.

"He asked me if I had discussed Lois with you. I told him without your consent I could not disclose what had been discussed. After a short silence your ex-husband added, 'Lois Bender is getting a divorce, and we are going to be married.'"

In that brief exchange, Dr. Quine revealed that the last several years of my marriage had been a farce, all those years when my husband assured me there was nothing between him and Lois. *How could I not have known?* Having been lied to and deceived by my husband—that was the worst part. I felt as if I had been cast in an R-rated movie or was a character in one of those sleazy stories printed in cheap love story magazines. *How in the world could I have been so blind?* I had caught them embracing and kissing more than once, and yet, I believed him when he said there was nothing to it.

I could accept that he fell in love with another woman easier than I could accept all the lies. *Why couldn't he have been truthful with me, especially these last few years when he knew I was struggling with the decision to divorce?* And I had been so afraid of hurting him, believing divorce would be traumatic for him. And all that time, he and Lois were wondering how much longer I would hang on to the marriage. Then I heard an echo: *I-never-did-love-you.* Lord, but I felt terrible.

I couldn't study that night or the next day. I wrote how I felt, how soiled I felt thinking of the times I had instigated sex when he didn't seem interested. He had probably had sex with her that day. No wonder I would cry sometimes after sex and not know why. I thought of those years when they were carrying on, of the many days and nights he spent with me while he yearned to be with her. I wrote my feelings down, hoping it would help diminish the ugly pain I was feeling. Realizing how I had used denial to my own detriment, I should have known years ago; I simply hid from the truth, denied it was happening, did not want to know. I was paying a big price for that denial; it would have been easier if I had acknowledged it years ago. I knew this pain would teach me to face things as they unfolded in the future. I would deal with my reality and not hide from it. *No wonder I had felt unloved. I was.* I had to understand my part in all of this, so I would not be an angry, bitter woman the rest of my life. Using denial to escape pain was no longer going to be something I needed or wanted. If I let myself feel the pain, I would be able to experience joy and an appreciation for beauty which I had never really taken in. Living with my feelings numbed was no longer an option nor did I want it to be.

To add salt to my raw, wounded feelings, when Sue came home the next day after visiting her Dad, she said, "Dad told me to tell you Denise is my half-sister." I stood there silently for a moment before retreating to my bedroom.

Denise, Lois' daughter, was ten-years-old. That means they were seeing each other for more than five years before we left Joliet. Dean had gone with me to visit Lois in the hospital to see Denise when she was born. We even had a toast later to the new baby with Lois and her husband, Walt. I saw what I wanted to see and blinded myself to what I wasn't ready to deal with. *My God, I lived with that man for so many years and was anesthetized the whole time,* I thought. He said he never loved me; I guess I really never loved him or I wouldn't have tolerated such an empty relationship for so long. And Walt, a nice guy, what was he thinking during those years? And Dean couldn't even tell me himself—had to have Dr.Quine and Suzanne tell me. What a wimp.

He wasn't honest with me during our marriage so, of course, I shouldn't expect him to be now.

Suzanne Is Eighteen 1968

While I was learning to deal more appropriately with life, Sue was experiencing what should have been a carefree, happy time for her. Her prom was on the first of June; she and Mike looked so grown up that night. We took pictures, and they drove off. I felt like I should have been more 'with' her. I knew my sadness and lack of enthusiasm was bound to affect her enjoyment of this memorable evening.

One week later she turned eighteen. And just five days after that, she graduated from high school. She told me where to find the best seat and said to come early so I'd get it. We had gone through some rough times getting to this day, and I didn't want to miss any of it. That night I was the first one to arrive for the graduation ceremony; the doors weren't even open yet. I got the seat Sue had described and she spotted me the moment she walked through the door with the graduating class. No one else could know all that was behind the big smiles we exchanged at that moment. She had actually made it, regardless of what was going on with her parents.

It helped her that she had Mike to talk with. During most of her high school experience, they had been dating and were planning to be married in August. She had quite a summer with her eighteenth birthday, the prom, graduation in one month, and a wedding to look forward to.

Mitchell Is a Veteran

The day after Sue's birthday, Mitchell was honorably discharged from the Marines. He was now a Viet Nam Veteran. That was not something to be proud of at that time; many people considered Viet Nam veterans to be traitors. There were no bugles blown, no cheering and no pats on the back when these soldiers returned home from the battlefield. In fact, some people spat on the men in uniform, if they had served in Viet Nam. The animosity toward our soldiers was very damaging to them individually. They had been at war, been shot at, killed men, and had seen friends killed as they fought side-by-side. To be treated as scum upon their return to the States, was crushing. It took years before that destructive attitude toward the veterans of the Viet Nam war changed; it added to the trauma these brave men had experienced. It was to be several years before Post Traumatic Stress Disorder (PTSD) was recognized as a Psychiatric Diagnosis. Once Mitchell read that PTSD was an acknowledged medical condition, he realized that he was affected and had been fighting it on his own. This motivated Mitchell to get the kind of help that he needed to begin his recovery.

In the meantime, Mitchell kept his status as a Viet Nam vet hidden. I was surprised several years later when I heard him acknowledge voluntarily that he was a Marine and a veteran of the war. As years passed, he became proud of his service to his country. It became a vital part of his life, helping him in his professional career and molding him into the confident person he is today. He will forever carry the deep scars which are part of every combat veteran.

Mononucleosis 1968

Mitchell was discharged in June, and Suzanne and Mike were making plans to be married in August. I was in my last semester at Florida Atlantic, and I was feeling extremely tired. I had gone with Sue to pick out her wedding dress and was so exhausted that I could hardly keep up with her. It was raining, and I wondered if I would make it across the street as we headed to the car. That was unusual, because I am naturally a high energy person. I complained of my lack of energy to Dr. Quine, who told me I needed to be careful, or I was going to get sick. That was already happening. I was diagnosed with mononucleosis a week later and told to get twelve hours of rest a day. That was just not possible with my school schedule. I was in my last semester, expecting to begin my Master's soon after graduation; I couldn't let anything prevent me from graduating. And my daughter was going to be married in less than a month.

I was able to help Suzanne make the reservation for the reception and went over the details of the food and beverage she wanted served. That is about as far as I got in helping her with her wedding. I was hospitalized the next day because of Sue's intervention. She had called the doctor and told him that she thought I was not resting or eating as I should, and that she was worried about me.

When I went in for my appointment, I was sent directly to the hospital, where I spent the next two weeks. I had pushed myself more than I should have. My liver was so swollen that I was not allowed out of bed until it was back to normal size and functioning properly. I guess that is what a forty-three year old gets for hanging out with college students. Mono is referred to as the young person's disease or the kissing disease. Neither of those categories applied to me.

I had taken my mid-terms just before I was hospitalized, and I was able to keep up with the assignments while sitting up in bed. I mailed my work to the appropriate professor when finished. I spoke daily with the Dean of the English department. The Dean assured me that I would graduate as planned.

An Unexpected Visitor

While I was in the hospital, my ex-husband, Dean, showed up at my bedside with a dozen red roses. He had never, ever given me even one daisy much less a dozen roses. *There must be something on his mind,* I thought, *other than my health.*

After an awkward silence, he said, "Lois is having second thoughts about us getting married and wants to talk with you." Just a week earlier, she had moved to Fort Lauderdale from Joliet with two of her four children, leaving the older two with their dad.

I was flabbergasted. *Lois wanted to talk to me about marrying my former husband whom she played around with for years while I was married to him?* She was my friend and his lover at the same time, and wants to ask me for advice. This is too bizarre.

As soon as I could find my voice, I said, "No, I can't do that." The last thing I needed was to see Lois and discuss her problems regarding her relationship with Dean. I didn't want to be bothered, and I didn't care what they did. But he pleaded with me (his behavior reminded me of a child's begging), and I finally agreed to see Lois. What the hell, I thought, let her come see me. After all, I'm in a better place than she is, even though I'm bedridden and look like I've been dragged behind a truck.

I said, "Okay, when does she want to come?"

We set an approximate time and he left. Immediately, I called the nurse and asked her to get rid of those flowers, to take them to someone who would appreciate them.

When Lois came into my room, I almost felt sorry for her; she looked awful and must have felt worse. *How could she ask me for help? This really was too much*—my former friend coming to me for solace and advice, because she didn't know if she loved my former husband.

After perfunctorily greeting each other, she said, "Thanks for seeing me. I need to talk to you about my situation. I don't think I love Dean and here I am in a strange town. I don't know anyone and don't have enough money to live on my own. I don't know what to do."

Boy, you surely do know how to create a mess, don't you? You don't know if you love him and have taken two of your children from their dad and their friends, and now you don't know if you love him? You two ought to get along just fine!

After cutting off my nasty thoughts, I said, "Why don't you get a job, get the kids in school, and put off making a decision right now? Give yourself time and get more comfortable with your new surroundings. Maybe you could stay with him until you get on your feet. That way you could find out what your feelings are. Or maybe he would help you financially until you can start working and support yourself. You need time."

I was playing therapist to her. She *probably doesn't have what it would take to act on the suggestions I've made. Frankly, I didn't give a damn!* Not a lot more was said. She didn't respond to what I'd suggested and left after thanking me. I lay back in my bed to rest and shook my head in disbelief at this bizarre turn of events.

Suzanne's Wedding 1968

Suzanne and Mike handled all the details of their wedding, except for the couple of things she and I'd already done. They ordered the invitations and the flowers, hired the photographer, and managed the myriad details that a wedding entails. Sue was barely eighteen and working full-time. I was proud of both of them; they had stayed within the agreed upon budget and handled everything on their own.

Juanita, my sister, came down to visit us a week before the wedding. It was one of the best things that could have happened. Her presence was a great boost for Sue and wonderful for me. She and Suzanne brought some of the wedding gifts to the hospital, so I could see Suzanne open them. Considering all of the tasks she was managing, Sue was quite solicitous of me. It must have been difficult for her, worrying about her mother rather than having her mother to lean on during her wedding preparations.

The doctor let me leave the hospital on Friday, the day before the wedding. I had to promise to rest twelve hours a day. That was not difficult, since I didn't have enough energy or stamina to do otherwise. But I was determined to attend the wedding. Haydn (Juanita's husband) arrived the day before the wedding; he drove Juanita and me to the church early, so that we could be with Sue as she dressed. When we walked in to the bride's dressing room, there was Lois helping Sue put on the traditional garter. I kept walking without even speaking and went over to the window to give myself a moment to collect my wits. I really felt violated. That woman usurping my place with my daughter on her wedding day! I wanted to shout at her, "You can have my husband, but leave my daughter alone!"

Juanita was soon standing beside me and asked, "Who is that?"

"That's Lois," I whispered.

"If I'd known that I wouldn't have spoken to her."

When we turned around, Lois was gone. I acted as though everything was fine; I surely didn't want to do anything to dampen this day for Suzanne. The wedding was lovely; Suzanne was beautiful, and I caught the bouquet. Actually, Sue turned around and threw it directly to me.

Lois and Dean were married the following Friday; nothing they did surprised me or upset me. I had better things to think about now. I thanked God that I had spent those years in therapy—that I was comfortable with myself and didn't have to spend energy on that part of my life any more.

A Slow Recovery

I had Meals on Wheels delivered to me for a time, until I was strong enough to cook my own meals. It took me six months to totally recover. I had a couple of months before classes started at Barry, which was a blessing.

When I first returned to school, I had to sit down and rest mid-way up the twenty steps leading to the library. It was shocking to me to be so easily fatigued, but I gradually felt better, grew stronger, and that crisis was soon a thing of the past also.

During September, I sold the Ford Grand Marquis that I had been driving and bought myself a Volkswagen, anticipating the sixty miles a day I was going to have to drive to classes in Miami. I also had to move, because I had rented my present apartment with the agreement I would stay only six months. So, in my new VW, I found something which would do, and moved my things once more. It wasn't too big a job because I had very little furniture, but it was an emotional thing for me, I needed to be settled, to begin to feel I had a home.

Unexpected Honor 1968

Soon after the move I received my diploma in the mail. As I removed the diploma from its envelope, I was totally surprised to see that I had graduated summa cum laude. Ironically, I had to look it up to see if it was above magna cum laude. I had never given a thought to such an honor. I just entered each class determined to get the best grade that I could. Receiving this honor was a validation of my abilities. It rid me of any lingering notion that I was not "smart enough" to take a college course. This had been my mind set just a few years ago; my therapy and my concurrent four years of college had dispelled this notion. For some time I sat thinking about what it had taken for me to earn that piece of paper, and I thought of all I had learned during four years of therapy. I wasn't sure which had been more difficult and which had been more rewarding—college or therapy. I still had further to go in both areas.

The next day, as soon as I was seated with Dr. Quine, I said, "I got my diploma in the mail yesterday and I earned honors." I had been looking forward to sharing this news with him.

"You graduated cum laude"? He asked. I smiled and shook my head.

"Better than that."

"Magna cum laude?" Again I indicated no.

He hesitated before he asked, "Summa cum laude?" I smiled as I nodded.

"Wonderful. Wonderful! You can be proud of earning that honor with all that you have gone through these four years. That's fantastic."

It was good to have someone who had been there with me and knew some of the hills I'd climbed.

Classes at Barry

My classes at Barry started the next Monday. My first day was exciting, although quite draining. Barry was a small Catholic college (it is now a university). The social work classes were clustered in one area with twenty of us in the class—all scheduled to take the same class at the same time, no electives. We were to attend classes three days a week, and the other two days we served an internship.

Our schedules were planned for the next two years, no variation. We could state our preferences for the type of placement we preferred for our interning, but that didn't guarantee we'd get it. I wanted so much to be placed in a clinical setting, preferably in Fort Lauderdale at Henderson Psychiatric Clinic, but that was not to be; I was placed at Juvenile Court in Miami where I saw the young offenders, sometimes alone, sometimes with their families. The experience was okay, but it was not Henderson Clinic. I also had that drive to Miami, while Henderson was just a few blocks from my apartment. Three of my new friends were placed at Henderson. I was envious.

Research was one course that we had to take all four semesters, leading to a research paper the second year. That was entirely new thinking for me, and I learned to like it. We twenty students were a very competitive group, with ages ranging from early twenties to late forties. We were assigned a lot of papers—from two pages to fifty. When I wasn't in class or at my placement, I was in the library. Weekends were spent studying and writing papers. There wasn't much time for socializing. I was one of five women who ate lunch together every day we were on campus. One of the women was also from Fort Lauderdale;

we rode together the days we had classes. Because her placement was at Henderson, I drove alone the two days I was at the Miami Court.

We started our internships in November; there were four of us at the Court with our supervisor, Dr. Gibbs. Following each one-hour session we students had with our clients, Dr. Gibbs spent half an hour with us. It was a very good system for getting used to being a therapist. It would take years before I felt fully competent as a therapist, but I was on my way. I really like it.

There were no classes in the summer, and I got a job working at the Family Service Agency in Ft Lauderdale. I actually got paid those few weeks I was there, although it seemed easier than the position had at the Juvenile Court in Miami. My supervisor, an older woman, taught me a lot, and I felt good about my first job as a professional. I certainly enjoyed having the extra money.

I had all I could do to keep my head above water that first semester at Barry, and neglected both Sue and Mitchell more than usual. I had so much studying to do, so many papers to write, and clients to see at the placement, plus all the driving, and seeing Dr. Quine twice a week, there was no time for much else. When I was able to get off the merry-go-round for a brief respite, a sense of aloneness would hit me. I realized that, aside from my studies and responsibilities connected to school, I didn't have much to hang onto. I knew it was good that I was engrossed in being a student, but I also knew I was in a financially precarious place. I was approaching my mid-forties with no health insurance, no savings, and only my belief in myself. If I could just stay well, I would be all right.

The first semester ended, and the second one went a bit smoother. I attended my first professional workshops and conferences. Good speakers—psychiatrists and social workers who were well-known and had written books and articles. Those events were stimulating and educational. They helped us students begin to see ourselves as professionals. I was soaking up all the information I could, how the different theories worked, and how individual therapists bent those theories to suit their personalities.

My Second Year at Barry 1969

At the same time I finished my first year at Barry in June 1969, I finished five years of therapy. I had a good relationship with Dr. Quine, liked him a lot, and knew he liked me. I thought if Dr. Quine liked me, I couldn't be too bad. I had more confidence in myself. I was more at ease with my cohorts as well as with my superiors. I was still struggling with feeling lonely; aware of wanting to have a social life; wanting a relationship with a man; wanting to have some fun. However, I was enjoying learning and associating with people whom I found stimulating. These experiences had been totally missing in my former life. And most importantly, I knew my educational goal was within reach. That more than compensated for the material possessions I lacked.

In the fall, I resumed the mad rush of keeping up with school work and classes. I worked on my thesis whenever I could spare a few minutes. I had titled it "Communication Patterns of Married Couples Who Seek Counseling." I needed to be ready to gather the data by the end of the semester. I was looking forward to that part of the project.

My studies pretty much consumed me, but I was aware of the big events that were taking place in the world. The summer of 1969, Neil Armstrong and Buzz Aldrin landed on the moon. As Neil stepped onto its rough surface, he said, "One small step for man; one giant leap for mankind." A concerted effort had been made to be the first country on the earth to reach the moon and the USA had succeeded.

My Note Taking 1970

I continued taking notes about what happened in my therapy sessions. I began the note-taking in the middle of my first year with Dr. Abren. I found that I was unable to focus on my studying immediately after a session, and it was helpful if I wrote down the salient points— thoughts that kept interfering with my concentration. As time passed, I wrote a more complete recounting of my hour with him. I continued doing so when I began seeing Dr. Quine. I would return home and immediately write down the most meaningful parts of the session. It cleared my mind, so that I could focus on studying. One day, in early 1970, I told Dr. Quine about my note-taking.

"Could I read them?" he asked.

I hesitated before I said, "I will bring them to my next appointment."

Faculty at Barry

I was placed in Miami again for my second year internship and was so disappointed. I was with Jewish Family Services—at least it was in a clinical setting. Again, it meant driving to Miami five days a week. Mr. Barr, who was responsible for our placements, had a mind-set against those of us who wanted to be in clinical settings. He favored the social services setting, such as working in the black neighborhoods, or with retarded children, or with adoptions agencies. Also, he knew I was in therapy and made remarks that let me know he really did not believe in such "tripe."

What destructive measures are sometime taken by people who are in positions of power! Here I was, within a few blocks of Henderson Clinic, and he refused to place me there. He knew how badly I wanted that placement.

However, other faculty were giving me strokes and talking with me positively about my work. Dr. Adler was our research professor; he liked my writing and was complimentary of my progress on my thesis. Sister Demarilla spent time with me, and she told me why she thought I was going to be a good social worker. The casework instructor, Dr. Kennedy, talked to me privately a few times and made me feel secure about the direction in which I was heading. I was still somewhat unsure of my self-worth, and soaked up those reassurances.

Mitchell and Suzanne

During this time, Suzanne was working for GMAC and Mike continued working for his dad on their newspaper. They seemed to be managing married life okay.

Mitchell continued working in the Ft. Lauderdale area. He had a motorcycle, and a girlfriend, and seemed less agitated.

Sue and Mitch were considerate of me; we ate meals together whenever we could, usually at Morrison's Cafeteria or other restaurants where it wasn't too expensive. Even with my HEW grant, I had to be frugal.

Therapy and School

I was eating lunch one day at school with the four women with whom I always ate, when Rachel (who was notoriously outspoken) responded to something I'd said.

"You shouldn't be so melancholy. You shouldn't let school rule your life. Let people see that you can be happy. Lighten up!"

And she is going to be a therapist, I thought. *She certainly has a lot to learn.* Since I could think of no nice response, I said nothing.

When I told Dr. Quine about this event, he said, "You should tell her that you have a therapist, and when you want her impressions you will let her know." I was so glad I had Dr. Quine with whom I could discuss such things. He understood me, always helped me feel better. He encouraged me to move forward, to not to let others overwhelm me, and to stand up for my rights. I was learning.

My fourth and last semester at Barry began in January 1970. I enjoyed doing the interviews for my thesis, but it was a very time-consuming process. I discovered that I was able to apply some of what I had learned in those research classes. More and more I understood the value of studying research. Clinical work, I realized, is also a kind of research—delving into another's life and analyzing that data in order to help the client make changes. Two years earlier I had questioned the value of so much research.

Dr. Quine was relentless in keeping me working on those things that were still disturbing to me: my standing in my family of origin; my lingering feelings of being inferior, memories of childhood which still upset me. All of these emotions and thoughts had to be discussed and rehashed multiple times. I can see now how the repetitious reviewing of these remnants of inappropriate behaviors held over from childhood took away the power that they had exerted over my personality. Reliving and expressing the sadness and hurt gradually made those memories impotent; their negative power and influence over me were fading. However, at the time it was devastatingly difficult to deal with these feelings; it is such a lonely journey even with a therapist to help guide you. That is why, during analytical, long-term therapy, it is expected that the patient will become quite dependent on the therapist. The therapist is aware it will work itself out—the patient will not be dependent forever. It's like a parent and child relationship. The goal of the parent (therapist) is to assist the child (patient) to the point where the child is independent, but the child is dependent upon the parent during the process.

Job Searching 1970

The fourth semester was coming to an end; I frantically worked on my thesis, typing it and getting it bound. What a relief to have that finished; it had seemed to be a monumental task when first told what it entailed. Now, I began looking ahead to finding a position as an MSW—Master's in Social Work. I sent out my thin resume, hoping someone would want a forty-five year old, with no experience, but eager to work and learn. I sent one to Henderson Clinic—where I had wanted to intern, and where Dr. Quine worked. But West Palm Beach Mental Health Center and Hospital was where I really wanted to work. I sent my resume to them first. I heard from both clinics about two weeks later, asking for interviews.

I had a two hour interview with Dr. Vogler in West Palm, toured the new private mental hospital, set to open in a couple of months, and met several staff members. The Mental Health Center was going to be part of the hospital when it opened, and the job would involve working with in-patients and their families. The interview, the setting, and staff members increased my desire to begin my career in West Palm

This job would be a new start for me and I would be close enough that I could see Dr. Quine occasionally; the kids and I could see each other often, yet not be on top of each other. I had reached that magical plane where I wanted to be somewhat independent of Dr. Quine. I wanted my own place, like a kid who wants to move away from parents in order to establish her individuality.

Aside from worrying about getting on the staff at West Palm, some good things were happening. There was a euphoric atmosphere at Barry; we second year students were nearly finished and filled with anticipation. Most of us were having interviews and dreaming of working in a setting of our choice. Some students wanted to work with mentally challenged children, some with the elderly, and others with the disadvantaged. I wanted to work in a clinical setting with "good old neurotic adults." And that is not a pejorative use of the word neurotic. Neuroticism is a matter of degree.

With all else going on in my life, I had managed to find time to have an affair. We were introduced by a classmate. He was a handsome lawyer, a great dancer, and a good sexual partner. However, he didn't have any common sense, and his values and view-of-the-world were very different from mine. We avoided talking about life's serious issues. I just enjoyed my time with him without worrying about anything else. It would soon be three years since my marriage disintegrated, and this was the first man I dated more than once. I hadn't dated many men even once. Even though I knew it would not be a permanent, lasting relationship, it helped fill the void I had felt for some time. Plus, for the first time in my life, I knew what good sex was, which helped me with my personal and sexual identity as a woman.

As the time approached when I expected to hear from the West Palm Clinic, I became anxious. When another week passed without any word from them, my anxiety rocketed. When I saw Dr. Quine, I said, "They don't seem to appreciate how difficult it is to wait when the decision is so important."

"They don't know how you react under stress."

"Do you think I'm overreacting?" I asked, knowing I probably was.

"Well, it isn't the only job out there, you know."

I didn't answer, and thought, *it's the only one I want.* He was right, but it was nearly impossible for me to change that idea, even though I knew that Henderson Clinic was still an option. It was also close to where I lived. When classes were over, theses had been accepted, and some students knew where they were going to work, I became more aware that I'd not heard from West Palm.

Graduation

Glenna came for my graduation; it was nice to have her with me showing support. She, Mitchell, Suzanne and Mike attended the ceremony. Mike was the photographer for his dad's paper and took some great pictures of me walking across the stage, and coming down the few steps with a satisfied look on my face. What an evening! On the one hand, graduating meant the culmination of six years of sacrificing and working to the breaking point, moving from one ugly apartment to another, studying and studying. On the other hand, I had learned so much—the sciences, Spanish, psychology, literature, sociology, history, English, research, and even math. I appreciated my education more than any twenty-something kid ever would. All six years had been concurrent with my agonizing therapy. No wonder I felt overwhelmed with emotion!

With each passing day, I became more frightened that I wasn't going to be hired at West Palm. I began to wonder what I would do if they didn't hire me. Where else could I go and get the experience I wanted? Finally, I talked again to Dr. Quine about not hearing from Dr. Vogler. He suggested I call and inquire.

I did so the next morning, and Dr. Vogler said he had about decided I was employed elsewhere. It had been two weeks since our initial interview, and he had written to setup an appointment for a second interview and had not heard from me. I hoped he didn't hear the big sigh that escaped my lips. We made an appointment for the next day. I was so relieved and, again, full of hope. I took Glenna out to eat, and became an effervescent hostess within the hour.

Later, Dr. Vogler told me the politics were such at the hospital that he figured some disgruntled employee had seen to it that his letter to me had not gone out.

My interview went well. Quite the confident woman, I wrote in my journal, "I was at my best." I would know in a few days about the job. Sunday was Mother's Day—Mitchell, Suzanne and Mike came for dinner. It was nice being together, however, my mind was elsewhere much of the time.

When the phone rang on Monday morning, I heard Dr. Vogler's voice. He said, "We want you to come to work with us, if you are still interested."

Oh, my God, am I interested?

I tried not to shout and answered, "Yes, I am still interested."

An ecstatic feeling rushed through me. I was going to work where I knew I would be challenged to keep learning. I was finished with school, going to work at West Palm Beach Mental Health Center and Hospital, where I would get excellent supervision, and I would even get paid. I would no longer have to spend every evening and weekend studying and writing papers. I was leaving Fort Lauderdale and my proximity to Dr. Quine. I was finally leaving home; I was forty-five years of age.

I felt better about myself than I ever had. I was moving to West Palm Beach to begin my new life. I knew I had worked hard to arrive at this day, but I also knew I had not accomplished this by myself. A number of people had helped me, and I had been blessed with the intellectual ability, the motivation, and the perseverance to succeed in what had been six years of sacrifice, hard work, and neglect of my son and daughter. *Thank you, God, for all your blessings.* I knew not everyone could have done it, and was grateful that I could.

Letter from Dad 1970

After my graduation, Dad wrote me a wonderful and unexpected letter. He wrote, "I am glad for you and proud of you that you have an MSW and that you have a job."

What a tremendous pat on the back that was. I couldn't recall ever before receiving recognition from him, except in first grade when he'd looked at my papers and told me how good I was doing. It was worth more to me than had he sent me a thousand dollars. At the end of that letter, he signed, "Lots of Love 2 my Katie Pearl, Dad." Bless him. Maybe he couldn't say "I love you", but he could write it. After I wiped the tears from my eyes, I re-read that line over and over, savoring the love he expressed in those few words.

I planned to drive to Fort Lauderdale every other Saturday to see Dr. Quine. I knew I was not quite finished with therapy, but I was over the hump—far enough along to be okay with seeing him every couple of weeks. It was much different from needing to go twice a week.

West Palm Beach

I made the big move to West Palm Beach in May 1970. It was only fifty miles away, but much further in the sense of what it meant to me. At last I was a professional woman earning enough money to live on ($7,200). I was in a new world, and I liked it. There were psychologists, social workers, psychiatrists, nurses, and aides on the staff. My office was near the in-patient unit and right across the hall from one of the psychiatrists, Dr. Alegra. I was to work closely with him and another psychiatrist, Dr. Menendez. Both were Cuban and had done their internships at the Menninger Clinic. At different times over the next couple of years, they each would be my supervisor, and I would learn a great deal from them.

My first day on the job was exhausting; my anxiety level was over-the-top. There were so many new people to meet, including my first clients in the new setting, and my first session with my supervisor, Mrs. Danser. She was perfect for me at that time, and I learned much about my profession from her. By noon I was exhausted. About two o'clock, Mrs. Danser came to my office and told me I could go home early. I was relieved and delighted. She was a very kind, perceptive woman.

My New Life 1971

I began riding my bike eight miles every morning before work. I continued refining my therapy notes, and started putting the first couple of years in book form. I didn't say "I'm writing a book." That seemed presumptuous to me. Writing helped take up some of my free time, but could not keep me from being aware of my aloneness. I wanted someone to share my life, but had not met a man whom I considered to be a suitable candidate. My affair with the lawyer ended when I moved to West Palm; I was glad I'd experienced it, but glad it was over.

I was forming friendships at the clinic. Mona Ludwick was one of the nurses I worked with. She and her husband, George, had three children and lived in Tequesta, just north of West Palm. Remembering that Dr. Quine told me to "just be yourself, you're not so bad," I began to see that most people liked me.

By early 1971, I was on a team with Dr. Menendez, a nurse, and a couple of aides; Dr. Menendez was friendly, knowledgeable and patient with those of us who were eager to learn from him. After we had been working together six months, he said, "You are something else; I like your work." I soaked up such reassurances and built on them. But he flirted with me, which I had difficulty handling. I found him charming and desirable, even though I knew he was married and had four daughters. By then I had enough sense to act appropriately; I decided not to take his flirting seriously.

I also learned from Dr. Alegra. I was extremely fortunate to be associated with two men who knew a lot more than I did, and who were glad to have an eager social worker to mentor.

I often stayed up later than I meant to writing on my manuscript. Finally, I acknowledged that it was going to be a book, and I would try to get it published.

A young man who had just received his doctorate in psychology from Florida State University joined the staff at the hospital. We formed a marital therapy group with four couples a few months after he arrived. We worked well together, and I learned more about group dynamics from that experience.

It became clear to me that there was so much more I needed to know. What complicated creatures we human beings are! And I was trying to better understand the complex system created by two of us living in an intimate relationship, such as marriage.

Continuing in my personal growth, I realized my contentment was much more in my own control than I had believed in years past. I was no longer a feather out there to be blown about by others.

I was trying some new things including running parenting groups at surrounding churches. The meetings were usually well attended, and I felt good about the work I was doing in them. Inpatient work was extremely challenging, but the experience was valuable. There is no better way to learn about human beings than to work with those who are the sickest.

I had whole days when I felt comfortable with myself and with being alone. Still, some days I felt adrift. Perhaps I should say I had days of NOT being lonely, which was a big improvement for me.

In March I moved into a nicer apartment. I had lived in so many apartments since my divorce that moving was almost routine. I would pack the kitchen stuff and linens into the Volkswagen, haul them and my lamps, my little knick-knacks, and my personal things to the new apartment, unload them and tack my few pictures to the walls. Someone would help me with the couple of pieces of furniture that I owned, and I was set for another few months.

Mitchell and Suzanne

I didn't hear much from Mitchell that winter. Soon after my graduation, he moved to California. Then a letter came in March, saying he was moving to Chicago; he must not have liked California. I knew he was searching for something meaningful in his life and thought of him often. But there wasn't much I could do to help him.

Sue, Mike and I got together frequently; she and I met at a mall to shop and have lunch on some weekends. We had a good relationship and I enjoyed her company. However, she didn't talk to me about her relationship with Mike. Her work at GMC was going well, she was making almost as much as I was with my Master's degree, and Mike was doing well with his father.

A Short Romance

One of the nurses, Faye Aberly, with whom I worked, had sclera derma, a fatal disease in which the organs thicken and gradually lose their ability to function. Her husband, Fred, called me to tell me that she had a heart attack and died. I had met Fred several times and found him very attractive. He was a Rhodes Scholar and had a good position with Union Carbide. Soon after Faye's death, Fred came to my apartment to visit me. The attraction was mutual, and we soon became sexually involved, even though I knew he had not had time to recover from Faye's death. I knew she had not been able to have sex with him for more than a year which partially explained his rush.

Pushing aside my good senses, I quickly fell in love with him. It was contrary to my better judgment and in spite of my supervisor's warning about him. She had seen his wife for supportive therapy and knew much more about the situation than did I. She told me to be careful and to go slowly. I was so hungry for a loving relationship, that I didn't heed her advice. As Dr. Quine said, I was "in love with love." He was right. I didn't love Fred; I hardly knew him. But I surely did enjoy our times together.

After a couple of months of dating Fred, I attended a ten day workshop for Social Workers at Smith College in Massachusetts. When I left, Fred told me he was going to date other women while I was gone. We had discussed it, and I knew it only made sense. He was going to take care of my plants, so he had a key to my apartment. I asked him not to read my manuscript, which I put aside where I felt it would not tempt him. I told him he could read it when it was finished.

The second night I was gone, he called me, and the first thing he told me was that he had read the book. He also told me that he had a date the night before and had a good time. I realized how inconsiderate he was of my feelings; a more considerate man would have waited until we were together to tell me these things.

The time at Smith was valuable to me in my professional and personal growth. We were kept busy all day in classes studying individual therapy and group therapy. I soaked it up and realized that, in addition to good supervision at work, this is where learning takes place—at conferences and workshops. While a master's degree provided the basics, there was so much more to learn. Also, socializing with other participants felt great to me. We had our work in common, but we were from many different backgrounds; each person brought his point of view to the discussions.

First thing each morning, we had a two hour group therapy class with about twenty participants. The leader, Dr. Platt, was a well-known man in the field who had published several books on the group therapy. Sitting in a circle where we could see each other, we were learning by doing and by listening to Dr. Platt. I was very comfortable and did not hesitate to speak up when I had something to say. During the last session, Dr. Platt asked us to select the person whom we would want to run the meeting if he wasn't there. Much to my surprise, I was the overwhelming choice. I was taken back and later realized that people respected me, and that I had much to offer.

Fred met my plane when I returned to West Palm, as we had planned. It seemed he couldn't wait to tell me that our relationship was over. I was not really surprised; there had been plenty of warning signals, and I had tried to heed them. This time I had recognized them as they happened. I had learned that I must have my eyes wide-open and look both ways to successfully survive all of life's experiences. When a truck is barreling down on you, stop and let it pass. Even so, it was hard to be back without the excitement of having Fred in my life. I realized how much time I had been spending with him; now, I was able to concentrate more on my book.

A Ph.D.? 1972

During one of my infrequent sessions with Dr. Quine, I told him, "I'm more and more aware of how much there is to learn in order to help the families and individuals who are my clients."

"Have you ever thought about getting your Ph.D.?" I didn't respond verbally—just frowned at him.

I wanted to disregard such an idea. I enjoyed my freedom from studying all the time and enjoyed my life as it was. But he had planted the seed, and the soil was fertile. That weekend I sent for a Florida State University (FSU) catalog where a doctorate in Marriage and Family Therapy was offered. I wanted to just take a look.

When I received the FSU catalog, I decided to send in an application to enter the doctoral program for the fall of 1972. I figured I could easily take that step and wait and see what happened. Mailing the application didn't commit me to anything; I just wanted to see if I could get in. Then I could decide if I wanted to take the next step.

Update At Home

I had Christmas early with Suzanne and Mike, flew to Chicago where Mitchell met me and drove me to Dad's home. I saw all six of my siblings and enjoyed the visit. But I wrote in my journal, "I feel sort of alien in my own family." I knew that would change as I became more secure with the new me in relation to each of them. I felt so different; and none of them seemed to realize how much I had changed. What had I expected? I knew I had to work it out myself, and it would take me more time.

After the beginning of the year, Sue told me she and Mike were getting a divorce. She didn't give me many details. She had received a raise, and soon had her own apartment that she shared with a friend of hers. The divorce didn't seem to have affected her as much as I would have expected. I hoped she was not postponing the grieving.

Mitchell had moved to Forks, Washington that was located in the extreme northwest corner of the state. He was a logger, working and living the life he told himself he liked, but he admitted it was hard work and dangerous. I heard from him infrequently, but regularly. He sometimes had a girlfriend and sometimes not. I really didn't know much about what he was doing, but hoped he was not going to stay on that job long.

Looking For a Publisher 1972

That summer I finished my manuscript and began sending out synopses to publishers. I had gone to the library, found lists of publishers, and decided on about fifty that might be interested in publishing my book. I sent out seven synopses at a time and usually received at least one request for the manuscript, which was encouraging. I knew it was difficult to get a book published, so I was not discouraged, but I was determined to do the best I could.

I continued sending synopses and manuscripts to publishers, stashing the rejections in a shoe box. With each request for the manuscript, I responded with sustained hope. That kept the refusals from being devastating. Some publishers enclosed explanations of why they didn't want to publish my manuscript; others sent encouragement and some said nothing.

I Move To Tallahassee 1972

After receiving my acceptance from FSU, I spent a lot of my thoughts and energy figuring out how I could afford to go back to school for a minimum of three years. I wrote Juanita and Haydn and asked if I could borrow $200 to $300 a month until I could get used to the regime. I figured I would be able to work part-time and pay my expenses after the first semester. They were able to help me, so step by step, I committed myself to three more years of no income, studying, and being a penniless peon—after two and a half years of being a professional woman with a bit of money in her pocket.

It was difficult for me to move to Tallahassee, an eight hour drive from West Palm Beach. I was enjoying my work and my friends. It would be scary to be alone in a strange city where I didn't know a soul. But I was not going to let those fears deter me. I was thinking of this move as a process. I could always take one more step, or not take it.

In early spring, I bit the bullet and drove up to take a look at the campus and to meet some of the professors. It took all the courage I could muster, but I found myself in my VW Bug heading for Tallahassee.

The next morning, I pulled out of the Holiday Inn parking lot onto Bronough Street, just a few blocks from the campus. I was surprised when a driver let me go ahead of him and even smiled at me. That was certainly different from West Palm—a considerate driver, one plus for Tallahassee already. I parked by the administration building and began my initial trek across campus. It was a pretty setting with different foliage from that found in West Palm. Large camellia bushes lined the walkway as I strode bravely toward the Bellamy Building. The azalea bushes were vying for attention with their bright lavender, pink, red, and white blossoms. Dogwood trees spread out their gorgeous white limbs over all those colorful shrubs making a most impressive picture for a woman taking it all in for the first time. My initial fears were losing ground; such a beautiful place couldn't be too bad.

At Bellamy I met the head of the department, Dr. Watts, a man about my age. I also met three professors and some students. I even attended a party at one of the student's home that evening, which was helpful in making me realize how easy it was going to be to get to know the other students.

While I was in Tallahassee, I found an apartment near campus and reserved it for the middle of August. I wanted to move up a week before classes began, so I would have time to orient myself. I was pleased that I had made the trip. Now I was actually looking forward to returning in a few weeks.

Separating from my patients was difficult; it was my first experience at telling patients I was leaving them. Terminating patients before they are ready has to be done carefully. Even then, many will take it as abandonment. Those two and a half years at the mental hospital were great preparation for the next three years of study. It was as if someone else had been in charge of my life for several years now. I had switched directions several times; each change furthered me along a path which, I believed, had been sculpted for me. My part had been to make the right choice at each fork in that path. Here I was, beginning a doctoral program which a few years ago would have been implausible.

I gave up on getting my book published; I had to move on. I was glad I had tried. I had done my best and accepted the fact that it didn't get published. There were still two manuscripts outstanding, but I wouldn't worry about them. The publishers would return them in time. I packed my shoebox full of rejections along with my synopses and my manuscripts, knowing I had to put that project aside and focus on the three year journey which lay ahead.

My good friends, Mona and George Ludwick, helped me move. We rented a U-Haul, loaded my belongings in it and took off early one morning in mid-August. George drove the truck, Mona and their three kids rode in their car, and I followed in my VW, also packed to its limited capacity. All of my possessions and I were en route to one more apartment where I would live for the next few years.

What mixed feelings I had—leaving my friends, my job and all that was familiar, heading to a city where uncertainty would again be my companion. I still felt somewhat anxious, especially about money, but hope and excitement were beginning to take up more space in my thinking.

We all slept on the floor of my apartment that night; we were exhausted from the trip and the move, so it didn't matter. The next morning we rose early to unpack the boxes and get things somewhat in order. We assembled the bed, put away the kitchen things, placed the couple of living room pieces I owned, and arranged study area to my liking. Again, we were so worn out that we retired soon after dinner. But that night we could sleep on a bed and a sofa instead of the floor. As I drifted off to sleep, I felt a deep sense of gratitude for Mona and George who had given up a weekend and worked hard to help me make my transition. They were good friends, and I hated to see them drive away the next morning. I took a deep breath and went into my little one bedroom apartment with its bright red carpet. The only decent-sized window looked out onto the radiators of the cars lined up a few feet away. But it was home.

I spent the week before classes orienting myself to the town and the campus. I rode my bicycle around, getting used to the area where I would be living. I located the buildings where my classes would be held, the closest drug store, and grocery store.

A Student Once More

The first week of classes was somewhat traumatic, meeting so many new people, getting to and from the right buildings, trekking up and down the hills, and adjusting to the sultry heat. West Palm was so flat; I was not used to climbing hills. After the first day, my shin bones hurt with every step that I took, and I had blisters on both feet. Up and down the hills I trudged, dropping and adding courses, buying books, finding out the books for one course had not arrived yet, having to talk one professor into letting me into his class which was full.

Then there was the rain—when it rained, it poured. Many of us took our shoes off and waded through the puddles. I soon adjusted to wearing jeans, tee shirts, and sandals. What I looked like was secondary; I was a poor student once again.

At the end of the first week, I was already behind in the class for which I had no text, and I began wondering why I thought I could do this crazy thing. My first Friday night in Tallahassee was the worst; I cried myself to sleep. The next morning I told myself to calm down, I would adjust and, of course, I could do it. Just one day at a time, one exam at a time, one paper at a time, one hill at a time.

Horizon Press Calls 1972

One month later, I came home from an evening course exhausted, and I found a letter waiting from Horizon Press in New York. They wrote that they wanted to publish my book. I was used to refusals and thought it must be from one of those presses who wanted me to pay for my book being published. I lay the letter on the desk and went to bed. The phone rang the next morning while I was getting ready to leave for my first class; it was Mr. Reagon with Horizon Press.

"Hello, is this Ms. Kate Young?"

"Yes."

"I've had a hard time locating you and am glad to finally get to speak with you. We want to publish your book this spring, and I want to talk with you. I am sending you a contract which I hope you will sign and get it back to me as soon as you can. I will call you in a few days, when I know you have the contract, so we can discuss it and a few things about your book. We have decided on a different title. How do you like, *My Own Woman?*

"I like it, better than *A Woman Alone.*"

"I'm glad you like it. We are excited about your book and look forward to getting to know you. I'll call you in a few days."

I hung up the phone. I had given that project up, and now a real publishing company wanted to publish my book. I was shaking. A publisher liked my book. And I'll get money for it. Who can I call? I wish I could talk to someone who knows me. Thank you, thank you, thank you, Lord for giving me what it took to write it.

I had wanted so badly to have my book published, had done my best to make it a reality, and had accepted the fact that it wasn't going to happen. Now, I had difficulty believing it was going to be published, and I would be paid for it. I didn't have much time to digest the good news; it was time to go to class. I kept wondering whom I could call. I just had to share this good news with someone.

As soon as the class was out, I called my sister, Glenna. She had read the manuscript and given me encouragement along the way. She was delighted for me. I told some of my classmates later even though I didn't know them that well. I just wasn't able to keep this good news to myself.

Mr. Reagon kept in regular contact with me over the next few weeks. He asked me if there was such a word as *nurturance*. I assured him there was. The only change he requested was that I clarify what happened in an event to which I had alluded, but had never disclosed the details. That was not a big problem, although I would have rather not exposed quite so much of myself. But I had told everything else, so what was one more personal experience?

Back To Business 1973

I soon got back to the grind of classes. Qualifying exams were coming up, and I was worried about them; I studied every minute I could. We took the much-dreaded exam the end of January 1973, and we all passed. Afterward, we settled down, thinking they surely won't flunk us out now. I realized much later that the exam worked as their filter—a way to weed out students who weren't working out.

Soon after the exam, Betty Friedan came to campus. She was short, probably no more than five feet tall, plump, and very Jewish. She was an excellent speaker. I had read her book, *The Feminine Mystique*, the month before.

My theories professor discovered that I had recently had a book published and asked if he could read it. Reluctantly, I took him a copy. A couple of days later, he called me to his office. He asked me if I'd read Friedan's book. When I told him I hadn't, he reached up and handed me a copy from his shelf and said, "Here, read it and come back in when you've finished it."

When I returned to his office a few days later, he told me that my book was an example of experiencing what Friedan had written in theory. Her book had a profound influence on me as it did on millions of women. I never felt the same about male-female roles and relationships after reading it. I became aware of how women were not seen as equal to men in our culture. After the publication of Friedan's book, women began to want and demand equality. Her book was one of the motivators of the revolution that began in the sixties and is still influencing American men and women today.

Between semesters I moved into a nicer apartment in the same complex. It was larger—with a small dining area and a window looking out on a nicely landscaped lawn which I could see from where I studied. It created a better atmosphere than the dark dungeon I'd been living in.

Update on Suzanne and Mitchell

Mitchell continued working as a lumberjack in Forks, Washington. I knew he was still unhappy. Knowing how dangerous that type of work was, I added it to my "worry list." It was a challenge to continually compartmentalize the things in my life that could get me down, if I thought about them too much. Staying focused on my studies and blocking out what I couldn't control kept me on track. That is different from denial, because I was conscious of what I was doing.

After Suzanne and Mike had divorced a few months earlier, she had gone out to Colorado for a few weeks before she moved back to Fort Lauderdale where she went to work waiting tables in a nice restaurant named Valley's. She seemed to be doing okay.

Ludwick's Tragedy 1973

When the second semester was well underway, I received word that Mona's and George's fourteen-year-old son, Kevin, had been hit by a car while riding his bike. He was not expected to live. I flew down to be with them and saw him during the last hour of his life. I couldn't afford the time to stay long but was glad I had gone. Later in the year, they came to see me for a couple of days and were able to share more of their experience and feelings about their loss. He was their middle child and only son. Life is difficult to understand as is death, especially at so young an age.

A Paperback Edition

As soon as I returned to Tallahassee, Mr. Reagon called to tell me good news. "Signet bought the rights to print your book in paperback. They are a good, solid company, and I am delighted for you."

"This is wonderful news." I had always hoped it would be in paperback because I think more women, who would benefit from it, could afford a paperback.

"It should do very well with them. And I think you will receive more from it than you do from the hard cover edition. Many books do better in that format."

"I'm really happy it'll be in paperback, and I know Signet is a good publisher. This is such great news; I thank you very much."

"We'll be talking again soon," he said and hung up.

I Go to Work 1973

At the beginning of my second semester, I began working part-time for Dr. Wilson, a psychiatrist. I saw patients he referred to me in his office. I was to work up to twenty hours a week. With that income and the promise of some money from the sale of my book, my finances were looking up.

Everything in life is threatening when there is not enough money—every unexpected expense can be a crisis: your car breaking down, the need for dental care, missing a few days of work because of illness, a professor asking you to buy one more book. I will always have empathy for those who barely make ends meet.

Time Out for Surgery

My gynecologist had been checking an ovarian cyst that had been causing me pain for several months. He had been assuring me it was benign. However, it began to grow and caused me an increasing amount of pain. Dr. Gere strongly advised surgery as soon as possible, which ended up being two weeks later. He told me he was worried about malignancy, because of the sudden rapid growth and because it was unusual for a woman my age to have that type of tumor.

I was struggling to keep up with my studies, and my new job; I could ill afford taking off several weeks. But I knew I had to do it, so I conferred with a couple of my professors about taking an incomplete on papers they had assigned. One was happy to accommodate me, but the other one was adamant that she accepted no excuses for late papers. I wrote the paper even though it meant some long nights. I felt sorry for her being so rigid and totally lacking in compassion. I figured I could keep up with the assignments after I returned from the hospital.

I'd told my kids, but hadn't said anything to my siblings about my upcoming surgery. I wanted to talk with them after the fact, but knew I shouldn't do that. I decided to call my brother, Clay, rather than one of my five sisters. I would let him notify them. I thought I was being very philosophical about the whole thing; only when I began to explain to Clay what I was calling about did I realize how exhausted and fearful I was. I was overcome with emotion and began crying and trying to explain to him that I was simply tired, that I was okay. I asked him not to tell the others that I was crying; it was just that I was tired; I was going to be fine. Let our sisters know and tell them I will be in touch. I'll have someone call them as soon as it is over.

That afternoon I entered the hospital, answered all their questions, got hooked up to the necessary paraphernalia and lay back to finally rest my mind and body. It was mid-December; Christmas was around the corner, and I had done all I could to prepare myself for the possibility that I might have to deal with cancer, but my mind had a hard time letting go of the worry.

As I lay there contemplating possibilities, I heard familiar uneven steps coming down the hallway. It sounded so much like Clay with his prosthesis, but he surely wouldn't have tried to come to Tallahassee. I had only called him that morning. The closer the steps came, the more familiar the sound became until I saw him in the doorway. He had come to be with me even though he had his own work to do, four children at home and his wife, Rose, to consider. And it was near Christmas with all the extra events that come with that time, especially for someone with children. Clay and his family lived a couple of hours from the Chicago airport, they weren't wealthy, and I knew he didn't like driving into O'Hare. He had sacrificed to come to Tallahassee so that I wouldn't be alone.

He was back in my room the next morning in time to wish me well as they came with the white gurney and whisked me away. In 1973 the procedure was done abdominally, which takes much longer to heal than the vaginal or laparoscopic surgeries of today. A few hours later, I was back in my room. Clay was right there when I opened my eyes. He kept telling me that I didn't have cancer. I should've been all smiles, but I kept crying and hanging onto the nurse's hand. Anesthesia affects me that way—I'm tearful and love everyone. Later, I rejoiced, knowing I was fortunate. A weight had been lifted from my shoulders.

After two weeks of recuperation, I began seeing my patients again and concentrating on the coursework which had piled up. I spent Christmas in town with my good friends, Sally and John Hanson. Suzanne came up from Fort Lauderdale; I was cancer-free and had one more semester behind me; there was much to celebrate.

Fired 1974

A couple of months later my phone rang at 10:30 PM. Who *would be calling me this late? It can't be good news.* "Hello," I said anxiously.

"This is Dr. Wilson. I'm calling to tell you I won't need your assistance any longer. You can come in tomorrow and pick up your personal things."

"You can't do this over the phone and at 10:30 at night." I was stunned. Not only about what he was telling me, but also the manner in which he was doing it.

"I'll talk to you about the details tomorrow when you come in." And with that, he hung up on me.

He had never given me any indication that he was in any way dissatisfied with my work. I had been seeing around fifteen patients a week in his offices and often I felt that he resented writing that big check for me each week. I decided he had found a way out.

Here was another man who was such a wimp he couldn't tell me something unpleasant face to face. Later, I found out that he had hired a young man with a master's and no experience. He could manipulate him easier and pay him less money.

It was a blessing disguised as misfortune. Several of my patients remained with me. Another psychiatrist, whom I had met years earlier when he had visited mutual friends in West Palm, let me use his office in the afternoons for a small amount of rent. I was financially better off because I kept what I earned and didn't have to give sixty percent of it to someone else. The added bonus: I didn't have to put up with Dr. Wilson and his neurotic behavior anymore.

Looking Ahead

At the end of that semester, I drove my little VW to West Palm and visited the Ludwicks. I also went to see Drs. Alegra and Menendez and made plans for my return that fall. They were good psychiatrists and wanted me to join them when I finished my coursework. They had purchased a building and were saving an office for me. I had made an agreement six months earlier, without considering any other opportunity, to return to West Palm to work with them. I liked both men; we had worked well together at the hospital. I was fortunate to have such a lucrative position waiting for me as soon as I finished my studies. This time I wouldn't have to go through applying for a job and agonizing over whether or not I was going to be hired.

In July we had our comprehensives, the written exams covering the coursework of the past two years. Everyone dreaded them—cramming ahead of time and writing as fast as you could for two days. We had to wait a couple of weeks to find out how we did, but we all passed. Now I knew I would make it.

Dr. Bill Nichols, my major professor, agreed that it was safe for me to leave the campus before I finished my dissertation, even though many students reach that status and never complete the degree. He told me he didn't have any doubts that I would finish mine as fast as I could. I had titled it, "Depression in Married, Middle-Aged Women," and had been working on it as much as time allowed during the last semester.

Back To West Palm Beach 1974

I found myself not wanting to leave Tallahassee. It was the state capitol and I had become used to the slower pace, the southern influence, and the proximity to two universities. But I had promised the two doctors I would join them; I had to go. I was tearful much of the time that I was throwing my stuff into boxes.

The next day, as I drove south, I recalled with what apprehension I had made the first trip to Tallahassee, and now I was sad to leave. The re-entry to West Palm was even more difficult than I thought it would be. The life I returned to didn't seem to be the one I'd left two years earlier. After Tallahassee, West Palm seemed harsh, so much cement and none of the foliage I'd become used to—the live oaks, azaleas and the dogwood trees. I missed the university and the Capitol City atmosphere. People in West Palm expected a certain brand of scotch when they visited; there was more emphasis on how much money you had and less academic and political talk. I missed Tallahassee and my friends.

I was aware of my aloneness, of my desire for a loving mate whose presence would make this transition easier and who would understand why I missed Tallahassee. I wasn't thinking a mate would be the answer to any problems I ran into, but I knew the kind of man I wanted would make it easier. I just wanted someone to love.

I Visit Dad

Before I began working in West Palm, I went to see Dad whose health had been failing. He lay in bed most of the time I was there. He used a wheelchair when he went to his meals or to the bathroom. He looked like he had shrunk—he seemed so small and hunched down when he sat in that chair. But he liked to reminisce and tell some his stories to me one more time. I enjoyed listening to them, just knowing what it meant to him.

While I was there, the farm manager came in, and Dad, who was in his chair, wheeled himself out to the kitchen to greet him. As he turned and headed back to the living room he said to the man, "Come on in, there is someone I want you to meet." He wheeled right up to me, turned around and proudly said, "This is my daughter, Dr. Kate Young." He said it with such pride.

I was never more surprised. He had always acted as if he couldn't quite remember what I was studying and wasn't too impressed. I had no idea that he knew I would have a title. He knew I still had work to do before I was through, but he also knew he wouldn't be around, so he just didn't wait. Bless his soul. He was obviously proud of me. It meant so much to me that he knew and cared. It was the only way he could tell me—indirectly. What a perceptive, loving man he was under the crusty shell he had created around himself.

I had a good visit with my sisters, Dorothy and Betty, who lived nearby, and spent several hours a day with Dad. I recorded him one afternoon when we were talking and he was in good humor, telling his familiar stories. I also got him on tape reciting long poems he still knew almost word for word; poems such as: *The Rime of the Ancient Mariner* by Coleridge and *The Wreck of the Hesperus* by Longfellow. There was surely nothing wrong with his mind. During that short visit, I realized anew how much I loved him.

I was so glad that I visited him when I did. He died a couple of months later on December 14th of heart failure; he was eighty-three years old. He didn't hug us or tell us he loved us; he was often angry and grumpy as he aged; he wasn't one for easy conversation. But he was a loved and loving Father. He and Mother had worked hard all of their lives, taught us good values and character traits by their examples as well as their teachings. They were highly respected in their farming community. Love of family and respect for others had been instilled in us seven kids as well as integrity, honesty and the intrinsic value of each individual.

Dorothy, who lived near the folks, had made it possible for Dad to stay in his home. She checked on him regularly; she cut his nails and his hair for years. She came home from her office at noon and took his mail in to him and gave him lunch. She was a wonderful daughter (and sister) who never expected payment of any kind; she just did it. He hired a woman to come in when he became more disabled, but Dot still did many things for him, and I have always felt she didn't get much recognition from the rest of us.

West Palm Beach 1974-1975

Back in West Palm, I was soon up to my eyebrows building my practice, starting groups, working with the Ministerial Association, meeting with the other staff members at the hospital, continuing work with the in-patients, and, above all, working on my dissertation. Doing it away from campus added stress and expense; I had to communicate via phone and ran up some pretty high bills. It would be so much easier today with email and fax. I also had to fly to Tallahassee a couple of times to meet with my committee. Of course, Dr. Nichols was always available and encouraged me along the way.

I took my electric typewriter to work each morning and brought it back in the evening. It was heavy and cumbersome, hard to lift in and out of the trunk of my little car, but I needed it there in case I had half an hour I could work on the dissertation, and I needed it at home as I spent most evenings typing.

Drs. Menendez and Alegra were plotting and planning for the expansion of our practices. I was eager for the day when I could give up the work at the hospital and devote full time to the practice. I joined Newcomers, gave a talk to the Woman's Club, and became acquainted with several ministers—anything I could to become better known in the community. Three psychiatrists (all of whom were male chauvinists) and I made a presentation on depression in women for the Chamber of Commerce. I felt secure in my knowledge and figured I had the upper hand by being female—after all we were talking about women. I also made a presentation to the aides and nurses each week on some aspect of their work.

Although it was a pretty city in many ways, West Palm Beach just didn't cut it for me anymore. There were many things that I did like, such as being near the beach and Lake Worth. Every place you drove, you were surrounded with water. Many restaurants were on the water, gorgeous sunsets reflected when the seas were calm and always that ocean breeze was present. I knew both the doctors I worked with respected and liked my work; I was very fortunate to be asked to join their already successful psychiatric group. It was a big plum professionally and financially for me. Nevertheless, I missed Tallahassee.

My Defense 1975

I finished my dissertation in May and flew to Tallahassee to defend. When the plane landed, and those old pine trees whizzed past my window, I knew I had to move back. I felt I was home. Everything practical (and I am quite a practical woman) said, "Don't leave a good thing, you are almost fifty years old and financially you can't afford to leave such a great opportunity."

But I knew in my soul I belonged in Tallahassee, not in West Palm Beach. My mind was made up; I could never be happy in South Florida again.

On the big day for the defense of my dissertation, I met Dr. Nichols at his office. We walked together to the Dean's office where the defense was to be held. I had on heels and a dress and told Bill I felt good just being dressed up—it was so different from walking around in jeans and tees. It was as though I had gone through a fast transition from being a student to a professional woman again.

The defense went well and soon it was over. I was asked to leave the room; they would let me know when to return. It wasn't long before Bill opened the door and said, "Come in, Dr. Young."

No more papers to write, no more exams to be taken, no more studying evenings and weekends. No more having to please the professors, some of whom were difficult and could hardly handle the power they had over the students. I felt like a prisoner who was released after three years of not seeing the blue sky.

And I was coming back to live where I was supposed to be, where I wanted to be, with my friends who knew me as I was in the present. With the live oak trees, the hills, the canopy roads, where people were more genuine and more laid back, where the city was small, but offered so much culturally, with Florida States' excellent music, film and theater departments. I missed living so near the coast but the atmosphere in Tallahassee more than compensated for that. And, after all, the coast was less than an hour away.

I Leave West Palm

I returned to West Palm Beach, where I faced the unpleasant task of telling the two psychiatrists that I was moving back to Tallahassee. I did not look forward to that. But I didn't have someone else tell them, nor did I do it over the phone. I did it face to face.

However, telling two male Cuban psychiatrists news they didn't want to hear was more difficult than I had anticipated. They simply could not understand why I would leave all they offered me. I could not explain it well in concrete terms; it seemed so much an inner knowledge that I had without reasons they would consider valid. I told them the lifestyle suited me better; I liked the change of seasons, and I wanted to be near the academic setting. But nothing seemed to make sense to them until I lied and said I was going back to find a husband. I knew they would see that as legitimate. They never treated me the same after that; they simply couldn't accept the audacity of a female underling turning her back on their generosity.

At Home in Tallahassee 1975

I sold my office furniture to the psychiatrist who was going to use my space, said my goodbyes and left two weeks later. How I enjoyed the trip back to Tallahassee in my reliable VW. I had done what my soul told me I needed to do. I knew it was right for me. I would miss seeing Mona and George, but I knew they understood.

Good fortune smiled on me again. Mary Hicks, a former professor of mine, was leaving for a two week trip a couple of days after I arrived in Tallahassee. She arranged for me to stay in her house and dog-sit while she was gone. This gave me time to locate one more apartment. I also taught her classes in her absence. That felt very strange so soon after acquiring the title to hear the students call me "Dr. Young." I had my fiftieth birthday during those two weeks. That birthday seemed like an introduction to the first part of my second life. The first fifty years were, hopefully, the hardest. I looked forward to the next fifty with my identity well established, my realistic self-concept intact, and I planned to face reality with enthusiasm.

I applied for every job close to something I would want to do and focused the rest of my time on my practice. I accepted the offer to write a paper on marriage and the law for the University and the Governor's Commission for the Status of Women. I was to explore the legal requirements for marriage in Florida and to make proposals for change. I was to present the paper, *Marriage and the Law*, to the committee from the university and members of the Legislature. It was very time-consuming; I spent hours and hours in the Law Library researching the topic so I would know what I was talking about. They paid me a pittance considering the hours I spent working on it, but I was rewarded, because they liked my paper when I presented it in October. It had given me something constructive to do while I slowly built a practice. It was later published in a compilation of articles regarding marriage and divorce.

I Visit Mitchell

I attended a conference in Salt Lake City, where I read a paper I developed from my dissertation. When the conference was over, I went to Seattle to visit Mitchell. He had moved to Seattle the year before, after he quit his job as lumberjack in Forks, Washington. I had not seen him since Christmas 1972, when he met me in Chicago. Three years was a long time not to see my son; I hoped I would never have to go so long again. Now that I was through school, I would be able to manage to see my kids more frequently.

Mitchell had a nice apartment within walking distance of the University of Washington, which was important since he had gotten rid of his old car. He was proud to show me the beautiful university campus and introduce me to some of his friends. I got reacquainted with him again; he was continuing with his studies, varying his load according to how many hours he was working. We went to Pike's Market and bought enough fruit, fish and vegetables to feed ten people. Everything at that market was so scrumptious looking that I just kept buying one more thing. It was a good visit and wonderful to be with Mitchell again after so long.

My Own House

Soon after returning to Tallahassee, I began looking for a house to buy. Dad had left me a little money, and I wanted to use some of it as a down payment on a house. I decided on a small three-bedroom house with lots of trees and flowers in the tiny back yard. It had a cottonwood tree which brought back memories of the one we had on the farm. I failed to remember how messy they were, but it wouldn't have mattered if I had. The couple who had owned the house sold me their dining room furniture and all of the outdoor furniture and equipment, including a mower. I was really a proud homeowner—my first house as a single woman.

Glenna came down to help me settle into my new home. She recovered a daybed I had, fixed the drapes which I had inherited from the previous owners, and helped me shop for a few things I needed for the house. It was great having her with me at that time; she was and still is a great decorator. I talked to her about my discouragement in ever meeting a man whom I would be interested in. It seemed impossible sometimes that there was any man out there with whom I would want to share the rest of my life. I surely hadn't met any that even tempted me. And yet that hunger would not let go of me.

Life is Good

I began the New Year 1976 with more self-confidence, optimism, and eagerness than I'd ever felt before. I was able to repay Juanita and Haydn from the money I received from book sales. I was earning money again, had paid for my schooling, and was buying a house. I liked my work a lot, and I had fun things to do with friends I liked. I was fifty years old without much money, but sitting on top of the world. I knew I would soon be saving for retirement; I knew how to be quite frugal.

I joined a Toastmistress Club in an effort to overcome my fear of public speaking. I enjoyed it, even though I was at ground zero as far as ability was concerned. The members were encouraging to those of us who were beginners.

I felt enthusiastic about building my practice. Bill Nichols let me work out of his office. He used it weekends and evenings, so it was available mornings and most afternoons. He would not let me pay him rent, nor money toward the utilities. He and I were colleagues now; he was no longer my professor, but still my friend. It helped me very much to not have any rent while I established my practice. I took his advice and was selective regarding my clientele. I didn't work with children or teen-agers nor did I take psychotics. I limited my practice to good old adult neurotics. Remember, neuroticism is a matter of degree; we all have our place on the scale. And neurotics are usually hurting when they come for help, which motivates them to work toward improving. I knew all of this from experience.

I also liked to do marital counseling, often ending up with either the husband or wife getting into individual therapy. Most of all I liked working with adults who were unhappy and really wanted to change; to know themselves better; to understand how they got where they were and what they needed to change in order to get more of what they wanted out of life. These were long-term clients who were willing to invest time and energy and to endure the pain and loneliness which that type of therapy demanded. Not many people grow dissatisfied enough with their lives that they will make sacrifices for a goal that is so elusive. Or they think their unhappiness is someone else's fault and therapy would be wasted on them.

I also began teaching a course on Human Behavior for the School of Social Work at Florida State. I enjoyed the teaching, and if I had been younger, I would have taught for a few years before concentrating on a practice. I taught that course for three semesters before they wanted me to teach a different course, which I didn't feel adequately prepared for, so that was the end of teaching Social Work.

Suzanne and Mitchell 1976

Sue came for a week's visit between jobs. She wrote frequently and would occasionally mention going to school full-time; she was taking a course or two at the Community College (where I had begun) whenever she could.

Mitchell became discouraged at the beginning of the spring semester at the University and withdrew. He planned to study for the Real Estate exam. I had to let both of them find their own way; I went to school later in life and hoped they would do the same.

Body Language

I continued going to Toastmistress and had offered to do a four hour workshop on body language in June, in conjunction with a conference being offered by Florida State. When they asked me, I agreed to do it knowing I would have to do some research on the subject. Not too long after that, I found out there was a four-week series on body language to be held on Wednesday nights in May by a colleague whom I knew slightly. I could get all of my research done in those four weeks. Each Wednesday night meeting was to last three hours, so I would surely gain enough knowledge for one four-hour presentation.

My practice was growing; I was seeing twenty clients a week which was full-time for some therapists. I still had time to do other things—to socialize with friends and to go to the coast to stay overnight with the Hansons on the weekends. There was always something going on down there, and I enjoyed it even though most of the folks were married couples. I was used to that, but I still had yearnings which I kept bottled up most of the time. Sometimes I let them sneak out to invade my thoughts when I was by myself, especially at night.

On May 19th, Bill Nichols called and wanted to talk with me. I was hoping he was going to tell me something great, like the University was opening up another faculty position, and I would be a likely candidate. But that was not to be. He told me he and Alice had decided to move back to Michigan as soon as the semester ended. What a disappointing message. I knew he was unhappy with the way things were going at the University, but had hoped it would turn around. He had become so important to me in my few years in Tallahassee. There were times when I would have floundered without his support, or at least it seemed so. He was always there for me to bounce things off of and to discuss a problem when I had a difficult decision to make. It just wouldn't be the same once he was gone.

At the Hilton Hotel 1976

I left Bill's office and broke into tears before I could reach the car; I wanted to go home, but this was the night I had to attend that series of presentations on body language. I had already missed the first one, so I had to go to the rest of them. I didn't have time to go home and touch up my face or regain my composure; I just drove the short distance to the Hilton Hotel where the seminar was being held.

As I entered the room, I looked around for an outlet so I could plug in my recorder which I had with me. I spotted one on the other side of the room, and walking over I said to the man sitting near it (who had his name tag on), "John, would you move over so I could plug in my recorder?" There was an empty chair next to him, and of course, he moved, letting me sit by the outlet. During the break, two women came over and hovered over John. I was hoping to have a conversation with him, but they obviously knew him and wanted to chat. I went outside and took a short walk, thinking about what kind of a man he might be. He seemed to be someone I might like to know better—straightforward and pleasant. *Oh, well, he's probably married.*

The presentation was fast-moving and interesting, so the time went by quickly. I was glad that I had forced myself to go. I felt fortunate to have heard of it, as it was the perfect preparation for my upcoming workshop. I was gathering my belongings together after the presentation was over when my friend, the co-presenter, came over to chat with me. As we conversed, she asked me, "Are you dating anyone?"

"No, I'm not dating anyone." I was always a bit annoyed when asked that because I had dated very little during the past few years, and the question irritated me. "I met an interesting man tonight, but he's probably married, they usually are."

"What's his name?"

"John Kerr."

"Oh, he's not married, he's divorced," she said enthusiastically. "Come on and I'll introduce you."

"No, no. He met me, we sat by each other."

"Come on, he's right over there. We'll just talk with him a minute." She was insistent and took hold of my arm.

But I was also determined. "No, I'm going home; if he wants to talk with me, he knows my name." With that I picked up my recorder and my purse and left by the side door. I didn't like to be the aggressor with a man that I'd just met.

Mid-morning the next day, I checked my messages, "This is John Kerr. I sat by you last night, and I was wondering if you'd like to go to dinner sometime. I'll call you back."

I hung up as I thought: *Now don't go getting all excited; you've barely met him. He's probably not at all what you've imagined. You don't even know what he does or how long he's been divorced or much of anything, really. He may not call back.*

But he called back after lunch. "This is John Kerr again. I wonder if you'd like to go to dinner with me tomorrow evening."

"Oh, I'm sorry, I'm busy tomorrow night, but I'm free Saturday and Sunday nights." I wanted him to know that I'd really like to go out with him.

Without hesitating he said, "Then how about Saturday night?"

"Yes, I would like that." I was excited as it had been a long time since I'd had a real date.

When I saw him drive up Saturday evening, I peeked out the window to see what he looked like; I couldn't remember very well from Wednesday night because I sat next to him and not across the table where I could have seen him better.

Our First Date

After dinner at the Brown Derby, we went back to my house for an after-dinner drink and more talking. I found out a lot about him that first evening. He was a professor of Marketing in the School of Business at FSU, having been hired there right after receiving his doctorate at Indiana University. He was born and raised in Fort Wayne, Indiana. His father had worked most of his adult life for Lincoln Life Insurance and was recently retired.

His mother died at the age of sixty, and his father was now remarried to Maverne, whose deceased husband had also worked for Lincoln Life. John was an active member of First Presbyterian Church, having joined after he was divorced two years ago. He had been twice married and divorced and had three children. His fourteen-year-old daughter from his first marriage lived with her mother and step-father in Maryland. He didn't see her much, but she visited him for two weeks during the summers. Schelley, nine, and Alex, six, lived in Tallahassee with their mother, Betty Ann. They spent one night a week and some weekends with him.

When I heard he had been divorced twice, my educated antennae flew up. But from our talks, I found out he had attended a group for divorced people for two years at his church that was led by a psychiatrist. He had come to understand some of the mistakes he had made previously in choosing a partner. The best sign that he was ready for a healthy relationship was that he didn't blame the divorces on the women. He had learned that he must've done something wrong for his two marriages to have failed. For one thing, both of his wives were only-children. When I told him that I had six siblings, I hadn't known that in his mind, my stock went bounding upwards.

He was interested in the fact that I had grown up on a farm and that I had only recently received my doctorate in the Social Sciences. He left my house that evening without even hugging me, much less kissing me. That was the first time that had ever happened to me. I didn't know whether he simply was not attracted to me or if he was a rare gentleman. I say *rare* because it was the mid-seventies and most men I'd gone out with expected to go to bed after the first date. That was one reason I hadn't dated much in the past few years.

After the next Wednesday night meeting, John and I went out for a drink and talked another hour or so. I was impressed with him and his background; he seemed to be the kind of man I might really like. But I refused to think about that. Before we said goodnight, he asked me if I would like to go to a dinner dance that Saturday night. So that meant I could throw out the possibility that he wasn't interested.

My Very Own Office

I was continuing with Toastmistress and gave a couple of speeches out in the community, primarily as a means of getting to be known as a therapist. It certainly wasn't because I liked to give speeches, although I was improving. At least I no longer visibly shook or lost my voice entirely when I spoke before a crowd.

I'd been using Bill's office for several months, but was now earning enough money that I could afford my own space. I found an office in a large complex occupied primarily by state workers. I had fun decorating it and felt really good about being that much more independent. It was not an ideal setting; the acoustics were poor, but it would do for the time being. I needed help moving but didn't think it appropriate to ask John to help me; I didn't know him that well. So I moved myself on a Sunday with my Ford Pinto which had replaced my Volkswagen Bug. The Pinto had just a little more power than the Bug, but not much.

When I got to the office with my first load, I couldn't get into the main building. I began looking around to see if anyone else was working on Sunday afternoon and found one man bent over his desk. I went around and knocked on his window hoping he would have a key. He went with me and got my door opened, for which I was grateful. That is how I met Bill Furlong, CPA, on whom I called when I needed help with my income tax later that year. I got to know his wife, Jane, who was also a CPA. They have done my taxes ever since.

John and I went for a drink the next two Wednesday nights after the seminar and dated at least once in between those nights. By mid-June I had begun to count on continuing to see him and knew that was very dangerous. After all, I had just met him a month earlier. I didn't want to like him too much. Our relationship might end abruptly and I didn't intend to be overly involved. He had asked me to go to church with him, which I declined, telling him I would be glad to later, but not now. He seemed to understand. I had to protect myself from getting in too deeply, had to hold onto some of my old routine.

I did my body language work shop later that month; it was very successful. I couldn't believe how relaxed I was in front of nearly forty people. I was aware they were enjoying it and so was I. That was the part I was most happy about; I had actually felt self-confident giving a four-hour workshop for forty professional people.

The Fourth of July 1976 fell on a Sunday and, since it was the bicentennial of our country's independence, First Presbyterian was celebrating by joining two other downtown churches in holding a joint worship service in the nearby park. I told John I would go to that service with him. His kids, Schelley and Alex, went with us, making it even more special. The service was unforgettable; the combined choirs were spectacular, and I was so glad to have been there for such a memorable experience. I had wanted to become involved with a church again, and I decided that day that if John and I broke up, I was going to begin worshiping again on a regular basis, but not at First Presbyterian where I would have to see him with someone else.

John Kerr 1976

I hadn't told my family that I was dating John. But when they called me the afternoon of the Fourth to say they missed me at the second family reunion, I told them about him. They wanted to know what he was like.

"Well, he is about five feet ten inches tall, has a charming smile and beautiful teeth, very blue eyes with smile lines at the outer edges. He has brown hair and a bald spot on top of his head, where bald spots usually are. He is trim and slim, is a professor in the School of Business at FSU, has three kids, is from the Midwest and educated at the University of Indiana. He has one brother, Roger, who is a trust officer in a bank in West Virginia. He is gregarious, sociable, affable and ingenuous. He likes people and people like him, including me."

I didn't try to go into the most important part—how he treats me. It would be difficult to put into words how he was so thoughtful in the little ways that told me much about his character. He was not sending me flowers or romantic cards, no 'courting' as such, no attentive behavior that would stop if the relationship ended in marriage. The words that I most often thought of were "genuine" or "unpretentious." He didn't know the meaning of "guile."

From the first night I met him he treated me with consideration. One day we met one of his former girlfriends who was real gushy and almost snuggled up to him—totally ignoring me. John reached over and put his arm around me. "This is my friend, Kate Young." That told her a lot and she didn't hang around. Men I had known before would have enjoyed having two women paying attention to them. John always thought of my feelings in those kinds of situations.

That summer was so much fun. It was hard for me to keep in mind it might end. I had to keep reminding myself that I was doing okay before I met John, and I had begun to be pleased with my life. I can be happy without him; I have friends, work I like, and I have proven to myself that I'm capable of being alone and quite content. I am not sure how well this reminding myself of these facts worked, but I tried. I didn't talk about him to others, and if asked, I tried to brush off the fact that we were dating.

By August we were seeing each other three or four nights a week. Nearly every Friday afternoon, as early as we could, we headed for the coast with a bottle of wine, some cheese and crackers, picking up fresh shrimp on the way down. We sat out on the porch at Sally and John's place at Shell Point and never tired of simply talking—what could be a better setting for falling in love?

Tom and Abby Potter

John had talked a lot about his good friends, Tom and Abby Potter. One Sunday afternoon we took Schelley and Alex and went to visit them at their home on Lake Bradford. John thought so much of this couple, I was afraid I might not find them to my liking. Those fears disappeared that afternoon. They were gracious hosts and were so easy to be with. I was impressed.

Tom was a retired Air Force Colonel who, after retiring had knocked on John's office door at the University and asked him, "Can an old fart like me get into your Honors program?" They had talked for a couple of hours that day, sharing their Air Force experiences. They were good friends by the time Tom left John's office.

Bill and Maverne 1976

Later that month his father and step-mother, Bill and Maverne, came for a few days to visit with John. John had rented the house where we stayed at the coast for that week, and was taking Schelley, Alex and Jennifer—who was coming to visit her dad the same week.

I was looking forward to meeting his folks, but I had a conflict; my trip to New York to read my paper, *Women in Divorce*, for the American Association of Sociologists, was scheduled on that same week. John asked me to spend as much time as I could with all of them and he seemed disappointed that I couldn't come until the end of the week.

The first night after I joined them I knew he cared a lot for me when he said with much feeling, "I missed you so much, honey." That helped assuage my doubts, but I still felt something could happen and tear us apart. I simply couldn't believe that I could have found my man. And we still had not used the word "love." We were both being quite cautious, each afraid of getting hurt.

We celebrated John's forty-fourth birthday that week; we had discovered that I was a little more than seven years older than he. Our ages had absolutely not entered our minds at all. We enjoyed each other so much; chronological age often doesn't compute.

That Sunday, when John asked me to go to church with him and his folks, I was more than happy to go; I felt secure enough to risk what that meant to me. I liked it that he attended church regularly and took his kids when they were staying with him. First Presbyterian was very different from the church where I had grown up or from any church I had attended previously. The music was superb, the talented organist taught at Florida State, the minister was an effective preacher, the people were friendly, and there was an emphasis on social outreach. I realized that some of the difference was in my readiness to absorb all that I could and take part in what was available. I also liked the diversity in the congregation.

I had begun accepting the fact that I was emotionally involved with John to the extent that if he, for any reason, decided to look elsewhere, I would be devastated. I enjoyed seeing how he made everyone feel welcome and at ease. He was much more gregarious than I; I liked that about him a lot. I was in for a bad time if he told me it was over; I had not wanted to become so vulnerable. I wouldn't say it even to myself, but I was so in love, it was frightening. The deepest pain in life is because we love.

Football Games

One day in mid-August, John said, "I received the football tickets today." He didn't say 'our' tickets nor had he mentioned our going to the games together, so I contacted Sally and John and asked if they could get me a season ticket by them, I just wasn't going to sit home and mope. The next time John and I were together I said, "I'm getting season-tickets with the Hansons, probably not..."

He loudly interrupted me, "What do you mean, you're getting tickets with the Hansons? I told you I had our tickets."

"You said you had the tickets, and I figured you weren't asking me for some reason."

"Who else do you think I'd take? Of course, you're going with me."

Not only was I relieved to be going with him to all the games, I knew he saw our relationship continuing at least through November. Lord, how much reassurance did I need? My past had taught the lesson well, don't assume anything, ask for clarification if you doubt. I should have asked him when he said the tickets, but I was determined not to push him, not to push myself into his life without being asked. Anyway, I was a happy football fan, and we certainly did have fun watching our team, whose new coach, Bobby Bowden, was coaching his first year at FSU. It was another first for me; I had not gone to a college football game before.

John explained a lot of the plays and rules, which I had never understood when I had watched on TV. As if the games weren't enough, we got in on all the pageantry, the thousands of fans gathered for a few hours of solidarity, the tremendous Florida State band which was part of the show, and the tailgating with friends.

The tailgating started three hours before the game was to begin, so we could get in on all the excitement and conjecture about what the score would be, and enjoy good food and drinks. These pre-game festivities were always accompanied by the Fight Song blasting away from someone's boom box.

My Practice Grows

My practice had mushroomed, for which I was very grateful. I was seeing twenty-five or thirty clients each week and found it hard to believe that less than eighteen months ago I was out beating the bushes. Bill Nichols referred several students to me; I had two family practice doctors who were referring to me and I was beginning to get referrals from previous clients. I liked being a therapist; it was perfect for me. Dr. Quine had suggested Social Work which introduced me to the therapy world, and it was he who had encouraged me to get a Ph.D. Those choices had made it possible for me to be doing what I came to believe was my destiny.

A Day to Remember 1976

One beautiful fall day, John and I had driven to our favorite small restaurant in a quaint coastal spot called Spring Creek. We took a bottle of wine since it was a dry county. They would open and serve the wine, but the customer had to bring it. We felt especially close during our drive back to town—talked about our children, the upcoming holidays, the football games and our work. Later, after making love, the words "I love you" were whispered involuntarily by my lips. John didn't say anything for a second, and I wondered if I had really been the originator of those three small words. Then he looked at me and said, "I love you, and I have for quite a while, but have been afraid to say it to you." We were overcome with emotions, ecstatic with joy.

I had wanted to wait until he told me he loved me; the words had come from somewhere deep within me but not consciously. Our subconscious is less inhibited than our conscious mind. We had known for some time that we loved each other, but having been in unhappy relationships and knowing how painful divorce was, we were cautious. Now that we could finally talk openly about it to each other, we became rather like teenagers. We were absolutely giddy, madly in love.

It was a fun time for us—we were uncomfortably hyper with excitement and agitation. It's that period of time when lovers see the other as being perfect, no warts and no blemishes. We knew it wouldn't last, and decided we would be glad when we could get our feet back on the ground. We were becoming exhausted with all the emotions we were experiencing, even though it was exhilarating. We soon began making plans to get married.

The Holidays

On the Sunday before Thanksgiving, I joined the First Presbyterian Church with stronger commitment than I ever had for any other church. I had found the church where I belonged even though it continued to be John's church in my mind for a long time. It was a downtown church, a small historical building, the oldest public building in continuous original use in Tallahassee. It had been built in the 1830s and had a balcony for the slaves. It was quite plain with no icons on the walls. The windows were plain opaque glass. It seemed somewhat solemn; I found it conducive to worship. It was a friendly congregation. The church was recognized as a liberal church; I liked it very much.

When we returned home one evening, a notice of an attempt to deliver flowers was hanging on the door knob.

I wondered aloud, "Now who could have sent me flowers? It wouldn't be Suzanne, they are going to be with us, and I don't think it would be Mitchell. Who would it be?"

With that John said loudly, "I sent them! Why wouldn't you have thought of me, I'm the one who would send you flowers?" He sounded irritated.

"I've never received flowers before as a romantic gesture; I guess I'm just not used to being treated so thoughtfully and lovingly as you treat me." I couldn't explain it any better; it seemed to me that logically I should have thought of John immediately

Suzanne had met Sal Presti in Ft. Lauderdale a couple of months earlier. I had not met him yet. But she brought him to my house to celebrate Christmas with John and me. He worked for the A&P grocery store; he was older than Sue, but that didn't seem to matter.

Schelley and Alex were with us part of the day; it was a memorable first Christmas for John and me. Suzanne and Sal seemed to enjoy themselves. I wished she lived closer, now that I was at a place where I had more time available to spend with her. She continued taking courses at the Community College. She was working some for her dad in his accounting practice. Of course, John's kids were happy; they were seven and ten, and it was Christmas.

"Our" House 1977

We decided to get married March 18th, during John's spring break. We enjoyed thinking about it, telling friends and family, plotting and planning.

In January we bought a house in Betton Hills and sold my house on Ivan Drive, although it had been less than a year since I bought it. I wanted to begin our marriage in *our* house, not *my* house. Looking back I realized that we made quite a few big decisions together so easily—the ability to do so continued throughout our marriage.

Neither Suzanne nor Mitchell said much when I told them John and I were getting married. Mitchell had not met him yet and Sue only briefly. They were used to my being alone; now it would be quite different. We couldn't possibly know how much John was going to impact the three of us, how much better our lives would be with him as part of our family.

John and I closed on our house in mid-February and moved my household the next weekend. John kept his apartment, for when Schelley and Alex were with him. We felt they were too young to see us sleeping in the same bed before we were married.

My Cup Runneth Over

We spent the next weekend in Atlanta, where my national organization, AAMFT (American Association of Marriage and Family Therapy) was meeting. We went a day early so we would have an extra day to simply enjoy. We loved driving out-of-town, meeting each other's friends, visiting new places, and just being together. My agonizing trip to self-realization had certainly been worth it—I was now who I had been born to be. Sometimes I thought of Dr. Quine and knew he would be pleased. So would Dr. Abren.

As soon as we got home, we got our marriage license. After that we went to the jeweler and chose our rings. We picked out simple ones; we didn't consider anything else. We went to Moon's jewelry store and found the rings without shopping around. That was John's modus operandi which never changed. I'm afraid I learned to shop quite differently as time went by.

John and Kate Kerr, March 18, 1977

March eighteenth dawned just like any other day, except for John and me. We were married at seven o'clock in the evening in our new home with twenty-five good friends and family members present. As we were getting ready back in "our" bedroom, the new pair of panty hose I had purchased turned out to be too small and I tore the crotch out of them in order to get them on. John kidded me about that many times over the years.

Sue and Sal, Schelley and Alex, Glenna and Phil, and Bill and Maverne were the family members there. I could have invited all of our family members, but, at the time, we didn't consider it—we didn't even talk about it. In my mind, it was a second marriage, and we just needed to keep it low key.

During the ceremony John cried, actually sobbed. He could hardly say "I do." Schelley and Alex were somewhat subdued at seeing him cry. Afterward, John's folks came up, and John embraced his dad and cried some more. Then Suzanne, Alex and Schelley came up; Schelley asked me why their dad was crying. I told them he was crying because he was so happy. I'm not sure if they understood that or not. Suzanne gave me a warm hug, she was glad to see me happy, even though she was not sure about John yet.

We had our reception at Brother's Three Restaurant for about seventy people. Afterward, the twenty-five who were at the ceremony came to our home for a buffet dinner which Glenna and Phil had arranged. It was the perfect ending for a memorable day. Later, I wondered at my lack of planning. I was pretty blasé about it all; the details had not worried me much.

The next morning Sally and John had a champagne brunch for us. It was a scrumptious breakfast with eggs Benedict—a memorable send-off for us. We were as happy as if we'd had two or three hundred people at our wedding and a sit down dinner at an expensive country club. We felt very married.

Soon after breakfast, we left for Atlanta where we were going to spend a few days looking for furniture and relaxing. Bill and Alice Nichols rode with us as they were flying out of Atlanta. We stopped on the way at Plains, Georgia, President Carter's home town, to have a picnic lunch which I had packed without the other three knowing it. I'd even included a bottle of champagne. We had our champagne lunch on Sunday afternoon in the town square on picnic tables provided for tourists.

John and I were so tired by the time we got to our hotel, we didn't even go out to eat. We had a snack and went to bed. We lay close to each other with his arms around me as sleep took over. I dreamed I was married to the most wonderful man, and we were going to spend the rest of our lives together.

1971 Kate in West Palm Beach

1974 Dorothy, Clay Vonnie (back row), Kate, Glenna (middle), Betty and Juanita (seated) after Dad's funeral

1974 Kate visiting with family after funeral service

1975 Kate back in Tallahassee

Chapter 4

A MARRIAGE OF SOULS

We spent the first week of our marriage in Atlanta purchasing a few pieces of furniture. It was not an onerous task for us; we enjoyed the idea of converting our recently purchased house into our home.

We were invited to Janet and Mike Adamson's home (Janet was Maverne's daughter) for dinner the second night we were in Atlanta. It was a memorable evening and a great way for me to get to know John's step-sister and her husband. We had cocktails and were getting acquainted when the electricity went off. The power didn't come back on all evening; the meal they had planned had to be altered. It didn't matter what they served, the evening of candles and a cold dinner with an aura of being pioneers made it a fun evening.

After the few days in Atlanta, we returned to Tallahassee and settled into living together. We were busy before we met, now it was somewhat daunting deciding what tasks to eliminate. John soon gave up coaching youth basketball, and I stopped serving on the Ethics Committee for AAMFT which entailed a two-day trip to Washington every couple of months.

Our Home

We paid fifty-three thousand dollars in 1977 for our house in Betton Hills. It was relatively small—sixteen hundred square feet—had three bedrooms and one bath.

I became aware of how women were not treated as equals when John and I applied for a loan. During the process, the loan officer talked directly to John. He never even glanced at me; it was as if I wasn't there. As the loan officer finished, he asked, "Do you have any questions?"

By now I was pretty upset and spoke up immediately. "Yes, you have treated me as if I wasn't here. I'm an equal partner in this deal, and I expected to be treated as such. We'll go through with the loan this time, but if I'm treated as second-rate in here again, we'll take our business to another bank." I said it in a nice, controlled voice, but he knew I meant it.

Another time an airline stewardess asked John, "Would you like a *Forbes,* Newsweek, or *Money* magazine?"

She then turned to me. "Would you like a *Ladies Home Journal, Good Housekeeping,* or *Cosmopolitan?*"

"No, Ma'am, I'd like a *U.S. News and World Report* or a *Business Week* if you have one. And I'd like to suggest that you don't assume all women read only the magazines you offered me. It is an insult to us when you make such a distinction between male and female intelligence." Again, I used a soft tone, but was serious.

John and I had agreed that the only way society was going to change its attitude toward women was to point out to anyone who offended one of us that an error was being made. Occasionally John was the one who spoke up.

Those are just two examples of subtle putdowns that demonstrate how our culture treated women differently. Betty Friedan's book, *The Feminine Mystique,* motivated women to want and demand equality. Her book was one of the instigators of the revolution that began in the sixties and is still influencing American society today.

Bill and Maverne

John's Dad and Maverne came for a visit after we were settled. They were married a few years after John's mother, Edna, died. Maverne's husband, who had worked for the same company as Bill, had died several years earlier.

Bill was somewhat reserved, a nice looking man, rather quiet, conservative in his lifestyle, and a gentleman with integrity and high moral standards. He wrote letters to us frequently and kept in touch occasionally with phone calls. He did have the reputation of being a bit frugal.

Maverne was a lovely, gracious woman with beautiful white hair, full lips and a ready smile. She was interested in family events and wanted to be kept abreast of what each member was doing. She liked sports when she was young and had been a star on a women's basketball team. It was not difficult to like them.

John and Mitchell Meet 1977

A few months after we were married we attended a conference in San Francisco. After the meeting we flew on to Seattle to visit Mitchell who had not met John yet. I was glad we got to see Mitchell on his territory; it allowed us to see how he lived and it might have been more comfortable for him to meet John this way. Mitchell took us to the salmon hatcheries where they had a simulated river which the fish swam up to spawn; spectators could watch the salmon as they made their way upstream. We had a cocktail at the top of the Space Needle, a ferry ride across Puget Sound, and a tour of the beautiful campus of the University of Washington.

Mitchell planned a daytrip into the Cascade Mountains. He had purchased a large salmon, head and all, which he stuffed and wrapped in aluminum foil to take with us along with all the paraphernalia one needs for a cook-out in the mountains. The best part of the trip was the time by the mountain stream where we cooked the stuffed salmon and picnicked. Salmon never tasted better, and we enjoyed the beautiful weather with perfect temperature until the sun went behind the mountain about 2:00 PM. Suddenly, the temperature dropped twenty degrees; we all rushed to put on the jackets which Mitchell had warned us we would need.

Our time with him went well; I was glad to get to be with Mitchell again, and John came home with good feelings about him. I think Mitchell liked John well enough for having just met him. Mitchell was still earning his meager living working wherever he could find a job. He read extensively, had great recall, and was an interesting conversationalist. John told others that Mitchell reminded him of a young Eric Hoffer, the longshoreman who was also a philosopher; John told me on the way home he thought Mitchell should have been a professor.

Our First Christmas as Family

John was beginning to know my grown children, and I was doing the same with his children—Schelley and Alex, who were nine and six respectively when we married. They stayed with us one night a week and every other weekend. Schelley was especially well behaved, a good student, creative, and affectionate. Alex was very different from his sister; he was mischievous, less eager to please, and more likely to get into trouble. However, he outgrew "testing the limits" by the time he was in middle school. We enjoyed both of them. John ate lunch with them at school when his schedule allowed.

Suzanne, Schelley, and Alex were with us for our first Christmas as a married couple. We had dinner at Tom and Abby Potter's in the afternoon. Sharing dinner with them on Christmas and Thanksgiving became a tradition for our families, alternating between our two homes. We felt like family toward each other. They had six children, most of whom were married, and some of them were always able to be home for the holidays. Abby and Tom liked to entertain and did so easily and graciously.

Old Records Die Slowly

Not long after we were married, John was late coming home one evening—later than I had expected. I became anxious wondering what was keeping him. When half an hour went by and rushed toward forty-five minutes, I began to panic. I was not concerned about his having had an accident; I was imagining him with some woman. I began to pace back-and-forth on the driveway, my anxiety and fear running through me. When he drove up, I pounced.

"Where in the hell have you been? I've been…"

He interrupted my hysteria with, "What do you mean? I told you yesterday that I would be an hour late because of a faculty meeting."

I remembered as soon as he told me and relief rushed over me. I began to cry and finally was able to say, "I know this really has nothing to do with you. I realize now that I was reacting to things from the past. I remember that you told me you would be late, and I'm sorry I jumped on you, but I couldn't help myself."

Some old records die slowly. They must be allowed to rise up out of the depths, be exposed, and understood for what they are, then thrown into oblivion. Trust is built over time.

John understood my emotional sprees, even when they were inappropriate. From that day forward, I was able to live in the present with my trustworthy husband. We both had experiences in past relationships that influenced us that first year we were together. Perhaps that was a good thing; it helped us understand each other at times when the past played tricks on us. John also had his way of over reacting to things I did. One time he became furiously angry and screamed at me. I really didn't know what I had said that provoked such a violent reaction.

"What are you so upset about? I love you and don't know what I said, but I didn't mean to make you so angry." I was able to stay cool until he regained his composure.

His demeanor changed from being on the attack to being contrite and apologetic. Softly he said, "It's not about you. You didn't say anything terrible, but it reminded me of other times when I did have reason to be angry, but didn't feel free to express it. Now it seems those old angers come out at you when they really shouldn't."

We sat on our deck and talked about what had just happened. I know that my training and experience as a therapist, as well as my deep love for John, helped me respond in a way that was calming, rather than provoking. A trust grew between us, the depth of which neither of us had known before. Those disturbing kinds of episodes happened several times in the first year of our marriage, but each succeeding year, they occurred less often, until by our third or fourth year of marriage we very seldom had to deal with them at all.

We enjoyed our deepening intimacy and protected it mightily by facing our negative feelings as they arose rather than stuffing them into our bellies to ferment.

My Office Building 1979

Throughout this busy time in our lives, my private practice had continued to grow; I was seeing as many clients as I could handle. With confidence that my reputation as a therapist was established, I decided I could afford a nicer office, one more to my personal liking. I had been looking around and was quite discouraged with what I was finding. That same week Bob Miles, a psychiatrist whom I had known since I had worked for Dr. Wilson when I was a student, called and asked me if I would be interested in buying office space together. What timing! We decided that day to look into building a small office building. John agreed with me that owning our office building made good sense financially.

We found the perfect lot on Delta Boulevard and agreed on the builder. I helped design the building so the client could come into the waiting room through one door and leave after their session through another door. We rented out the front of the building, which included three nice-sized offices, a waiting room, and a rest room. I handled everything from collecting the rent and paying the bills to watering the new shrubs and trees. I didn't mind; I could do it as I pleased. Bob sold his half to me after ten years when he was facing a divorce and wanted to consolidate his holdings.

We planted a live-oak tree in the front part of the parking lot, and I watered it two or three times a week. I went out in my high heels, dragged the hose across the parking lot and watered that little oak tree. In the fall the leaves all dropped off, and I thought it was because winter was coming. I continued religiously making sure it had enough water, even though I would get mad sometimes when my shoes got splattered or when the hose got a twist in it and I had to go down and straighten it. Working with long watering hoses has always been a test of my patience.

One morning in early spring someone from the front offices left a note on my bulletin board telling me a man had carried away my oak tree. I thought they must be playing a joke on me, but I dashed out, and sure enough the tree was gone. I couldn't believe my eyes. I immediately called the Tallahassee Nursery where I had purchased the tree.

"Mr. Prosser, my oak tree you planted for me a few months ago was carried away this morning by someone and…"

"Oh, Mrs. Kerr, I should have called you; we took it away because we noticed it had died, and we're bringing you another one this afternoon."

I had learned something new: healthy live-oak trees shed their leaves in the spring not in the fall. I worked out of that building for twenty years, selling it in 1999 to therapists who had been renting the front offices. I didn't mind leaving the building so much, but felt sentimental about that tree.

Chamberlin Drive Home 1983-1984

John and I had many intimate talks about our days' events, future plans, hopes, and dreams. We also had conversations about building a new house or adding on to the one we had. John wanted to add on, so we consulted with the man who did carpentry work for us. He said it couldn't be done because of lack of space on either side of our lot.

We purchased a lot on Timberlane Road. After our architect, Al, looked at our lot, we three sat down and discussed the kind of house John and I wanted. Al took notes as we dreamed out loud and gave him our intended budget. He made some preliminary sketches and consulted with us several times over the next few months; each time the plans grew more gorgeous, but we knew the price was going up also.

Al sketched a beautiful deck which wrapped around the pool and had different levels with lighting to highlight the trees that were to be left standing in the yard. We asked about the price again, and he assured us it would be within our budget. We weren't so sure.

Several days a week I drove to the lot from my office, trying to get a feel for how it would be to live in that area and in that house. I had doubts which wouldn't stop nagging at me. After Al added the deck, I began worrying about taking care of such an expanse of decking, the larger pool, and a house which had become larger than we had intended. I wanted us to have less upkeep, spend less time taking care of the home, not more. We began to admit the house was not going to be built for the amount we had specified, even though Al kept assuring us it would be within budget.

Al was ready to begin; he had the drawings and building specifications finished, but I was still struggling with my doubts. I went out and sat on the lot one afternoon and finally came to a decision. That evening I said to John, "I have something to tell you that will surprise you. I have decided we shouldn't go ahead with the house even though everything is set to begin."

He was dumbstruck. "What made you come to that decision?"

"I'm sure, and I think you are too, that the house he has designed will cost a lot more than we planned to spend. It'll take more money and energy to keep it up than our house does now. That's exactly the opposite of what we want.

"You're right, but you sure have surprised me. I know we've been talking about it being more expensive each time he comes. I just didn't know you were ready to give it up."

"I've been going out there trying to get a feel for living there. I decided today, it just isn't worth it."

John shook his head and looked at me with a slight smile. "You're something else. I wonder what Al will say. Do you think he might be able to add onto this house?"

"That's what I'm hoping. I know you wanted to do that from the beginning. We'll see what he says when he comes tomorrow evening."

So, the gorgeous house shown on Al's drawings which we had pored over for the past several months was not to be. The cost of his time would be minor compared to the amount over budget that we knew the house would have cost.

The next night before Al could unroll the plans, John said, "Al, we have something to discuss with you." He had been eagerly waiting for our okay to go ahead with the house and sat down with hesitation.

"We've been having doubts about going ahead with the dream house which you have created for us on paper," I said. "You have done a beautiful job, and we like the house you have designed, but we are having second thoughts."

John quickly asked, "Would you look at this house and see if there is some way we could add onto it?"

Al didn't react as negatively as we had feared he might. In fact, he went right out and started taking measurements. It always surprised me how easily we all switched our attention from a new house to a remodeled one. John and I knew we had made the right decision.

We went through the same steps we'd taken before in designing the new house, except this time it was on a smaller scale. Again, Al came up with some unique ideas we really liked. The contractor had said we didn't have space, but Al found ways to add seven hundred square feet to our existing house. The three of us became as enthusiastic about the plans for our "made larger" house as we had been for the new one.

In June 1983, everyone was ready to begin; John and I moved into a furnished apartment, for what we hoped would be three or four months, but ended up being nine months. We didn't really mind, because we were so excited about what was happening to our little sixteen-hundred square-foot home.

John knew the manager of the apartment we rented; he made arrangements for her to pay our utility bill, so we didn't have to disconnect and reconnect. She agreed to add it to our rent.

One night when John was out of town, I got home quite late and exhausted after having to hospitalize one of my clients late in the day. As tired as I was, I had to stop and pick up something to eat on my way home. I was looking forward to getting changed, eating my sandwich, and going to bed. I opened the door and switched on the light, except the light didn't go on. *Drat, I thought, the bulb is burned out.* So I switched on the kitchen light, and it also refused *to go on. It was 9:00 PM and I had no electricity.*

I called the manager, and she readily admitted she had forgotten to pay our bill. *Why do these things seem to always happen when John is out of town?* The utility company agreed to come out and turn my electricity back on. I ate my sandwich in the dark and waited. The electricity was on by 10:30 PM, and I was soon in bed, none the worse for the experience.

It was exciting to see the framing of the addition. When it was nearing the time to put in the fireplace in the library, John and I met at noon one day to pick out the brick. I thought there would be ten or fifteen bricks to choose from, but there were dozens of different ones. We had only one hour so we couldn't deliberate long. We chose a few in the color we liked. John held one up and asked the name. When the salesman told us it was *The Presbyterian,* we said, "We'll take it."

That Thanksgiving, Sue and Sal from Ft. Lauderdale, and Glenna, Phil and Aunt Clae from Illinois, came to celebrate the holiday with us. The apartment we were living in was so small that we decided to have our Thanksgiving dinner at a country club which served an excellent buffet. It surely was different eating Thanksgiving dinner in a restaurant. It was a lot less work which we all thought was great. Of course, there were no leftovers to enjoy either.

When Sue and I were alone she asked, "What would you think if we moved to Tallahassee?"

"I would love it. Are you thinking about it?"

"I'm thinking about it, but haven't mentioned it to Sal yet." We said no more about it.

Back in Our House

Even though the addition took longer than we had expected, the time went by quickly and in March 1984 we eagerly moved back home. What fun that was! Our old bedroom had become our walk-in closet and housed our dresser and chest of drawers. We especially liked the many windows and sky-lights, the stained glass windows, the cozy library with the new fireplace, and the dressing area off of our bedroom. For the next nineteen years, John would say, "I like our house, Kate; I like our life together." We liked it and were very happy there for as long as we both lived. So the nine months of being displaced was easily forgotten.

I Teach the First Year Medical Students

I taught the first year medical students at FSU for several years; it was in the early eighties, before FSU had a medical school. The students spent their first year at Florida State, then went to the University of Florida for the rest of their training.

The course included communication with emphasis on how to listen to their patients and interpret their non-verbal messages, to consider the patients' lives, to see each patient as a whole person, and how to communicate with and respect their spouses' needs. My goal was twofold: to help the young student know how to relate to their patients as human beings and not as a diagnosis, and to help them with their relationships with their spouses, since it's a well- known fact that doctors have one of the highest divorce rates. I received good feedback from the program director at the University of Florida. He told me that there was a noticeable difference in the students who had taken my course and those who hadn't. His remarks were quite complementary.

Schelley and Alex 1984

The same spring that we moved back in our newly remodeled house, Schelley graduated from Florida High School. She and Alex attended the Florida State Developmental Research School from kindergarten through high school. She was happy to be finished and looked forward to starting at Florida State University where she received her degree in communication four years later. She was a good student but eager to be out in the real world.

Her first job was with the State in the Department of Transportation, Public Relations Bureau. She had two more jobs with the State. One was with the Lottery where she wrote their newsletters, and the other was in the Governor's office as a computer consultant. When she left State employment, she went to work for the Open Text Company as a technical writer. She is still with them today and works from her home which she finds convenient. She is also on the Board of Directors for Big Bend Cares, a non-profit organization which helps and supports people who have Aids. She is their Public Relations chairperson.

Alex graduated from Florida High in 1987, three years after his sister. He tried college, but after one semester, decided to join the Navy. He was sworn in on February 8, 1988. He had his basic training in San Diego and was deployed in April 1991 to serve six months aboard the aircraft carrier Eisenhower. They were anchored off the Gulf Coast during the Gulf War and were involved in a skirmish during Desert Storm.

When they returned to Jacksonville, Rae Keith was there to meet Alex. He had met her in February 1991, just two months before he was deployed. They had written each other during the time he was gone, and the relationship had grown through those months. He was honorably discharged from the Navy in April 1992.

Alex received his bachelor's degree in Hotel and Restaurant Management from Florida State University in 1996. Rae earned her Master's in Accounting from Florida State and passed the CPA exam that same year.

One month after graduation they were married on May 24th in the Pisgah Church, an historical church at the edge of Tallahassee. Rae was a beautiful bride in her bouffant dress, and Alex was the handsome groom. The reception was held at Oven Park with good food, plenty to drink, and good music for dancing. We combined the Strubbe/Kerr Reunion with the wedding festivities, so all of the family came and stayed for the weekend.

Family Reunions

Reunions were a big thing in our family. Dad's family held reunions from the time I was a small child, always on the first Sunday in August. They were held at his Aunt Ella and Uncle Jim Durbin's house, because they had a beautiful spacious yard with plenty of shade trees. We kids were not allowed to go in their house out of consideration for them. Those reunions with the extended family ceased in 1975 after Dad died.

Dorothy had our siblings who lived within driving distance (all except Vonnie, who lived in Arizona, and me) come to her house on the Fourth of July 1976. They decided to get together every year on the weekend after the Fourth. Thus, our reunions (we seven siblings, spouses and children) were conceived. We met for a week-end rather than a day; because some of us had to drive or fly quite a distance, and we needed more than one day to catch up on each other's lives.

We held the reunions the first few years at Glenna and Phil's, Juanita and Haydn's or at our house, because we three had pools and that made a nice place to gather on hot July days. The year after John and I moved back into our house, we were the hosts, happy to show off our 'new' home. Juanita and Haydn brought fresh-water bass Haydn had caught in Georgia. We decided to cook them in the new microwave-oven which we had only used to heat a cup of coffee or a bowl of soup.

I carefully piled enough fish for the twelve of us (Glenna and Phil didn't come that year) on a large platter and set the timer for about three minutes. I had heard that the microwave- ovens performed miracles. So, after three minutes, I took the platter heaped with the fish and proudly headed for the porch where we were going to eat. Blood seeped onto the white platter before I got to the serving table. I turned around and headed back to the kitchen trying to act cool. "I think I need to cook it a bit more."

After another three minutes, I again went forth with my offering. This time, I realized as soon as I stuck the first one with a fork that it was far from being ready to eat. A little less cool this time, I muttered under my breath as I headed back to that dumb oven, "I guess I should read the directions."

That oven might be miraculous, but it wasn't magic! I finally cooked the poor bass in the old fashioned oven which I knew how to operate. To compensate, we had an extended happy hour.

Later years we held our reunions at different resorts; we took turns being in charge of making the arrangements. We had reunions in many different locations including Sedona, AZ, Estes Park, CO, Door County, WI, Phoenix, AZ, French Lick, IN, Wilmot, OH, Pheasant Run, IL, Bull Shores, AR, and in the State Parks of Kentucky.

Clay always brought a large cooler filed with cold drinks. He also brought a lot of food—snacks and fruits, candy and nuts. We girls made comments about "all of that stuff" Clay brought, but we enjoyed every bite of food and every can of diet soda. After a few years, we counted on him bringing those goodies. No more whispered remarks about "so much junk food!"

About five years ago, we began meeting in Rockford, IL, since the majority of the siblings lived in that area, and it had become difficult for some to travel far. In 2010 we had it in Toulon in conjunction with Dorothy's ninetieth birthday. We plan to have it in that area from now on because it is easier for most who live in Illinois and Indiana. Getting together to celebrate being with each other has kept us closer than if we got together only for weddings or funerals.

At one of the reunions held at Juanita's and Haydn's, she gave each of us a gift—something with a personal meaning behind it. My gift was a pair of tap shoes. (I had often said I would like to be a tap dancer.) That was all the encouragement I needed, and at sixty-eight, I took tap dance lessons from a woman who was in her early seventies. The biggest problem was that the lessons were at eight-thirty in the evening, and after a long day at the office I would feel so tired, that I didn't see how I could do it. But once we began dancing, I felt energized and came home ready to practice.

I couldn't practice on the deck or on the cement floor in the garage because it was either too hot or too cold. I got a large piece of plywood, but that didn't work either. So I practiced on the hardwood floor in the kitchen. After two years I got myself a sexy costume and performed for the family at the reunion. I was not a great dancer, but I surely did enjoy trying. Needless to say, we had to have the kitchen floor refinished.

Mitchell Accepted at Purdue 1986

Mitchell and Suzanne were able to attend the reunion occasionally. Mitchell went from one job to another for several years, after he got out of the Marines. In addition to his experience with logging in Forks, WA, he was a short order cook, drove a cab in Lake Tahoe, parked cars, sold costume jewelry, made a stab at photography, tried selling real estate, and even tried his hand as a car salesman, but he was never happy with any of those pursuits. He probably made his living the longest working as a cook. He was a long-distance driver with the Mayflower Moving Company for two years. He went all over the country and never told us he didn't like it, but never said he liked it either.

However, in November 1982, he wrote, "I very much enjoyed our last talk. It was the first time that I mentioned that I didn't like what I'm doing (loathe it). That was a relief to vocalize, but having done so seems to have made the situation somewhat worse. As long as I pretended that it was okay... Well, now I'm forced to confront my feelings; I'm somewhat at a loss as to my future. Just knowing I won't be in this truck much longer is a treat." He quit soon after that and got an apartment in Seattle hoping to live a more normal life. He began taking courses at the University of Washington while earning a meager living as a cook.

When Post-Traumatic Stress Disorder (PTSD) was first recognized in the medical field as a diagnosis, he was immediately interested. He knew he had most of the symptoms listed. He felt relieved knowing his condition had been recognized as a legitimate medical problem, and knowing he was not the only one with his haunting problems. He eventually got in group therapy offered at one of the Vet Centers, which had also just begun to sprout up around the country. The groups were (and still are) run by combat veterans for veterans who suffer from PTSD. He was admitted to one of the groups in Seattle and became a loyal participant. After one year, he was asked to be the leader's assistant. He liked that a lot; it encouraged his decision to major in psychology for his Bachelor's degree. He had found his pathway into the mainstream.

By 1985, he was a full-time student and talking about graduate school. He had written papers on PTSD and wanted to focus his studies in a field where he could use his present knowledge and his past experience.

Mitchell received his Bachelor's degree later that year from the University of Washington. He wanted to go to graduate school and hadn't decided where that would be. Then Mitchell attended the first annual PTSD meeting held in Atlanta. Charles Figley, professor at Purdue University and the PTSD expert in the U.S. had organized the meeting. Mitchell knew of him and wanted very much to go to Purdue to study under him. So he attended the conference, introduced himself to Figley and told him he would like to come to Purdue to study with him. After they had talked awhile, Figley asked Mitchell to send him his paper on PTSD which Mitchell had written for one of his classes. He wasted no time sending the paper when he returned to Seattle.

A few days later, he got a phone call early in the morning. "Hello, Mitchell, this is Charles Figley. I like your paper a lot; it tells me, not only that you can write, but also you already have a good grounding in the dynamics of PTSD. We want you to come to Purdue, but not next fall; we would like for you to get here in time to start next month."

Taking a deep breath and trying to sound calm, Mitchell said, "I'll be there, whatever I have to do, I'll be there." Then he asked, "When do classes start?"

"The first day is January 10th, four weeks from yesterday; I hope that is enough time for you."

"Yes, I'll be there. I'm delighted to be accepted and I appreciate your calling me; I'll be there before the 10th."

"You may call me later if you have questions; I'm glad you can make it and look forward to working with you."

"Thanks again." All kinds of things rushed through his mind. *How will I pay for it? Will I be able to get loans? Will my old car make it to Indiana? Can I get out of my lease here? What will I be able to take with me?* The important thing was that he was going to Purdue for graduate work.

Suzanne Moves to Tallahassee 1985

Suzanne made some changes in her life during those years also. She and Sal were married in 1981. The wedding was held in Sal's sister's new home. Suzanne looked very pretty, and I hoped she would be happy. At one point during the evening, I went over and sat beside her Dad and Lois. I told them that I wanted them to know they needn't feel guilty about what happened years ago, and I hoped they were happy together. I wouldn't have done that if I hadn't sincerely felt it. Therapy helps in many ways as did my being in a good marriage. They told me they appreciated it, and I could tell they were sincere by the tears in their eyes.

Sue and Sal lived alternately in Ft. Lauderdale, Atlanta and Tallahassee. She took courses at the community college when they were in Lauderdale, earning her AA in Computer Science. She worked part-time for her Dad in his successful accounting business and continued taking courses toward a Bachelor's degree.

In 1985, Sue and Sal moved to Tallahassee. They lived in an apartment not too far from our house. She enrolled in a couple of courses at FSU. It seemed like things were going along okay. But at dinner with us one evening, Sal told us he didn't like Tallahassee, and they were going to move back to Ft. Lauderdale.

"Sal, why don't you wait until Suzanne finishes her courses and then move?" I asked.

"I don't like it up here, and we're going back to Ft. Lauderdale," he said with finality.

"You must not want Suzanne to get her degree or you'd wait until this semester is over." I so seldom confronted him, but I was really upset. He was indignant that I would think such a thing. He got up and left in a huff. She reluctantly followed him.

The next morning we tried calling Suzanne; there was no answer. We drove over only to discover they had moved out. Everything was gone, the apartment was vacant. We were very disappointed; it seemed he called the shots, and she felt compelled to go along.

Within a month Suzanne returned to Tallahassee without Sal. After breakfast the morning after her arrival, she turned toward John and asked, "May I stay with you and Mom while I finish my degree?"

"Of course," John said without hesitation.

It would take her a year to finish if she could get enrolled that spring, which she managed to do. She told us her divorce from Sal was final, but she had still found it frightening to walk out on him. She had packed up and left while he was at work. She said she didn't think he would attempt to follow her, since she would be living with us. He might be able to manipulate her when they were alone, but he knew better than to try anything with the three of us together.

She was right. He never attempted to get in touch with her again. She finished her degree by the next spring (1987) and spent the summer taking the three extra courses she needed to sit for the CPA exam.

That fall she got a job with the State of Florida and moved into her own apartment. She settled in, adjusting to living alone and working full time as an accountant—no more working for minimum wage. We were so proud of her for hanging in there. She certainly earned that degree with a load on her back. Along with her other good qualities, she showed perseverance and determination.

About a year later, John and I were eating at our favorite restaurant, and Sue appeared at our table. "Come to my apartment when you're done," she said and left. By her demeanor we knew something had happened, and it wasn't good. We speculated as we finished our meal and drove the short distance to her place. As soon as we walked in she said, "Dad died." He was sixty-three years old.

Dean had been diagnosed with Lou Gehrig's Disease (ALS) several years earlier. She had driven down to see him the previous weekend and knew he couldn't live much longer. But even when we know death is approaching, it is a shock when it actually happens. We stayed with her for a while and talked; Mitchell called while we were there. They were able to offer some solace to each other. They asked me go to Ft. Lauderdale for the funeral, and I did. They felt my being at the funeral would help them feel a little less awkward, surrounded by Lois' family. I surely understood and didn't mind going. Dean, their Dad, was buried on Suzanne's thirty-eighth birthday.

Suzanne had divorced, moved, finished her degree, moved again, and her Dad had died within a relatively short period of time. Dealing with all life's changes can show us how much strength and resilience we actually have, especially when we are challenged by so many adversities.

On the more positive side, Suzanne found out that she had passed her exam—she was a CPA. The three of us went out and celebrated. What a tremendous accomplishment for her. Neither of my kids had an easy time getting their educations. They both took a course or two whenever they were close to a university to make it possible. They worked at menial jobs, anything they could find to make a meager living. Most often Sue had worked as a waitress, but also as a clerk and a receptionist. It had been a long, difficult journey; John and I were very proud of both of them. I was rewarded when they each, at different times, told me that knowing I had gone to school later in life had encouraged them to "hang in there."

Bill Kerr Dies 1986

One year before Dean died we received word that John's Dad, Bill, was in the hospital with congestive heart failure. It was soon apparent that he was not going to recover. He died in October 1986, at the age of eighty-three. He and Maverne had been good companions during the seventeen years they were married—Maverne would certainly miss him. We spent several days in Ft. Wayne with the rest of the family. Being together was good for all of us. I was glad I had known John's Dad; it gave a depth to our relationship that nothing else could have given.

Strubbe/Kerr Reunions

After Bill's death, Janet and Mike arranged the first Strubbe/Kerr reunion which was held in Big Canoe, Georgia. (Maverne's name was Strubbe before she married Bill). All five couples attended: three Strubbe families and two Kerr families: Barbara (Wilbur), Tom and Janet (Mike) from the Strubbe line; John (Kate) and Roger (Joellen) from the Kerr. We met in different locations until Janet and Mike built their lake house on Goodwood Lake in Ninety-Six, South Carolina. Yes, the name of the town is Ninety-Six.

Janet organizes our get-togethers year after year; Mike is the chef. They plan the meals as a team—Mike does the grocery shopping and cooking while Janet is busy with the myriad other things entailed with hosting a three-day invasion of loving relatives. We are served great buffet meals—breakfast, lunch and dinner every day. It is all done in such an unobtrusive manner that the food seems to magically appear. The rest of us are grateful for their hospitality. The family surprised me in 2005 by celebrating my eightieth birthday (a month ahead of time) with a present, a cake with candles, and fireworks.

Birthdays

John surprised me a couple of times on my birthday. He told me two weeks prior to my sixtieth birthday to keep the morning of June 25th clear. About six in the morning on the big day the phone rang. I jumped out of bed, picked up the phone, and a voice said, "Happy Birthday, Kate. How would you like a hot-air-balloon ride this morning?"

I was really surprised. We ballooned over the northeast part of Tallahassee, landing in an open area by a new winery. There was a table set with a champagne breakfast. It was quite exciting; the best part being that John had planned it and surprised me.

The second surprise was a year later for my sixty first. He and Suzanne told me we were going out to eat at a fancy restaurant, but first we stopped at one of our favorite lounges and had a glass of wine. Well, they had a glass of wine; I had a scotch and water. While there, John said he'd forgotten something, and we drove back to the house to get it. I went in with them and they managed to let me walk down the hallway first. As I turned to go into the kitchen about fifteen people sang out, "Happy Birthday!"

Tables were set by the pool and the catered dinner arrived as scheduled. I was really taken back, could hardly believe John and Suzanne had pulled it off. It was a lovely evening; the dinner was great, and the whole thing was memorable for me. I had dressed up thinking we were going to a special restaurant. I wore ivory-colored silk slacks with a satin blouse which matched the slacks perfectly. I had my hair pulled back with clips and felt really good about how I looked. I was sixty years old and felt about forty—frisky and sexy.

John and I continued being aware of how much we enjoyed our lives together. We considered ourselves extremely fortunate; we liked our jobs, had a nice home, and were healthy. We didn't agree on everything, but there never seemed to be anything we couldn't resolve. I knew those lonely years, when I had struggled in therapy and school, had prepared me for the kind of marriage I had with John.

Our Travels

One of the many things we enjoyed doing together was traveling. Our first trip abroad was to London—we played it safe and went where we could speak the language. During the next seventeen or eighteen years, we traveled to Germany, Hawaii, the Soviet Union, China, Spain, Africa, the Scandinavian countries, Scotland, Ireland, Italy, Eastern Europe, Israel, Egypt, Greece, Turkey, Hong Kong, Bangkok and Singapore.

We toured the Scandinavian Countries and China with Juanita and Haydn. It was great traveling with them, especially in China where Haydn, who made consulting trips to China, made all of the arrangements. It was a special trip with just the four of us and a guide.

We traveled some with our good friends, Moira and Urb Ozanne, including trips to Hawaii, the Soviet Union and Africa. The Soviet trip was planned for the week after the Chernobyl meltdown at Kiev, the capitol of Ukraine, so most of the people cancelled. The thirteen of us who did go flew over Kiev to visit Odessa and Malta instead. We also met the Ozannes in Scotland where Moira had been born and raised. They were great traveling companions as well as loyal friends.

John and I also traveled quite a lot in the United States. Because of our work, we were not able to take more than two weeks at a time for traveling. Many people would have waited until they could stay longer but we found two weeks adequate. We saw a lot of the world that we would not have seen had we waited.

In 1990, we met Mitchell in Washington, D.C., to visit the Viet Nam Memorial. It was a very emotional experience. Mitchell found a couple of buddies' names and placed meaningful tokens under their names, as many people do. He put a picture of one friend under his name, and as we stood there in silence everyone who came by bent down, picked up the picture and looked at it. That was a sobering experience for all of us.

Mitchell Accepts Position at Monroe, LA 1992

Mitchell had been dating Teddi, who was also a doctoral student in the same field at Purdue, one year behind Mitchell. Late that summer, they called to tell us they were going to get married. She came with him to visit in October, and we went to the FSU-Syracuse football game on Saturday. When I began to explain a play to Teddi, I soon discovered she knew more about football than did I. It was a fun weekend. But their relationship had some challenges; I hoped they could work through them.

Mitchell received his Ph. D. in May of 1992. Juanita and Haydn, Suzanne, Teddi, John and I attended. It certainly was a big day for those of us who were aware of the jagged, painful path Mitchell had traveled to reach this goal. When the seven of us we were together, Mitchell stood up and said, "I have a surprise announcement. I have accepted a position in Monroe, Louisiana." That topped off our celebration. Jobs were not plentiful at the time, and Mitchell was the only student in his small class at Purdue who had been hired so far. The search committee told him one of the things in his favor was the long road he had taken to earn his doctorate. They believed his experiences along the way would help him in his teaching in the field of counseling. His starting salary was $34,000 with the usual perks, including good health insurance and a retirement program.

He began teaching in July. He wrote to us how much he liked it adding, "I am a natural." (I remembered John telling me, after he first met Mitchell, that he would have been a good teacher.) Mitchell was forty-six years old and finally in a profession that he loved. No more fast-food cooking or driving cabs or parking cars. He beat my record by four years; I was fifty when I began my career. And Sue beat us both; she was only thirty-eight when she became a CPA.

Suzanne's Foot Surgeries 1992

Suzanne bought her first home that year—a two bedroom town house. Her Siamese cat, Mali, had several spaces where she could hide when company came or go to take a nap without being disturbed.

Soon after moving into her new home, Sue had surgery on her left heel. She was still using a crutch when she was in a car accident in which she broke three bones in her right foot. The hospital took many x-rays but none of her feet, even though that foot had become quite swollen and the left one was bandaged. She also had a broken rib and some severe bruises, so she stayed with us for a couple of nights.

After a week of hobbling around on crutches and two sore feet, she went for her check up on her heel. Her podiatrist took one look at the swollen right foot and ordered an x-ray. As soon as the x-ray was developed, he called in his partner.

After introducing him, he said, "Look at this. And she's been walking on it for a week!" The two doctors shared their amazement that she had been crippling along for a week with badly broken bones in her foot which had not been discovered by the hospital and had not been set.

We had not known the small bones in her feet were broken and slipped so that the broken ends were rubbing against each other. They did surgery that night, but put on a soft cast. The bones slipped apart within two days. After the second surgery, they put a hard cast on which worked better. The good ending is that her neglected foot has never given her trouble since.

Also in 1992, President Bush and the Soviet Union's Yeltsin proclaimed the end of the Cold War. The U.S. Supreme Court reaffirmed the right to abortion. Bill Clinton was the newly elected president.

Maverne 1993

The next month Maverne celebrated her eighty-fifth birthday. She looked lovely as always and was pleased that so many, almost her entire family, was able to come and celebrate with her. After Bill died, she continued to live in Ft. Wayne until it became difficult for her to live alone. None of her three children lived near-by. Janet and Mike helped Maverne move to a nice assisted living complex near their home in Atlanta where they could look after her.

A little less than one year later on March 29, 1993, Maverne died. She had recently been diagnosed with cancer, but died one evening from a heart attack after having played bridge in the afternoon. Her death left a big void in the family; she was a much loved mother, grandmother, step-mother and mother-in-law.

Ansley Katelin Suzanne Young 1993

Another chapter in our book of life began in the spring of 1993. Mitchell called to tell us Teddi was pregnant. That was a surprise to everyone. She had another year of studies at Purdue; Mitchell was in Louisiana, and they were not married. I had wanted a grandchild so much, and now it looked like that dream was going to become reality. At the same time, Teddi found out she had passed her preliminary exams which meant she was free to work on her dissertation without worrying about any more exams. She still had the responsibility of raising two boys.

In June we were with Mitchell and Teddi and were able to share in the anticipation of our granddaughter's birth. Yes, they knew it was to be a girl, much to their delight. They had decided to wait to get married until Teddi had her degree, and Mitchell was settled in his first professional position. It was fairly common in the 1990s for couples to have a child before they were married. "In my day" that would have been a real catastrophe. Teddi called to tell us they had the name chosen: Ansley Katelin Suzanne Young. I loved it; we would call her Annie Kate. She was due November 29th which seemed a long time to have to worry about Teddi in Indiana and Mitchell in Louisiana. But they kept busy; the time was soon upon them.

Teddi had some trouble during the ninth month of her pregnancy, because she had developed a hernia. She was ordered to stay off her feet as much as possible, because her legs and feet were swelling badly. But there was not much chance of that happening because of her responsibilities.

Although the due date was November 29th, Teddi called on the evening of the 8th and told Mitchell she was headed to the hospital. At 11:00 PM she called to tell us she was in the hospital and had just spoken to Mitchell who was already in Illinois.

The next day, November 9, 2003, I had clients from 8:00 AM until mid-afternoon. That was a good thing because it made the time pass faster. Mitchell called right after I got to my office: "We're still working on it. The doctor came in and broke the water. Teddi is really working hard. She is doing great. Everything is hunky dory."

The hours passed slowly so before my client arrived at 1:00 PM, I called the hospital. Mitchell said, "Everything is all right. It is just taking a long time. The doctor is here and said it won't be much longer."

When my next client arrived, I told her what was going on so she would know I was going to answer the phone when it rang. I usually didn't answer the phone when I was with a client, so I needed to explain. Thank goodness, she was one of my long-term clients who had grandchildren, so she understood. I was sixty-eight and had given up ever having a grandchild. Mitchell was forty-eight and Sue had not been able to have children, so this was a momentous day for all of us. I had my pen and paper ready so I could record our conversation when the time came. (I still used my short hand which I had learned in high school.)

When the phone rang, I grabbed it. Mitchell said, "Hello Grandma!" What sweet words those were to me. *Grandma, I'm a grandma.* Mitchell continued:

"She was born twenty minutes ago and Teddi is holding her. She is so alert. She has big blue eyes and is looking me right in the eye. She has hair and is holding onto me. She is a pretty little girl. She has dimples. She is so sweet. She is just looking around. She is so alert. She is a cutie. This little thing is something else. She has a good disposition. She grabbed my finger. She is something else. She is sharp and so alert. She is trying to smile. She weighs eight pounds and nine ounces. She is twenty inches long. She is perfect."

I had said all along that I wasn't going to go up to see the baby, but would wait until Christmas when they would be with us at our home. That would just be six weeks. But as soon as I hung up the phone, I knew I had to go see my granddaughter. I flew up the next day. As I entered the airport concourse, there stood Teddi with a pink bundle in her arms. Mitchell looked on proudly. Teddi handed me the baby. With tears welling up, I just stood holding my granddaughter close to me.

I got to meet Annie Kate's big brothers—Philip who would be eleven the next month, a tall, good looking boy with sort of a serious demeanor, and Michael, nine and a half, a little more playful personality, also good looking. What a big event for them! It turned their lives around for a while. During my visit, I didn't give them the attention I wish I had. There was so much attention being given to the baby that they must have felt pushed aside, especially Michael. Philip would still be the oldest, but Michael was no longer the baby. I'm sure it was a big adjustment for each of them.

Teddi did so well before and after the birth. With all that was going on in her life, she never faltered in her efforts to earn that doctorate which she did the next spring. From the time Annie was born until Teddi finished at Purdue, she carried Annie with her where ever she went—work, school or grocery shopping. Annie was a healthy baby, and I am sure it was because she was exposed to every germ early and built up a strong immune system.

Mitchell and Teddi got married in April 1994 in our living room. Annie was five months old at the time and made her presence known during the ceremony. Glenna and Phil, Clay and Rose, and Dorothy came down for the wedding. Teddi was lovely and Mitchell was handsome. We had the reception at the house following the ceremony. It was a perfect spring day, and we opened up the porch and pool area for the celebration.

The next day, the bride and groom went to Disney for a few days for their honeymoon, leaving the baby with us. I enjoyed every minute that Annie Kate was there, even at night when she would awaken me. I had set up the crib by my side of the bed, so when she whimpered, I awakened immediately. When I turned on the light, she would raise her head and smile at me. I wouldn't have cared if she had wakened me every hour. She learned to turn over during those few days with us; I captured her on my camcorder as she struggled and struggled until finally she flipped over.

As she had hoped to do, Teddi finished her dissertation in June 1994. That was quite amazing with all she had to deal with in addition to her academics. She applied for a position that was open in Monroe where Mitchell was finishing his first year. We all kept our fingers crossed and were tickled when she was notified in August that she had the job. It was a tenure track position which meant they would be able to be together and both employed in their chosen fields.

A Divorce and a Retirement 1995-1998

Their marriage was a struggle from the beginning. Mitchell was forty-eight and had never been married. Now he was not only married, but had a baby and two pre-teen boys, several pets and televisions.

He had never had a pet or a TV. Teddi was adjusting to living in the South, a new job, a new marriage and a new baby. Sadly, they separated in March, and after much pain and many tears, they were divorced in August 1995. They worked in the same department at the University of Louisiana at Monroe (ULM). It was an uncomfortable situation. They felt good about having tenure track positions, so put up with the unpleasantness.

As Mitchell and Teddi were beginning their careers, John was planning his retirement. He had taught at FSU since 1966 and decided to go on the phased retirement in the fall of 1995. We had talked about it for a few months and felt it was a good idea for him. He would be teaching one semester a year. He could do that for five years, but could stop teaching sooner, if he so desired. After three years, he retired completely. He felt he was out of touch with the students by teaching only four months of the year. He was a fully retired Professor Emeritus in May 1998. But he stayed involved with the church, the Chamber of Commerce, and served on several boards. He played golf three or four times a week; he was never bored.

We enjoyed college football. Together we watched Florida State football move from an unknown team in 1976 to being the National Champions in 1993. Going about three hours prior to kick-off, we met with friends from the School of Business for tailgating before we hiked over to the stadium in time to see the team warm-up. We didn't want to miss any of the pageantry. We sweated through some ninety-five degree heat and got drenched in some heavy rains, but we never had to contend with freezing cold or snow. I don't know of any other activity characterized as fun where we would willingly sit for three or four hours in that kind of heat and rain.

Visits with Family Members

In the fall of 1995, after John's retirement, Mitchell and Annie Kate visited us for several days. She was such a joy for all of us, and she really liked our pool. We had to keep the doors locked when she was inside; we feared she would get out and head for the pool. She was two and a half and thought she could do everything by herself. "I can do it!" was an automatic response when you tried to help her with anything. She loved our neighbors' cat, Snowflake. She said, "I just love Snowflake, she is such a 'wonnerful' cat." She still likes cats and dogs. They have two of each at home. While they were with us, Mitchell told us that he had begun working with the VA, treating Viet Nam Veterans who were suffering with PTSD. He was excited about the possibilities.

Later Teddi brought Michael, Philip and Annie for a visit; the boys didn't much care for Snowflake, but they surely liked the pool. They were now eleven and twelve and growing fast. Philip was as tall as I and Michael not far from it.

We also spent a few days at Gulf Shores on the Florida Panhandle coast in a place that Teddi had rented once before. Michael and Philip played well together—they were like a couple of puppies. Annie was so much younger that their relationships with her were different. Philip seemed more like a surrogate parent sometimes. He looked out for her when Teddi wasn't there. We all had a great time doing what people do at the beach—swimming, building sand castles, applying sun screen, sunning, eating, drinking, and playing cards.

Broken Ribs and a Broken Nose 1996

Our next short vacation trip was to attend the Strubbe/Kerr reunion at Big Canoe, Georgia. We were getting ready for bed the night before our trip, when I lost my balance while kicking my shoes off and fell backwards, hitting my back against the metal shelving, and breaking two ribs. John heard me fall, and came into the closet where I was sitting flat on the floor. I quickly said, "I'm okay; I didn't break anything."

Then I tried to get up and the stabbing pain let me know I was wrong. With much gnashing of teeth, I got to my feet, and we knew I had at least one broken rib. "I'll be all right tomorrow; we'll be able to go." I was trying so hard to be optimistic, but could no longer deny I was in trouble. We managed to get me in bed, and once I could lie still, the pain subsided. But if I moved the least bit the pain would grab me. I lay there long after John had fallen asleep, until I had to go to the bathroom. As soon as I made an attempt to move into a position to get up, I would gasp with pain. John woke up and came around to my side of the bed to help me, but that wasn't good either. Finally, gritting my teeth and inhaling deeply, I got to my feet.

I put my hand on John's arm for security, but when we slowly headed toward the bathroom, he seemed not to be with me. It became clear that he was lagging behind me. As I began to speak to him, he lunged forward with two or three quick steps and fell head first; his face hit the door jamb. He lay prone on the bathroom floor with his head in a fast-spreading pool of blood.

I moved as fast as my injured body would let me and called 9ll. After giving them the address and directions, I inched my way to the front door and turned on the lights. I shuffled back down the hall to check on John. He was still face down in a large circle of blood, making gurgling noises. I couldn't bend down to help him. I was panic-stricken.

I crept gingerly back up the hall to be by the front door when the paramedics arrived; they were at the door in six minutes after my call. When we got to John, he had raised up on his hands and knees and blood was dripping from his nose. The paramedics turned him over onto his back and did some perfunctory testing of his awareness, as I tried to explain what had happened. I knew it sounded far-fetched, and I was sure they thought we'd had a fight. After they determined that John was all right except for a broken nose, they told us to call our doctor in the morning and left us.

Painfully, we climbed back into bed. As I lay there trying to sleep, I thought about how John had fallen. I knew he had fainted because of the pain I was experiencing. He had fainted before in a similar circumstance, and I was sure that was what had happened. I knew we were not going to any reunion the next day; we went to the doctor instead. We had both been patients of Dr. Judelle since we were married, so he knew us quite well.

When he asked us what in the world happened, I said straight-faced, "Dr. Judelle, we had a terrible fight last night. John kicked me in the ribs, and I punched him in the nose."

His fallen facial expression told me he believed me. I dared not laugh, but quickly we told him the truth.

John had to have some tests, and I had an x-ray to be sure my lungs were not punctured. When we called to tell the family we wouldn't be able to come, they must have wondered if we couldn't have made up a better story than that. John wasn't hampered by his broken nose, but it took me a couple of weeks before I could comfortably go about my usual routines.

Life is Good

Early in the New Year of 1997, Mitchell rented a house in Monroe. He wrote that he had bought Barbie Doll sheets for Annie's bed. We visited him as soon as we thought he was settled in. Annie was growing up so fast; we wanted to see her as often as possible. She had a chalk board on an easel where she spent a lot of time practicing her writing. She was proud that she could write her name and numbers; she spent hours standing at that board entranced with her new abilities. Mitchell had given her two hamsters which she also played with a lot—letting them out of their cages more often than her Dad liked. She certainly had a mind of her own.

We always visited with Teddi too, when we were in Monroe. Michael and his friend won first prize for their science project while we were there. They had constructed a likeness of a volcano and explained some of the reasons for eruptions.

Annie Kate learned to swim across the pool that summer and even learned to swim on her back. If she wasn't in the pool, she wanted to play cards or Monster, which was her version of hide and seek. She was very loving with lots of hugs and kisses. We went to her fourth birthday celebration in Monroe in November. She entertained her friends at the Fun Factory and was queen for a day.

That fall I wrote in my journal, "Life is good. Sue is excited planning for the house she is building just off of Meridian Road, two miles from my office. Mitchell and Teddi are adjusting to the divorce. Annie's brothers are growing; Philip will be fifteen on New Year's Eve, and Michael is a healthy thirteen-year-old. Annie is in pre-school, taking dancing lessons and just being Annie.

In December I took her shopping for Christmas presents for her Dad and Mom. We went several places before she picked out a blue glass bird and a magnet with a deer on it for her Mom. She got a purple crystal rock for her Dad. She wrapped them by herself with her "I can do it" attitude. I filmed her on the camcorder while she put ribbons and stickers galore on each package. She was in what we called the Green Room, where I did all my wrapping. I left the paper, ribbons, tags, scissors, and Scotch Tape out all the month of December, so she had free rein with all of it. I stood where she couldn't see me and watched her. She sang little ditties and talked to herself as she worked. As much as she enjoyed herself, I think I enjoyed watching her even more.

Our lives were good. Bill Clinton had been re-elected president. The good economy was reflected in the higher prices we paid for the essentials. The average cost of a new house was $124,500, average income was $36,300, the cost of a new car averaged $17,300. A gallon of gas was $1.22. A postage stamp was 32 cents.

An Accident and a New Job for Sue

In February, after moving into her new house at 183 Ivernia Loop in January, 1998, Suzanne suffered a badly broken elbow, when she fell off the kitchen counter. She was standing on the counter looking for the directions to the garage door, which she had put in the cupboard above the refrigerator. Luckily the man who had come to help her with the door was still there. He called the ambulance and tried to reach me, but I was with a client and didn't answer my phone. They did reach John who met them at the emergency room. I went over as soon as I checked my calls and burst into tears when I saw her. I don't know why I cried. It was obvious that the injury was not life-threatening.

We were fortunate that Dr. Thornberry, the orthopedic specialist, was the doctor on call. He did the surgery later that evening and told us it was a bad break, but he hoped that she would have full use of the arm once it healed. A couple of years later, she had an ulnar nerve transposition on that arm. The ulnar nerve had become bound in scar tissue, and was causing her hand to become numb. Other than that small problem her elbow healed well, and she lost less than five percent of its function.

Sue took a new job with the Children and Families Department and received an increase in salary, so her new year started off great—new house, new job, and a healing elbow. And Mitchell had submitted his application for promotion and tenure. Good things were happening in my family.

St. George Island

In June we had our annual week on St. George Island in "our" house—One Particular Harbor (the rental we always used). It had four bedrooms and a large shaded porch, where we could see the porpoises playing in the ocean, and we could toss bread to the birds as they swooped down to catch it mid-air. Nearly every afternoon we walked or biked over to Aunt Ebbie's for ice cream cones. They had the most delicious ice cream, and the two big scoops we each received came in many different flavors.

We played a lot of cards, everything from Go Fish to Canasta to Rummy. Annie was quite a card player by the time she was five, having started with Go Fish before she was four. Two big brothers in the house made a difference in such things.

Mitchell came for the first part of the week; Teddi came down for the rest of the week. She had applied for a position for the fall of 1999 at Clemson, South Carolina and Valdosta, Georgia, which was a good thing for her, but it presented a dilemma for Mitchell. He knew she needed to do what was best for her career, but he was in despair thinking of Annie having to move so far from Monroe—over five hundred miles away.

Annie, who was there the full week, walked down to the beach and played in the sand for a while by herself (we watched her from the porch). If there were any other kids anywhere near her age, she was not bashful about introducing herself and entering into whatever it was they were doing. If they didn't respond to her gesture, she would leave after a brief time. Usually she made herself fit in.

A Football Game from the West Coast

Early in September John and I took a trip to Washington, Oregon, and Vancouver. While we were out west, FSU played Miami. We timed our day so that we'd be back in time to see the game on TV. We were running a little late and hadn't eaten, so we pulled into a grocery store to get something to take with us. We had our tailgate right there on the coffee table and watched while FSU beat Miami by a field goal in the last thirty seconds. We were two happy FSU fans.

My Car Accident 1998

Soon after returning to Tallahassee, I totaled our Cadillac. I was on my way to the gym early Monday morning and inexplicably ran a red light. I wasn't going very fast, but couldn't avoid hitting a car driven by a young man. Neither of us was hurt; both of us wore our seat belts. My knees were bruised which meant if I hadn't had the seat belt fastened I could have damaged them. The police attended the man first, and I sat there for probably fifteen minutes, very upset at the thought that I didn't stop at that light, and I could've killed someone.

A well-dressed middle aged man pulled up beside my car and came over to see if I was all right. "Is there anything I can do for you?" he asked. "Can I call someone for you?"

"I don't have my license with me. If you could call my husband he would bring it to me. We don't live far from here."

When John didn't answer the phone, the man said, "Where do you live? I will go get your husband." At first I thought that was too much, but he said he would be glad to, so I gave him the address.

"John is probably out by the pool since he didn't answer. The gate to the pool area is on the north side of the house. If he doesn't answer the door, he will be out there. Thank you so much."

It turned out that he and John knew each other. He was the president of a bank and on his way to work early on a Monday morning. He had stopped to help a woman in distress. Those acts of kindness help us keep our faith in humankind.

John comforted me when he arrived, and we did what had to be done with the officer. We spent the rest of that day with the insurance company, renting a car, and shopping for a new car. John joked with me, "The next time you want a new car just tell me." He was so good at such times, always considerate of my feelings. He would sometimes say, "Kate, what would you do without me?"

"I'd be lost," I'd answer, although he had said it in jest.

John's being retired helped at times like that. If he'd still been working, he would have been at the university. And when Alex and Rae were living in Jacksonville for a couple of years, he was able to go over and spend the night, so he and Alex could play golf the next day. I went with him when I could, which wasn't as often as I would've liked. Alex was a manager for a Bennigan's Restaurant, so he could get a morning off if he knew in advance. Rae was with an accounting firm—her first job after earning her CPA license.

Schelley and Paul's Wedding 1998

Schelley had been dating a young man, Paul Cassidy, whom we liked. We were pleased when they told us they were getting married. They had a beautiful wedding at Wakulla Springs Lodge on October 3rd, 1998. It rained that morning but was bright and sunny for the wedding, which was fortunate because they were married outside with the lake as a backdrop.

Schelley was beautiful with flowerets in her hair and a gorgeous gown. She and Paul made a good looking couple. Dinner was served at the Lodge followed by dancing. John's four siblings and spouses were present and a few of the younger generation. All of us stayed at the Lodge on Friday and Saturday nights. What a fun weekend. We wished the Cassidys a long and happy life together.

Mitchell's Bronchitis

About a month after Schelley's wedding, in late November, Mitchell came down with severe bronchitis. His lungs had given him trouble for years; they often acted up when he was under heavy stress. He was trying to reconcile himself with the fact that Annie might move from Monroe the next fall; he was having a hard time accepting that possibility. He called us one morning from the hospital where he had been admitted for tests. His x-rays showed something going on in one lung which was very frightening. We cleared our calendars and drove to Monroe the next day. Sue went with us. We drove to Teddi's and picked Annie up before we went to the hospital. She wanted to see her Dad, but by the time we arrived at the hospital, he was in a surgical room. We got permission to take her in for a minute. What an experience that was for Annie! Her mouth fell open, and her eyes were troubled as she took it all in. He was hooked up to all the stuff one gets hooked up to when such a procedure is to take place. It took some fast talking on his part to put her five-year-old mind at rest.

We were all relieved when the questionable place on Mitchell's lung was swelling from the bronchial inflammation. Mitchell was sent home to recuperate. John, Suzanne and I went to Annie's fifth birthday party. It was quite a party with fun games, including dunking for apples and pin the tail on the monster. Later, we went trick or treating with

Annie and a little friend. She fell asleep as soon as we got home, happily exhausted. We had a little birthday party at Mitchell's the next day for her. Her dad gave her a hamster with a cage, toys and feed. She was thrilled with her new pet which she immediately named Belle.

With the help of new inhalers and large doses of antibiotics, Mitchell was getting better but had no energy. We knew he mainly needed rest, so we left early the next morning for home after delivering Annie back to her mother. One more crisis was behind us but not for long.

Mitchell and Annie came for a week at Christmas; he didn't feel well when they arrived. The bronchitis had hung on since the previous episode and had begun to worsen again. The second day they were with us, he nearly decided to go back home to see his doctor but changed his mind. He kept thinking he was going to be better the next day.

His coughing woke me about 3:00 AM on the 22nd. I got up and stood by our bedroom door hoping he'd stop coughing, so that he could get some sleep. As I stood there listening, I heard the unmistakable thud as his body hit the kitchen floor. By then John was awake; we ran down the hall and found him unconscious.

He soon regained consciousness, and didn't argue when we suggested John take him to the emergency room. I got his and Annie's gifts packed, threw some stuff in a suitcase, got Annie up and ready to go. Mitchell wanted to be home where he could see his pulmonologist and be in his own bed, but we knew he couldn't drive himself. As soon as they returned from the emergency room, we finished loading the cars and left. Mitchell had been given a shot of antibiotics and a prescription. John drove Mitchell's car, and I drove ours with Annie in the back; Mitchell sat up front on the passenger's side.

We were through Pensacola when Mitchell started one of his coughing spasms, and as I had feared, he passed out right on the seat beside me. I carefully pulled over, stopped, and jumped out to go around and open his door. I had no idea what else I was going to do. His face was the color of liver, and I was really anxious. Thank God, he regained consciousness before I had much time to ponder, and we were back on the road. John had noticed that we had stopped and he waited for us a few miles down the road. Mitchell didn't pass out again, and the only other time we stopped was to get a quick bite to eat around noon. It took us over ten hours, and Annie never complained.

She was a scared little five-year-old; her father was sick, and she didn't quite know what was happening. But she could surely pick up on all the free-floating anxiety.

Mitchell saw his doctor the next morning. He was ordered to stay in bed, and again we felt that he would get more rest if we left. We had been tuned in to the weather reports which had been warning people to get on the road if they were heading east, because freezing rain was on its way. It was hard to leave Mitchell. I felt I could cook better chicken soup than he could, but I also knew he would be more comfortable and get more rest if we left. We had to leave soon if we were to avoid icy roads. We took Annie to her Mom's, grabbed several hot chocolate-chip cookies that Teddi had just taken out of the oven, hugged them Merry Christmas, and pulled out at 1:15 PM.

We stayed overnight in Mobile that night, as we were too exhausted to drive on to Tallahassee. Company was coming for dinner Christmas afternoon: Tom and Abby, Johnnye and Heinz, and their son Geoff with his two children, Emma and Jordan. Sue helped by bringing a couple of casseroles, and it all went smoothly.

Mitchell slowly regained his health and was able to stay free of serious bronchitis for a while. He and Teddi had become more congenial and had made the decision that he could have Annie during the summers, except for a couple of weeks. They agreed on how they would deal with Holidays and the other issues fell into line.

I wrote in my journal, "I am nearly seventy-four years old and life is good. I have learned a few things in the last few years, one of them being that crises come and crises go—one just has to hang on and get through them."

Trips to Monroe 1999

That spring Mitchell bought a three-bedroom house on a large lot at 3703 Westminster in Monroe. We went to visit and help him move in. I got the kitchen stuff put away, and John helped him move some of the furniture around and did odd jobs. Mitchell and I went shopping for some lamps and tables. It was wonderful to see him in a nice house that he chose and liked so much. We had Annie part of the time while we were there, which was great.

John and I celebrated our 22nd Anniversary in March, 1999,

marveling at the passing of time. We hoped we would have another twenty-two years.

John, Sue and I drove to Monroe a couple of months later. We had a flat tire on the eighty mile stretch between Jackson, Mississippi, and Monroe. It was about ninety-five degrees outside. There were no trees to give us shade. Suzanne had her cell phone with her and that saved the day. We phoned AAA, and a truck was dispatched to help us. When cell phones first came out, we thought they were just a fad, and we certainly didn't need one. We bought a cell phone soon after this incident.

Mitchell took us to see "Saving Private Ryan" which had recently been released. It was talked about as being one of the most realistic of all movies portraying D-Day. We agreed with the critics.

Teddi and Family Move to Valdosta 2000

Teddi found out that she got the position at Valdosta, Georgia, and Mitchell was in a panic. It was a big upheaval for him and for Teddi. She hated putting that distance (about six hundred miles) between Annie and her Dad, but she had to do what was best for her family in the long run.

Louisiana had a law that one parent could not take a child more than a hundred miles from the other parent permanently. But there was no way to enforce it, besides Mitchell knew Teddi needed to do what she was doing.

Teddi hadn't been notified that she got the job until the last minute. She had less than two weeks to move a houseful of furniture, get the boys registered for their school, get Annie settled in first grade and get oriented at the University. I was happy for her but sad for Mitchell and Annie who were going to suffer. Annie knew that when they moved to Valdosta her Dad was not going with them, and she would not get to see him as often.

Mitchell and Annie joined Suzanne, John and me for our week on St. George Island which coincided with the week Teddi moved to Valdosta. Annie knew when her Dad left that she was not going with him, and that John and I were going to take her to her new home in Valdosta.

She was subdued all day Friday. When Mitchell had to leave

Saturday morning, she clung to him, sobbing so that she could hardly talk. "Please don't go, Daddy. I don't want you to go. Please don't go."

We all went out to his car, hoping Annie would let go of him. But I finally had to pick her up and take her back upstairs where she continued crying for some time. There were no dry eyes—Suzanne, John and I were all crying as I was sure Mitchell was. He had given her a little toy, a Furbie—a silly little creature which talked. It was the current "must have" toy, and he gave it to her an hour before he left. She went back upstairs, got her blanket and her Furbie and lay down on the floor. She held onto Furbie as the involuntary sobbing slowly subsided. I felt so terribly sad knowing how she was hurting and how Mitchell must be sick at heart. He had done all he could and was powerless to comfort his little girl. That is one of the saddest of all my memories.

Later that night Annie woke me up. "I can't get a wink of sleep. Furbie won't stop talking, and I'm tired of it." We went to her room. I turned Furbie off and lay on Annie's bed with her. In just a few minutes, she was asleep.

The New Millennium

Life does go on. In September we picked Annie up and drove to Monroe. She and her Dad enjoyed the weekend; she didn't let him out of her sight. We went back in October taking Annie again. Mitchell had a party at his house for his graduate students and friends while we were there. Annie loved it. She so enjoyed helping to get ready; she pulled seventeen folding chairs from the patio and placed them in a circle around the chimenea which Mitchell had put out on the back lawn. She also helped put strings of lights over the bushes to make it look quite festive. As soon as the company gathered, Annie disappeared for a few minutes and returned with large mugs filled with water. She was quite the hostess. The weather was perfect, the moon was full; the party was a success.

Mitchell and Annie were slowly adjusting to life apart. They were with us Thanksgiving and were back with us for a week at Christmas. Annie got her Nintendo 64 and was so proud of it; she couldn't wait to show her friends.

Teddi, Philip, Michael and Annie came a few days later. We were always glad to be with them even if the time was short. We didn't see the boys much, so that day was special. Philip was seventeen; Michael, sixteen. They were both already close to six feet tall.

The week between Christmas and New Year's Day was full of speculation as to what was going to happen when the Twentieth Century came to an end. Much had been said and written about doomsday when all computers were going to crash at the stroke of midnight, ushering in the new millennium. Nothing like that happened, of course; the world continued to spin on its axis on January 1, 2000.

The Murrays, (Juanita & Haydn) and the Omansons (Glenna & Phil) were with us for New Year's Eve and New Year's Day. On New Year's Day, when we all gathered in the library to watch football games, Annie was out in the kitchen making noises that told me she was being the hostess again. Soon she came in with a tray loaded with anything she could find that looked to her like a treat. She served peanuts in the shell, raisons, pretzels, cookies and some crackers. She went from person to person offering her goodies. She set that tray on the coffee table and went back to the kitchen where we heard similar noises again. This time she brought in small cups filled with water. She'd celebrated her sixth birthday in November.

My Office in Our Home 2000

In the spring we decided to close in our porch and convert it to an office for me. I was paying four hundred dollars a month rent, since I had sold the office building. With my practice slowing down, we figured it would work out to see the clients at the house. Our builder gave us an estimate of $30,000. It would add more than that to the value of our house.

I moved my practice out of the office at 2014 Delta Boulevard and into that lovely space in our home at 2511 Chamberlin Drive on June 26, 2000. Two sides of the room were floor to ceiling windows with a view of the back yard. The shrubs and trees accented by the deck and pool provided a tranquil setting. It was a lovely room in which to work, and a relaxing space for the clients, as well as completely private. As a bonus, John and I had another sitting area for our house.

We had our annual physicals that spring, and both received our expected glowing reports. We again prided ourselves on our good health. We knew part of it was genes and part was luck, but we also knew that our lifestyle helped. We continued exercising and watching what we put into our bodies. John often said, "I'm glad we exercise, glad we just do it and never have to decide if we are going to or not." We still walked every morning together, and I went to the gym three days a week. He played even more golf since he was retired.

We Meet Madeleine 2000

We all enjoyed our annual week at St. George. On our second day, Mitchell told us that a woman he had recently begun to date might come by for an afternoon. She lived in Monroe but was attending a meeting in Panama City and would be relatively close by. That is how we met Madeleine Robichaux. She stopped by for a visit while we were on the beach. She and Mitchell had met when he was being interviewed as a prospective counselor for the court system to work with DUI drivers. Madeleine was an Assistant District Attorney and had been one of the interviewers.

Sue, John and I drove to Monroe for Thanksgiving. Annie was already in Monroe having ridden over with Teddi and the boys, who were spending the holiday with friends. Madeleine spent most of the weekend with us. Thanksgiving Day she came in carrying three different kinds of pies she had made that morning. She was raised in New Orleans with five siblings, so she knew what it was like to be part of a big family.

Mitchell had bought a Harley Davidson motorcycle that fall and couldn't wait to take all of us on a ride. On Saturday we took part in a caravan of Harleys riding into southern Arkansas. Sue rode on the Harley with Mitchell. John, Annie and I rode with Madeleine in her van. It was fun to meet some of the other bikers and get a better understanding of the social aspects of owning a Harley Davidson. We had a great holiday and after we returned home, John and I conjectured about the relationship between Mitchell and Madeleine; it was apparent there was good chemistry between them.

We had our usual Christmas gathering—Mitchell and Annie were with us for a week; Sue spent much of her time at the house also. We enjoyed all the extra food that is part of the Christmas season. We especially enjoyed the traditional Fannie Mae chocolates that we opened on Christmas Eve. Most of us liked Kate's fruit cake, too. The hours were filled with games, cards, movies, eating and visiting. Mitchell talked with Madeleine every day; she told him he couldn't go for a week again without her. It sounded pretty serious to John and me.

Vonnie, My Sister, Dies

Earlier in the year, we had learned that Vonnie (my youngest sister, married to Clark and living in Phoenix) had lung cancer. The cancer was inoperable when it was discovered. She went through a series of chemotherapy and radiation treatments in late summer and early fall. She was not able to tolerate further treatment and was under Hospice care before the holidays.

She managed to get her Christmas shopping done and to adorn her home with her wonderfully creative decorations, before her body would not let her continue. Vonnie died at 2:00 AM, December 27th, 2000.

The service was comforting. Her house was full of cute things she had made; she took after our Mother in her creativity. She was only sixty-nine but had smoked until just a couple of years before she became ill. It was especially sad for all of us that she had died so young and, obviously, from not being able to give up the habit of smoking.

Wedding Bells for Mitchell and Madeleine 2001

In February Mitchell and Madeleine rode the Harley to visit us— five hundred and fifty miles in one day. I had picked Ansley up that morning. We celebrated Mitchell's fifty-fifth birthday while they were with us. We got to know Madeleine a bit more. She had two children— Zach, who was eighteen and heading for LSU in the fall, and Wren, fifteen, who was to be a freshman in high school. Madeleine had an outgoing personality and was openly affectionate with Mitchell.

One month later, they called to tell us they were going to get married. John and I thought Mitchell had found a match—it seemed to us that they were good for each other. They certainly had a lot of the same interests, and their work meshed so well. There was no doubt as to the chemistry.

The wedding was on May 5th, Cinco de Mayo, 2001. It was held in Mitchell's spacious back yard which was decorated for the occasion. It started off to be just the immediate family, and, as so often happens, the guest list grew to include some of Mitchell's fellow professors, some of his students, his Viet Nam Vets and their wives, Madeleine's attorney friends, and a couple of judges from the court system. It was a diverse group, all of whom had a good time.

It sprinkled rain that morning which created great anxiety for a while. Before the wedding, the sky cleared, and the weather was beautiful. The cake, baked by one of the vet's wife, was delivered mid-afternoon. When I heard that a non-professional was baking the cake, I was skeptical. But, it was one of the prettiest cakes that I've ever seen, as was the groom's cake—a delicious chocolate cake in the shape of a motorcycle. As the cake was being arranged, cases of soft drinks, beer, wine, champagne and bags of ice were being delivered and put into the numerous large ice chests. Several large folding tables were delivered and set with white tablecloths. Citronella burners were positioned around the yard in strategic locations. John loaded the ice and drinks in the coolers; Suzanne and I made signs for parking and put them in place. Annie helped 'Poppy' ice down the drinks. Madeleine was racing back-and-forth from her house to "their" house, welcoming her family members as they began to arrive—taking care of the last minute details.

By 4:00 PM all was miraculously ready for the ceremony. I helped Annie get dressed. She had a gorgeous pale blue bouffant dress with satin ribbons. She said the dress made her feel like a princess. I had shopped with her for her dress. We found one that she liked and was appropriate, but was more expensive than I had anticipated. She liked it so much, and I said, "Okay, Annie, if you like it that much we'll get it."

As she took the dress off, she said, "My Dad would give me everything he has if I needed it. And so would you, Mimi. And so would Mama." I thought that was a child's way of saying, "I have three people who love me unconditionally."

By the time I got dressed, Madeleine's family had arrived and the party had begun. The combo, setup by the tables, was playing love songs; the guests were enjoying themselves. Madeleine's family members were introducing themselves to the diverse guests. We happily met most of Madeleine's family that day.

Madeleine's sister-in-law, Sheila, and Suzanne stood up with Madeleine; John and a good friend of Mitchell's, Jonathon, stood up with Mitchell. Annie and Wren were the ring bearers. Annie stood beside her dad; she was a very somber seven-year-old. The combo stopped playing when it was time for the service. The guests gathered around. Vows were exchanged and the groom kissed the bride. That was the signal for one of Mitchell's Indian friends, Gary, to play a prayer-song on his homemade flute. His music added that final touch to a beautiful and moving wedding.

Now it was time for feasting, drinking, toasting, and partying. There was abundance of food—broiled shrimp with Cajun sauce, crab salad, pates, and other delicacies. After many of the guests had left, about fifteen close friends and family members sat around a fire pit. One of Madeleine's relatives played the guitar, we sang and laughed and wished upon a star. Ansley was enjoying the party, but finally grew tired; she climbed onto her daddy's lap and, uncharacteristically, said she was ready to go to bed. The singing and storytelling went on for some time. What an unusual, casual, fun, wonderful outdoor wedding. We were happy to have Madeleine as part of our family.

Later that summer Mitchell and Madeleine rode their motorcycle to Sturges, South Dakota. Then they headed east to Illinois and met John and me in Toulon, where Madeleine was able to meet some of Mitchell's extended family. They stayed overnight with Don and Bonnie (Dorothy's younger son and his wife), who graciously entertained all of us for dinner that evening.

Tragedy Strikes the USA

On September 11, 2001, the world was stunned when terrorists flew two large jets full of passengers into the Twin Towers in New York City, and the third one into the Pentagon. The fourth hijacked jet, headed for the White House or the Capitol, crashed in an open field in Pennsylvania after the courageous passengers rushed the terrorists, causing them to lose control of the plane. This was another "day that will live in infamy" for our country. Over three thousand people were killed. President George W. Bush was in Florida at the time, and was not allowed to return immediately to Washington, D.C. because of the situation. All planes (except the military) were grounded for two days. No football games were played the next Saturday. The country and the world were mourning. No one could predict what the repercussions might be.

But we knew that our lives were changed forever. The Homeland Security Department was created; airlines were required to scan passengers' belongings, including their shoes. Airline passengers could carry only a few ounces of any liquid, flying became a hassle. More stringent rules regarding who could enter the White House were enforced; our society had become less open overnight. Fear was much more likely to thrust itself into innocent people's lives.

Our Lives Rush Innocently Into 2002

John and I were plotting a trip to Machu Picchu and the Galapagos Islands in the spring. I had wanted to see Machu Picchu for years. Reading about both destinations and planning for the trip were exciting.

Alex was accepted into Officer's Candidate School with the National Guard. It meant he would have to be gone for three months in the spring, but would be worth it in the long run.

We still managed to have Annie visit once a month. We loved having her, and she still liked to come. She especially liked going to Winthrop Park which was close to us, and she loved our pool. Sometimes she would hop into the pool within minutes of arriving. She never tired of playing cards. If it wasn't warm enough to swim she would ask, "Anyone want to play cards?" Sometimes I couldn't play when she asked, but John always said, "I'll play with you." He never gave up his competitiveness, even with an eight-year-old. If Annie won, we knew it wasn't because he let her. I guess that was good for her, as she had to learn to lose as well as to win. Her Poppy treated her in his own special way—stricter than I, but lovingly, and they got along very well.

We took Annie to Monroe as often as we could; we enjoyed the drive, and it was easier for us to drive there than for Mitchell to come to Tallahassee. When we visited that spring, we went to see the movie, "We Were Soldiers," a film about Viet Nam. I had to sit quietly a few minutes after the movie ended to get control of my emotions. Mitchell had seen it before and told us that it was the most realistic film about Viet Nam that he had seen, and that it depicted a battle very much like the big ones he was in. It was a powerful movie. I wonder what he felt when he saw it.

John and I celebrated our twenty-fifth anniversary on March 18, 2002. Suzanne had written to forty people, and surprised us with a card shower. We received thirty-five cards. That made the day special. Eight of us went to Anthony's Italian Restaurant for a celebration dinner that evening. We marveled at those years having gone by so fast and ordered time to slow down.

Our Innocence Stolen

In the late May, 2002 we had our annual physicals as usual. My results came back a few days before John's, and I had temporary bragging rights. When his results came we both eagerly opened it to see if his were as good as in the past. All was good except a notice that there were "microscopic signs" of blood in his stool. He was advised to get a colonoscopy, which he scheduled for July. Sue, John and I went to Valdosta to watch Annie play softball that Saturday.

The weekend of June eighth and ninth, John felt very lethargic and spent most of the week-end on the couch. He usually played eighteen holes of golf, walking and carrying his clubs, but on Monday he came home after only nine holes; he didn't have the energy to play the second nine. When this was repeated a day or two later, he called Dr. Judelle, who told him to come in the next day for a blood test. Two days later, Dr. Judelle called John and told him his blood count was very low. H put him in the hospital and ordered a colonoscopy as soon as it could be arranged. It was done a couple of days later at 9:30 PM by Dr. Reisman.

I was with John in the recovery room when the doctor came in. He stood silently beside the bed for a moment. John, showing his everlasting positive attitude, lightheartedly asked, "Did you find any polyps?"

Dr. Reisman said, "Yes, but that's not the problem. We found a tumor toward the end of the colon."

My heart began racing even more than it already was. I thought to myself, *they won't be able to tell us for a few days if it is malignant or not.*

John started to speak, "Is it…?"

The doctor interrupted, "Yes, it is malignant."

Silence. John and I looked at each other. *Maybe it's tiny,* I thought.

Dr. Reisman continued, "It's a large tumor." *Maybe it can just be cut out and that will be that.*

Finally, I was able to ask, "How long do you think it has been there?"

"It has been there a long time, maybe as long as five years." When neither of us said anything, he continued. "It is a stage four cancer. It has gone into the outer layer of the intestinal wall. We took out twenty lymph nodes; cancer was present in only one. There is a fifty-fifty chance that we got it all. Chemo will raise those odds to sixty-forty. We'll know more when the lab work comes back in about five days."

A few days later, Dr. Crooms did the surgery and removed the tumor and several inches of John's colon. His recovery was slowed somewhat by the fact that his blood count was so low. He received three units of blood which helped. The surgery was done about 8:00 in the evening, and by the time we got back to John's room, it was nearly midnight. John slept off the anesthetic the rest of the night, while I stayed by his bed in case he awakened. My mind would not stop racing. *What does this mean? If stage four cancer is the worst? Five years? In one lymph node? Fifty-fifty chance? Of course, John is real healthy, that should help.*

When John awoke, we talked for a few minutes, but he kept dozing. I knew I needed to get some rest so took Teddi up on her offer to come down and sit with John for a few hours while I went home to take a nap. Fear had gripped me and wouldn't let go, but I did get a couple hours of sleep.

The surgery had been on a Tuesday and the following Monday an oncologist, Dr. Soy, came in while I was out of the room. He explained to John what the treatment approach would entail. John took notes and told me everything the doctor said. I knew of several oncologists in town but had never heard of Soy. I was upset that we had not been consulted as to whom we wanted. But I didn't want John to know how upset I was. Trying to act casual, I made some excuse and went out in the hall. I headed for the nurses' station but broke into tears before I reached it. I knew I was crying for more than what John just told me.

The head nurse took me into her office, and within minutes Dr. Judelle came in; he must have been on the floor. I was so glad to see him and was soon able to stop my sobbing. I said, "I'm so worried—it doesn't sound good, and I just don't know what I'd do if he died."

He said, "He's not going to die this year—or next."

Yeah, but what about the next, I asked silently.

I met Dr. Soy Tuesday, one week after the surgery. He took time to explain the treatment regime he proposed. He was friendly enough and answered all of our questions, even if we didn't like what he told us.

John came home the next day. He was not on a restricted diet and had a bowl of his favorite banana-nut cereal. He ate and slept a lot for a few days and was soon pretty much back to normal.

His illness stunned me; I thought he would be healthy for years to come. Dr. Judelle told me he would never be cured, just in remission. We would always have to be wary. It had changed the way I thought about our future. But John was so optimistic, and I was working on it.

The next six months revolved around his treatment and how he felt. He tolerated the infusions well at the beginning, which made us hopeful that he would be able to complete the regime as laid out by Dr. Soy. It would mean he would not finish the treatments until after the first of the year.

Mitchell, Madeleine, and Annie came to see John. One of Madeleine's brothers had died of colon cancer in his early fifties, so I knew she could empathize with us. Suzanne spent most of the week-end with us also—having everyone with us that weekend helped, and I was able to throw off much of the paralyzing fear which had been with me since the day of John's colonoscopy.

Chemo 2002

John had his first chemo treatment in mid-July. He tolerated them very well and continued to feel positive about it. I, also, began to feel he would be okay again, even if not rid of the cancer; I thought we could at least keep it in remission. They placed a medication port under the skin on his chest—no more prodding around searching for a vein.

We cancelled our plans to attend the annual family reunion, a planned trip to Pennsylvania to visit the Potters, and our much-anticipated trip to Machu Picchu in October. We knew we would not be going on those trips regardless of how well John did with the chemo treatments.

Toward the end of July, I wrote in my journal, "The days go by. I am so aware of how much John means to me. It is hard to express in words how much love passes between us." Serious illness does bring our immortality to the fore.

Ian Paul Cassidy Arrives

Ian Paul Cassidy was born August 3, 2002. They had to do a caesarean because of Schelley's high blood pressure. Ian was in ICU for a little more than a day for observation, but he was fine and healthy. Schelley did well, considering she'd had a C-section. John now had a granddaughter and a grandson, and Alex and Rae's second child was due in February.

John Does Well

John did better than expected tolerating his chemo. We were able to keep up our normal social life—football games, Economic Club, Tiger Bay Club, Town Club dances, plays at Little Theatre, movies, and going to dinner with friends. We believed he was going to be all right. The holidays came swooshing through like a tornado. We enjoyed the usual gatherings and were able forget about John's illness for a while.

He played golf twice a week during the month of December— walked and carried his clubs. Of course, that was his only activity for the day, but that much was a lot. He took his last treatment in early January 2003. In my journal I wrote, "We are so glad to have it behind us. We feel very optimistic that he is okay, and we'll live accordingly. We have learned a lot from the whole experience. I am even more grateful for our time together and realize how lost I would feel if he was gone." The New Year promised to be a good one.

Tom Potter

Early on the 2003 calendar was the Potter's big celebration on January 18th for Tom's eighty-fifth birthday. That evening, Tom did not look well; he didn't talk much, nor did he get out of his big chair except to give a short speech which his family had asked him to do. He had had pneumonia a couple of weeks prior to the event and had not fully recovered. He stayed in bed all day the next day—a Sunday. Early Monday morning, his family took him to the hospital where he died at 8:30 PM.

John and I went to the hospital about 4:00 PM and were with the family when Tom died very peacefully and painlessly. He was one of the kindest, most loving and honorable men I ever met. John felt the same way. We knew Abby would be lost without him. They were married over sixty years.

Sarah Elizabeth Kerr 2003

As so often happens, a sad farewell is followed by a new arrival. Sarah Elizabeth Kerr was born on February 21, 2003. When John and I walked into the hospital room, in the maternity ward, Rae was in the bed, and Alex was sitting by her with Sarah on his lap. She was a cutie—lighter hair than Emma had when she was born and real fat little cheeks, another healthy baby in our family.

Life is Normal Again

We began planning a trip to Alaska for August, counting on John being okay. We thought Alaska would be a lot easier than a car trip. In my journal I wrote, "Will be a very nice trip. Life is good, difficult but good." I also wrote, "Annie is here this weekend. She is growing up; wears seven and a half medium shoe at age nine. She is playing softball again this summer, also takes gymnastics. Still likes to go to Winthrop Park to play and usually makes friends with someone. Today she didn't hesitant to ask a group of kids if she could play with them. She loves to go to Sunday school. I love to take her."

John and I met Roger (his brother) and Joellen in Charlotte for a couple of days of golf for the men and shopping for Jo and me. We stopped for the night with Mike and Janet in Atlanta on our way home. We had a great time with both couples.

Back To Chemo 2003

We'd been anticipating John's appointment with Dr. Soy on March 3rd when he would tell us what the CT scan indicated—how the cancer had responded to the earlier chemo treatments. We were full of hope. However, the report was not good. Dr. Soy said, "There is something irregular going on regarding the liver." He scheduled a PET scan. John was having some pain in his lower back, so we were legitimately worried. We had to wait again for the results.

Two weeks later, Dr. Soy told us, "Doesn't look good—a relapse of the disease. It is in the tissue up and down your back and throughout your abdomen." John looked at me with fear claiming his face, his eyes clouded with apprehension. I felt my body wilt. I took a deep breath trying not to look as scared as I felt.

"What do we do now?" John asked.

"We'll start another round of chemo using a different drug this time."

"How long will I have to stay on it this time?"

"You will have chemo off and on for the rest of your life. It may be all the time, but if you do really well, you'll be able to take a break from time to time. You have multiple tumors. Chemo will be an attempt to control the cancer, but we can't make it go away." He went on, "Chemo works fifty percent of the time in cases like yours." Dr. Soy spoke these devastating words as if he was telling us about a picnic he had attended.

We had begun to dislike him. His unnecessary bluntness at that time made us angry. The news was bad, but he could have given it to us in a kinder manner—at least pretended he was sympathetic. I'm sure much of our anger was at the situation, and we directed it toward the doctor.

John asked, "What is my life expectancy if I don't have more chemo?"

"Life expectancy without chemo is about two years."

I thought, *"He's not telling us the truth about that. John can't possibly live two years without treatment when cancer is already running rampant throughout his body.* Maybe that was the only way he knew how to try to be kind to us.

John had begun having dull pain in his abdomen two or three weeks earlier. I wrote, "I am so worried about John, my mind runs wild, what if, what if. The doctor's report is very threatening and we're scared."

Earlier, in his optimism, John had had the port removed; now he had to have it put back in. The chemo began a couple of days later on May 1st.

Mitchell, Madeleine, Annie and Sue came, all quite undone about the result of the CT scan. Mitchell and Madeleine brought their fifth-wheel camper, and we all spent the weekend at Torryea State Park, about ninety miles west of Tallahassee. On Saturday we went to see the Florida Caverns. Sunday, Madeleine hid Easter candy around our area of the campground. Annie and her friends (kids she had made friends with the day before) had great fun scampering around shrieking and laughing. It was a memorable weekend; John's illness was very much with us, but we were able to enjoy being together. Everyone put up a good façade.

The next week John became quite despondent. He said, "It seems that a lot of bad is happening, and the good is being withdrawn; we're going to miss so many things that we enjoy. And I don't feel really good anymore." I listened to him and agreed. I couldn't respond with anything cheerful, so I said nothing.

The next day he continued sharing his thoughts, "We have to face it, Kate. If I can't tolerate this chemo, that's it." I wanted him to tell me his fears but found it most difficult to talk about mine. Also, I didn't want to burden him with more than he was already experiencing. I lay awake the next morning trying to imagine living without him; it was like having a nightmare. Early mornings, when I awakened and couldn't get back to sleep, were the worst. Later, I wondered if it would have been better to express my fears to him more than I did. But, I did what I thought best at the time.

I would snuggle close to him and put my arms around him, knowing how much I would miss being in bed with him. We often said when we were lying close in bed, with sleep slowly approaching, that it was the best part of the day. It made my world safer—secure. Together we would always be okay. I could not believe this was happening to my sweetheart, yet I could not stop thinking about it. Sometimes I felt angry. *Why John, who was so happy in his life, who was loved by so many, still relatively young (seventy-one), and so healthy prior to this nasty cancer?*

We got an appointment at the Moffitt Cancer Center in Tampa for the end of May to see if they would suggest any different treatment. We were having a hard time accepting the finality of the report Dr. Soy had given us so dispassionately.

John lost interest in most world events. He didn't care to listen to the recent news of our invasion of Iraq which had taken place on April 19th. Within weeks our troops were in Baghdad. Most Americans did not believe we should invade, but Bush seemed hell-bent on the invasion. John's disinterest was a drastic change.

We picked Annie Kate up on Saturday and took her to the Springtime Tallahassee Parade. It is a big event in Tallahassee with large crowds gathered for the parade and for the events held in the downtown parks. She got right out in front of the crowd at the parade and grabbed all the beads and candy she could. I always liked parades, so I had a double feature—watching the parade and watching Annie's antics.

The sky had grown very dark in the northeast, and we wanted to run to the car as soon as the parade was over. But Annie wanted something to eat from the many vendors on the grounds, and I had promised her something before we headed home. John went on to the car, and by the time Annie got her hot dog, it had begun sprinkling rain. The car was about a block away, and the rain didn't wait for us. That cloud opened up, and we got a good soaking.

We had agreed to usher and serve communion the next day. John thought he would be able to handle it, but as soon as we entered the narthex, he turned to me and said, "Kate, I'm not going to be able to do this. Suzanne can bring you home, and I'll see you back at the house."

I watched him as he went down the steps and headed slowly for the car. His walk told me more than his words how dejected he was feeling. Annie was happy to take his place as an usher and I easily got someone else to serve communion. John enjoyed serving communion; how sad he must be feeling to have to give up this sacred ritual. Sue dropped us off, and Annie and I left to meet Teddi at our usual mid-way place after checking on John.

Dr. Judelle

The next day, John took the pain medication, which had been prescribed earlier, for the first time. He was losing strength rapidly and was not eating well. I was feeling so emotionally wrung out that I went to see Dr. Judelle. When I told him that I didn't know what I'd do without John, he said, "Your job now is to take care of John. That will be your focus. Later you can decide what you are going to do. Right now and for the next year or so, you will be busy taking care of John."

I was able to talk to him about some of what I was feeling. "John is my life. My life began when I met him. My life has changed so much since I've known him. I don't know how I will live without him. I love him so much…"After a short pause, I added, "An example of how my life is changing is the fact that I won't be able to tell him about this conversation. I don't want him to know how much I'm hurting. I want to minimize my pain when I'm with him; he has enough of his own."

Dr. Judelle repeated, "You will be focused on taking care of him now. Later things will come together, and you will find your way, or it will find you. You are intelligent, educated and attractive; things will open up for you." Somehow, I felt better; just talking about it helped.

John had reacted so adversely to the last treatment that Dr. Soy had decided to try a different drug. He told John that the pain he was suffering was from the cancer, not the drug.

Brant Copeland

Again the deep sadness I felt sought to consume me, and I went to see Brant Copeland, my pastor. I was able to cry and talk with him in a way I had not been able to before. He was a compassionate listener, and I was such an emotional mess that I couldn't remember much of what was said. It was comforting, just knowing he cared and was going to help me get through this.

Cancer Attacks Other Family Members

To make matters even worse, we found out our nephew, Dana Stonesifer, Clay and Rose's son-in-law, was in the hospital. He had awakened in the night with pain, which he thought might be a heart attack. They went to the emergency room where tests showed it was not his heart, but unsuspected cancer on his kidney and lungs. He went immediately to Iowa City where he was to have surgery to remove the kidney. He was a dentist who had experienced no symptoms until that night when he was awakened with pain.

Also, Betty's husband, Harold, had recently been diagnosed with aggressive lymphoma. The prognosis was not good for either of them. Harold was in his eighties, but Dana was in his early fifties. It was shocking news. Our family was hurting.

The Moffitt Clinic 2003

The closest cancer clinic for us was the Moffitt Clinic in Tampa, and we decided to go for a second opinion on John's treatment and prognosis. We saw Dr. Balducci, a very warm, caring older man. He said, "Go ahead with the treatment Dr. Soy has laid out, and have a CT scan when the three cycles are complete. If the tumors are shrinking, repeat the cycle until the tumors remain the same size. If they begin growing again, try another treatment." He agreed with Dr. Soy's prognosis, but he affirmed it in such a way that, somehow, it was more palatable. He gave us his cell phone number and said we could call him at any time if we had questions.

What a good feeling we had when we left Moffitt. It wasn't that he'd given us any more hope; it was his warm manner that was so different from Dr. Soy's. Oncologists should be required to learn how to talk with their patients with empathy and concern. Dying patients should not be treated as if they have already lost their ability to feel.

John couldn't take the new drug and was switched to a different one. As we sat in the study one evening, he said, "I know I may never feel good again. I am angrier than I was at first. I am angry, frustrated and depressed. I know I am dying." After a moment he added, "I try to put it aside. I want us to enjoy the time we have left as much as we can." I was glad he was expressing these feelings to me, but there wasn't much for me to say except that I understood. It is often better to say nothing than to try to minimize or soften such feelings. I couldn't imagine how he must feel; I couldn't even describe how I was feeling. I just knew I was becoming numb to some of my emotions, lest they overwhelm me.

A Big Decision

The day after his next treatment we headed for St. George for our week with family. John didn't feel well for the first three days and not much better the rest of the week. His head would not stop aching. We took walks along the beach and talked about whether or not to continue fighting the cancer. The doctor told us there was only a thirty to fifty percent chance that the treatments would help, and if they did, it would add only three to five months to his life. If he stopped the treatment John could expect to live up to six months, a more realistic estimate than the two years previously quoted to us. If he stopped all treatment, he might have a few months of feeling relatively well.

So we talked of stopping the treatments and having some good weeks versus continuing treatments, and living a few months longer, but not feeling well. When put that way, it wasn't hard to make the decision to stop treatment. John said he just couldn't make himself go through another one. We told the kids, all of whom agreed it was the best thing to do.

John and I talked a lot about our relationship. It was impossible for me to imagine life without him. He knew me and my kids as no one else did. We totally accepted each other with our warts and all. We had often said, "As long as we have each other…" But that was not going to be.

John began feeling better the further he got from June 12th, the date of his last treatment. He was able to play eighteen holes of golf riding in a cart, and we began eating out again which was something we had missed.

We Visit Family 2003

In April, when we found out the cancer had spread, we had cancelled our trip to Alaska. We decided to spend what time he had left visiting with family.

Before we headed north, we drove to Jacksonville to be at Alex's graduation from Officer's Training with the National Guard. John got to pin Alex's bars on, which meant a lot to both of them. We were proud of Alex and happy that John got to be there.

The next day we drove to Atlanta where we attended Patrick Strubbe's wedding to Erica. (Patrick was Tom's son, Maverne's grandson.) All the Strubbe and Kerr families were there, so it also functioned as a family reunion. It was a lovely wedding.

John and I danced for the last time that night. It was something I will never forget, because I knew we were likely not to dance again. I wanted to freeze the moment, stop the clock. I formed the silent message to myself: *don't let me forget how it is to have our arms around each other and moving slowly to the music. Let me remember how John smells, how it is to have my face next to his, and how it is to have his hand holding mine.*

One dance was it for John, but we had that one.

We drove from Atlanta to Lake Barkley, one of Kentucky's State Parks. We had stayed there one year for my family reunion. We had another long intimate talk as we sipped our wine before going to dinner. We had always loved being alone together on trips, always felt so close. He talked to me in terms of hanging onto my confidence when he was gone. He said, "We are so spiritually related that we will communicate with each other. I will always be beside you in spirit, I really believe that." We took a second glass of wine and went for a walk, holding hands as we usually did, sharing memories of past trips. We even had dessert after dinner—warm blackberry cobbler with ice cream, my favorite.

Our next visit was with John's Aunt Margaret and all of John's cousins and their families in Southern Illinois. They had a family get-together at Marietta and Maurice's as they always had when we visited. There was an abundance of good food, and Maurice froze the ice cream which Marietta had made. We always spent one night with them and one with Mary and Larry McClay on their dairy farm. (Maurice and Mary were John's first cousins.) Mary had made blackberry cobbler and had ice cream to put on it. We were living high on the hog for sure—blackberry cobbler twice within a week! Couldn't do better than that. When we left his family, we drove to Rockford, Illinois for the Appenheimer reunion.

The day after we arrived in Rockford, Betty called to tell us Harold had died. We knew it was imminent, so were not surprised. We were able to cancel the hotel reservations for the next two nights, and all of us drove south to Anawan, a small town near where Betty and Harold lived. It was not easy for John or me to sit through that funeral service. John had a hard time controlling his emotions which was quite understandable.

We left the church after the service and drove tandem with Juanita and Haydn to Bloomington, Indiana, where we spent a pleasant twenty-four hours. They had a beautiful home which echoed Juanita's personality.

John's Three Grandchildren

The next day we drove home; John was tired but played nine holes of golf the next day. He was taking three aspirin a day for abdominal pain, and he tired easily, but stayed upbeat most of the time. It was hard to believe he was terminally ill.

Schelley and Paul's little boy, Ian, had his first birthday August 3rd. Shelley and Paul had a birthday party which John was able to attend and enjoy. Shelley had arranged to have a photographer come to take family pictures. Ian will have those photos, so he will know what Poppy looked like.

Ian was fascinated with telephones; he and John had many conversations when Ian would pick up the receiver and start to jabber. John was undergoing his first rounds of chemo when Ian was born, so he never really felt up to par during Ian's lifetime, except for the few months that summer. John adored all three of his grandchildren, Emma, Sarah and Ian; he was saddened that he would not see them grow up.

Emma would be the only one of the three who would remember Poppy. John always carried her down the hallway where we had family pictures hung. He would point to each one and have her tell him who it was. She was only three but could name many of them.

When John became bed-ridden, Sarah was nine months old; she was the only one allowed on his bed, so he could smell her baby smell, touch her, and admire her fat little cheeks.

We Drive to Woodburn

John wanted to go to Pennsylvania to visit Abby Potter and Abby & Jim Werlock. He wanted to sleep at Woodburn one more time, so we drove up mid-August. We loved the drive; it was relaxing. Abby and Jim are good hosts, and made us feel so welcome. We went for a walk to look at their property which includes a waterfall and pond. We visited Tom's grave between Woodburn and the little country church. Abby Potter was much improved from when she left Tallahassee in May. She had gained a little weight and seemed stronger.

Taking Care of My Love 2003

John enjoyed our time there, but on the first day driving home, he had to stop and let me drive. He had diarrhea and severe cramping, so we stopped about 3:00 in the afternoon. He went right to bed and stayed until the next morning, except for a couple of trips to the bathroom. We got home at noon the next day. He had two more attacks that afternoon and had no energy after those episodes.

We celebrated John's seventy-first birthday in August. His kids and their spouses, Suzanne, Teddi, Annie, Emma, Ian, and Sarah all came to be with him. He enjoyed everyone being there, but was exhausted. He lay on the couch in the library most of the next week, watching some TV and enjoying the friends who visited him.

John hadn't been able to go back to church since the day he had tried to and had to return home. He missed it a lot. Bruce Chapman, the minister at the Presbyterian Center on the FSU campus, accompanied Brant in early September and served communion to John, which he especially appreciated. I stopped going to church, because I could not control my emotions when there, and I didn't want to leave John alone.

John's health declined steadily during the last three weeks of September. He lay curled up on the couch much of the time—curled up and covered up. He needed more pain medicine each week and had started using patches (which dispensed the medication over a seventy two our period) on his skin. He had gone from a fifty milligram morphine patch to two hundred milligram patches, plus four oxycodone tablets and fifty milligrams of an antidepressant. He ate less and less. By the end of the month, I was feeding him what little he ate; a typical day would be half a poached egg and a couple bites of toast.

John's brother, sister-in law, step-siblings and spouses—Roger, Joellen, Tom Strubbe, and Barbara and Wilbur Hunley—visited that month. John loved them but just wasn't up to visiting much. He lay on the couch and listened, dozing off and on.

During one of Brant's frequent visits, John talked to him about his daughter, Jennifer, from whom he was estranged. He had pretty much made his peace with it, but talking with Brant helped give him peace. She had caused him so much pain in the past that he had said he didn't want to talk with her again. I agreed—it wouldn't have done any good and would have been an emotional upheaval that he didn't need.

We requested Hospice services during the last week of September. The next day the nurse brought him three prescriptions and started him on liquid morphine. She put patches behind his ears for the nausea he had been experiencing. In the next day or so, John began hallucinating and thrashing about with his arms, pointing and looking about fearfully. He didn't sleep at all for more than twenty-four hours. He saw Indians out in the yard and men entering his room. He was very scared.

We knew one of the Hospice nurses, Martha Paradeise. She agreed that she would be the nurse who would respond when we called. She was so good with John, and he was always glad to see her. I let her know about his psychotic behavior. She came and sat by him trying to determine what was causing the hallucinations. She thought it might be the patches recently placed behind his ears for nausea. If we removed them, the terrible vomiting would return which might be even worse. Added to the difficulty of getting the right medication to help, he was no longer able to swallow a pill, and the tumor on his rectum disallowed a suppository being inserted.

Martha called a compounding pharmacist and described what she needed. He produced an ointment to be applied to John's skin. Thank goodness, it worked. No more psychosis and no more vomiting. The pharmacist had added Haldol, an anti-psychotic drug to the ointment.

October arrived with its gorgeous autumn coolness, always so welcome in Tallahassee. I didn't realize it was so nice outside until mid-month, when I got someone to sit with John while I kept a doctor's appointment. I found it surprising that it was October; it made me realize how totally my life had become confined to the house and taking care of John. It was not something that I found hard to do; it was where I wanted to be.

People would say, "It must be so hard for you and so tiring."

"It isn't, really. It's just what I do. It isn't hard."

I had become an automaton; my feelings were crammed way back some place, although I didn't realize it until later. I cried only a couple of times when the dams couldn't hold the pressure any longer, then tears would burst forth in sobs which got me through until the next time.

Janet drove down from Atlanta to spend a couple of days with John. She brought two large pork loins, stuffed and ready to cook. She also brought some soup and other things. She came down again about a month later, bringing food again. That was such a welcome break for me and pleased John. He and Janet had some good talks; they had always enjoyed each other's company. The food came in handy when my kids visited.

We had a desk and a work area in our bedroom, so I could do bookwork when John was sleeping. Once he was bedridden, I had begun to go through all of our records, all of the folders of papers such as insurance, retirement information, and financial records. I wanted to do that while he was able to help me in case I had questions. I had several candles burning much of the time which helped keep the odor of illness from taking over our home and they provided a soft light, even though John insisted that the overhead light stay on day and night.

Giving John his multiple medications, answering the phone, greeting people at the door, and seeing them out, bringing him the urinal, dripping water from a straw into his mouth about every ten minutes, and just spending time with him kept me busy. The days went by with little thought on my part about the passage of time. My body and mind were occupied with what was happening in that bedroom. I would have to reckon later with what was happening within my soul.

The first of October I had hired a sitter from a place Martha recommended, Home Instead, to sit with John from 9:00 PM until 6:00 AM. That gave me an hour to have a glass of wine and try to relax before going to bed at 10:00 PM. I had stopped sleeping in the same bed as John—he was awake half the night and wanted the light left on. I knew I needed to get my rest, so I would be able to care for him. I began sleeping in the nearby guest room which wasn't an easy transition for me—giving up sleeping beside my love.

The first sitter was a lethargic woman who sat down in the chair near the bed and went to sleep. I checked a couple of times and both times she was asleep, and John was awake. I called the next day and requested a different person. That evening a tall young African American man greeted me pleasantly when I answered the doorbell. Colon was a former football player. He stepped inside and removed his sandals before going further. In the mornings when he left in the darkness before dawn, he wanted all of the outdoor lights on and would check out the area before dashing for his car. He told me that he was "afraid of the wild critters."

John and Colon bonded the first night that he sat. I never found him asleep, although I went to check on John every time I awoke during the night. Colon had a good sense of humor and joked with John, so that John looked forward to Colon's arrival each evening. They talked and laughed until John no longer was communicative.

One night Colon awakened me to say, "John wants to see you, he's afraid he is going to choke."

I went to John's bedside, "Colon says you're afraid you're going to choke."

"Yes, I am. I'm afraid to go to sleep."

"I don't think you are in danger of choking. The doctor hasn't said choking was a concern, and Martha has never suggested that it might be a danger. So, I think you are okay. You aren't going to choke. I'll lie down beside you for a while. He soon drifted into a troubled sleep.

John had stopped eating anything and had not been able to drink for some time. We dripped water in his mouth as requested, which was often. He told me that Colon could drip the water better than anyone else. I was glad he liked Colon; it meant he could look forward during the day to seeing Colon that evening.

Sherrie from Hospice, who bathed and shaved John, came every other day. She also changed his sheets with a little help from me. It was tricky because John was uncomfortable when we moved him the least bit. He wanted me to hold his head with both hands which seemed to make him less dizzy.

Brant began coming by every day, usually late afternoon. One Sunday afternoon, when his wife, Andra, came with him, Brant reaffirmed John's Baptism. It was quite emotionally difficult for John, but something he wanted and appreciated. They served us Communion again in October.

Mid-October I wrote in my journal, "He developed a lump in his groin; more morphine; more oxycodone, and four hundred milligram patches. Yesterday a large and very painful swelling by his ear and jaw appeared out of nowhere. Martha brought us another medication for that and it's much smaller today."

Schelley, Alex and Rae had a long talk with John—lots of memories and sadness and tears. I was glad they had that time together. When any of his family came, I tried to stay out of the room so they could have some privacy. Betty Ann (John's former wife), also came to say goodbye. I thought it was good for both of them; they were able to close that relationship on a positive note.

Annie and Teddi came down to see John for "one last time." Suzanne came for a while, and we were all in the room with John. Annie was so somber. When I went to the kitchen, she followed me. "Poppy isn't going to get well, is he?"

"No, Annie, he isn't"

"He's going to die?"

"Yes, he's going to die." She was standing facing me, and we put our arms around each other. I tried to carry the conversation further, but she was unable to say much more. We wiped tears from our eyes. Annie was going to miss her Poppy. She was the only grandchild old enough to remember much about John.

John's Near-Death Experience

Roger visited again from Charleston, West Virginia. He and John had a good visit that afternoon. Roger went to bed early, since he was going to get up and be on the road by daybreak. At 11:00 PM Colon awakened me to tell me he couldn't rouse John, and it was time for his medicine. When I tried to waken John, he didn't respond. I gently slapped his face, calling his name more loudly. He seemed to be in a coma. He was breathing with difficulty, and his face, arms and hands were cold and clammy. He was sweating with his eyes rolled upward and slightly open. His breathing was becoming more and more labored with increasing time between breaths. I called the Hospice nurse and described what was going on. She agreed that he was probably dying.

I had promised Schelley, Alex and Suzanne that I would call them, regardless of the time if I thought John was dying so they could come to speak to him. I called each of them; they arrived before midnight. We all gathered around the bed and kept vigil together. John was totally non-responsive. His breathing became more difficult as the hours passed. We began timing the lapses between breaths; it had climbed to forty-five seconds. Each breath seemed so difficult for John.

About 3:00 AM, we were beginning to think about whom to call first and what the next day would bring when, suddenly, John began moving his head from side to side and making small sounds. His breathing became less labored and more regular. Then he said in a small whispery voice, *"Oh, it is so beautiful; it is so peaceful, so wonderful. I feel so strange…it is so peaceful that I can't describe it. It is just so peaceful; I can't tell you how beautiful it is; I feel so strange."* He repeated this with small variations several times before he opened his eyes and indicated he wanted to hug me which he did repeatedly saying how much he loved me. Then one by one—with Alex, Schelley and Suzanne, this behavior was repeated.

John had opened his eyes, but didn't really look at us. He held out his hands and said, *"Shall we?"*

We all held hands and he said the most beautiful prayer, parts of which included: *"Today we are joined together to celebrate the life of John Robert Kerr. He is joining the flock of millions and millions and millions of other souls who have gone before him, and he will be joined by millions and millions and millions of others who will follow him. It feels like going home. He was and is a true believer of what Jesus has taught us over the centuries…"*

We were all in a state of shock, so we couldn't recollect more, although he said quite a bit more.

After the prayer he began talking to us and making eye contact; he asked, *"Have I died yet? Have we had the service? We are going to have a wonderful service. Have I died and where am I? I feel so strange."*

In response to one of us asking him if he knew where he'd been, he said, *"Don't challenge me too much; I don't want to hallucinate again."*

"All of you were here, and I was floating to each of you; something unusual was happening." After a short silence he went on, *"Will you answer me a question? What would it be like to die? I am at peace with the world. I know all of you here support me."*

"If I have not died, what should I work on next? I have been through the severe pain route; what have you folks experienced? Were you expecting me to die?"

"Yes, we were."

"I thought you were since you were all here."

Not too much more was said, and John indicated he needed to rest.

The kids and I talked some at the door as they were leaving about 5:00 AM. We had shared something we would never forget.

Twenty-two More Days

Brant came later that morning, which was unusual because he usually came in late afternoon. We told him what had happened. He said it was the first time he had known someone who had lived to tell of an experience of that nature. I wished so much that he could have been with us and witnessed what happened. I regret that I hadn't called him, but I didn't call him because it was in the middle of the night. I also regretted that Mitchell didn't witness it. It was, without doubt, one of the most profound experiences of my life.

We resumed our routine of the Hospice aide coming to give him a bath and shave him, the Hospice nurse coming to see what meds we needed, and acting as the liaison between us and the doctor. I continued dripping water into his mouth, reading his cards to him, giving him his meds, greeting his visitors, and welcoming Colon for the night.

John lived for twenty-two more days. Twenty-two days of suffering and being confined to that sick body. It is beyond understanding why he had to live those additional days which were painful for him and all of us who loved him. He asked me only once if I couldn't help him die. "I'm in this sick body and can't do anything about it," he said.

I gave him another of his tranquilizers to help him with his anxieties, but I thought about it later. I wondered how long it will be before we are allowed to give that assistance to loved ones who are in the dying process and, for whatever reason, linger day after day when they are entirely helpless and so ready for death.

Alex and Schelley came to see their Dad nearly every evening. It's hard to lose one's father regardless of how old we are or how sick the parent is. Their mother, Betty Ann, came again to say goodbye. Suzanne came every afternoon after work.

Teddi and Annie came again also, on Annie's tenth birthday, which I had remembered but had done nothing about. Suzanne had bought her a cake and had a couple of gifts for her. Losing a beloved grandpa is hard, and she did love her Poppy. I am glad she was old enough to have good memories of him—all the card games; the many times we played monster when she and I would hide, and he would find us with shrieks and laughter; the splashing and dunking each other in the pool; helping him make deviled eggs and oatmeal; playing hide-and-seek in the house including one of the last times when she hid under the large, square coffee table, and he couldn't find her. These and many more memories will always be part of Annie.

John was less and less communicative as time passed; he talked very little to me but mumbled under his breath a lot. He didn't respond much to anything said or done to him. I looked into his blue eyes when I was giving him water and would tell him, "I love you so much. I will always love you." He would look at me, but make no response.

He became more demanding and when he wanted something, he would yell, "Kate!" He seemed irritated if I wasn't there immediately. He had no interest in anything going on around him; he was completely withdrawn, ready and waiting for death to come. He wanted no music, no news from outside.

Death came on November 11th, 2003. The usual routine defined the day with Schelley and Alex stopping to see him; they told me I needn't call them as they felt they had had their closure. He was very quiet all day. The Hospice aide had come and bathed him. Suzanne stayed when she came by.

At 6:00 PM, I called Brant and Andra, "It is time for you to come."

They were with us in a few minutes. Brand read a bit of Scripture, and said a short prayer.

John died at 7:50 PM on Tuesday, November 11th, 2003. Death freed him of his confinement, released him from that sick body. He was back in that place that he had said was too beautiful to describe. He was with those millions and millions and millions, whom he had expected to join twenty-two days earlier.

Brant said another prayer. Then he asked, "Would you like a few minutes alone with him?"

"No, that is not John." Brant agreed with me.

I called Martha who came right over and checked out all the medicines. She had made herself so available and had been so generous with her time. I was grateful and felt that all Hospice workers should be commended. Martha left when she had finished with her duties.

Brant and Andra stayed until the undertaker left with the body.

Brant saw to the details with the undertaker, so I didn't have to deal with any of it. I did not want to see them carry his body out. Andra, Sue and I went out to the sitting area in my office and waited. It was good to have Andra there; Sue and I were not very "with it." Andra had loved John, too. He had been on her board for the Presbyterian pre-school several years, so they'd had the opportunity to know each other. Brant had been a tremendous comfort for John and me. I cannot find words to express my gratitude for their love and concern through those last months of John's life.

After we had talked a bit, Brant asked, "Would you like for someone to stay with you or would you rather be alone?"

"I just want to be alone tonight." I was so wrapped in my non-feeling state that I didn't think to ask Sue if she would like to stay with me. I know his death affected her a great deal also, but I certainly didn't have much to give anyone those first days after John's death. Surprisingly, I went to bed in the guest room soon after they left and slept fairly well.

The next day I felt a lot of relief; my precious John no longer had to lie on his back, completely helpless, yearning for escape.

We didn't have his memorial service until Monday, November 17th due to the fact that there was an FSU football game on Saturday the 15th, and there would be no hotel rooms available in or near Tallahassee on the days before and after the game. Alex came on Saturday to help me with some of the preparations for the next few days. Mitchell, Madeleine and Annie arrived that afternoon.

Teddi, Michael and Philip came Monday morning. The boys looked so grown up in their suits and ties. Teddi and Annie stayed with Suzanne that night and the boys drove back home. Saying goodbye to John was hard for Teddi also. She loved John and, as the rest of us in the family, had gained a sense of stability from his having been a part of her life.

John's and my siblings and their spouses arrived with all their love and sadness which, mixed together, supported each other, including me. The service was memorable. Mark Adamson, Janet and Mike's son, played the bag pipes. It was his first time to perform publicly. Mitchell gave a meaningful elegy—an emotional one. John would have been pleased with the reception at the church and the one at our house for about fifty of our family and friends.

Suzanne spent as much time as possible that week at the house with me. Mitchell and Madeleine stayed an extra day. Madeleine hadn't known John as well as the rest of the family, but she was saddened by his loss and was comforting to Mitchell. Most of our family members left the next morning. Juanita and Haydn stopped for coffee on their way out of town. Now reality would take over.

I was a widow; John, my love, my companion, my best friend, was gone.

1977 Kate and John on their wedding day with Alex and Schelley

1978 Kate and John

1981 Kate, Suzanne and John

1981 Suzanne and Mitchell

1982 Kate in her office

1982 Mitchell and his moving van

1984 Alex's 15th birthday
with John and Schelley

1986 John and Schelley
on her 20th birthday

1987 John, Alex and Schelley at Alex's high school graduation

1987 Suzanne

1990 John and Tom Potter

1990 Vonnie, Juanita, Betty, Kate, Dorothy
and Glenna at the family reunion

1991 John and Kate at home

1992 Maverne's Family: Barbara, John,
Maverne, Janet, Roger and Tom

1993 Grandma Kate holding Annie, 3 days old

1994 Mitchell and Teddi's Wedding Day

1994 Suzanne and Annie

1997 Rae and Alex's Wedding Day

1998 Kate and John in Taos, NM

1997 John and Annie making oatmeal

1998 Schelley and Paul's Wedding Day

1998 Annie and Mitchell carving a pumpkin

2000 Annie sewing a vest for her Daddy

2000 Philip, Michael and Annie

2001 Madeleine and Mitchell on their Wedding Day

2001 Mitchell and Madeleine's Wedding Party

2003 John, Schelley, and Alex with Ian, Emma and Sarah

2001 Annie and Mitchell

2007 Tom, Wilbur, Mike, Kate, Janet, Joellen, and Roger
(back row), Donna, Tom's friend, and Barbara (seated)

Chapter 5

THE REST OF MY LIFE

As long as John was still breathing, I had purpose, but now, without him, what will my life be? He had been so much a part of me, how do I go on functioning? They say 'life goes on,' but what kind of life?

Why would a man, who was so happy with life on earth, have to die? Why does a happy couple have to be torn apart?

John and I never thought it had been mere luck that we met. We believed it had been providential. I knew when I fell in love with John I was vulnerable. Now look where I am—aching in my soul.

What is love anyway? Why risk it, when it can be taken away? Why should we love when it leads to feelings of loss and despair? It is as if John was loaned to me; then so cruelly snatched away. Right now, I'm not sure it was a good idea to love. We can try to imagine what it would be like to live without the one who has been your very life, but it isn't possible; it wasn't for me.

My mind grappled with the loss, the pain, the conflict within myself. During the first two weeks, I stayed busy writing thank you notes, answering phone calls, and getting the house back in order—as it was before illness and death took over. Finally, I could no longer avoid facing the daunting amount of paperwork and legal documents that required my attention.

Tend To Business

I contacted Bill Furlong, our accountant and my co-executor. "I'm ready to get started," I told him. He picked me up the next day, and we went to the social security office, the retirement office, the bank, and the insurance office. Thank goodness he accompanied me. The next day I couldn't remember half of what had transpired; I still felt as though I was operating on automatic. Bill helped me settle John's estate, and to this day, he continues to be my accountant, advisor, and friend.

I was able to handle the correspondence with John's long-term care insurance and his cancer insurance. I managed to get through each day, doing what needed to be done, even though I was not functioning one hundred percent.

Holidays 2003

In mid-December I returned to church; I believed that my emotions were under control. I had missed attending church and worshipping God. The sermon, the music, and the love expressed by my church family were vital to me. It was many months before I could get through a service without losing tears. I was so aware that John wasn't beside me.

My family and I got through Christmas without John (Dad, Poppy, Step-Dad, Step-Father-in-Law and Husband). Each of us loved and missed him. I decorated the house as usual, baked my traditional fruitcake, and wrapped presents. It was not the same, but no one expected it to be. And it kept me busy with "doing," so I didn't have time to do too much thinking.

A week later my sisters and their husbands, who had winter homes in Bonita Springs, Florida, stopped by on their way south. Glenna and Phil left the morning of New Year's Eve. Juanita and Haydn arrived that afternoon and stayed until the 2nd of January. Those visits were exactly what I needed. The holidays were behind me and I'd survived better than I had anticipated. Loved ones coming and going had made a difference. How fortunate I was to have such a loving family supporting me.

Grieving

I met with Bill Furlong once a week and with Felton Wright, my broker, a few more times to get things settled with John's estate. One day I'd think I was doing well, and the next day, the sadness would sweep over me; each time this happened, I felt John's loss as if for the first time. He wasn't around so that I could talk things over with him. That hurt the most.

After the last of the family left on January second, I wanted to talk to John about what had transpired, what I'd heard and what he'd heard, discuss our impressions and feelings. Adjusting to his absence would take a long time.

I spent days getting his record-keeping system converted to my own, so that I could find documents easier and manage the running of the household. I got paperwork done, but slowly. I did what I could each day and then rested, knowing I could do more the next day.

By the end of January, 2004, I wrote in my journal, "I think I have turned a corner in my healing process." A week later I wrote: "That corner must have been a turnabout; I am right back where I started. I think I've been trying too hard, wanting to say I'm doing great."

Well, I was doing great in the sense that I was actively grieving. I didn't try to be frugal with my tears. I did a lot of repeating of feelings and thoughts in my mind. Brant suggested I read *A Grief Observed* by C. S. Lewis. It is a small book, but very powerful. I read and re-read it, jotting down passages that I later discussed with Brant, who met with me several times the first month I was alone. *A Grief Observed* opened up a lot of issues I had not dealt with. I cried until I felt exhausted emotionally.

Those discussions with Brant helped me deal with my deepest feelings. I soon realized I was no longer angry at God. I began to accept that loved ones die; death is a part of life we have to deal with. No one is immune.

I began dealing more realistically with my grief. Life was not at all the same as it had been when John was alive. I would have to accept that fact. I knew the risk I was taking when I fell in love with John. When two people love each other, one of them is going to get hurt sooner or later. John was gone, so I was the one alone and in pain.

Not only had I lost my dear husband, but also our way of life. Many things we did together were no longer desirable for me to do by myself. We had eaten most of our dinners out, and that was not something I would do by myself. I would no longer go to Tiger Bay Club, which met once a month and included dinner and a speaker; I would no longer go to the Town Club—a social club which met five or six times a year for dinner and dancing to the Big Band Orchestra; I wouldn't go to the FSU football games, because it wouldn't be fun without him; and I wouldn't travel as much as he and I had, because without John it would seem empty.

Life changed in other ways, also. I became aware of a very subtle difference as soon as I began going out in public after John died. I was now a widow—a single woman. My interactions with men were not the same; rather, I perceived them to be different. There is something about being a married woman which acts as a notice to other men that she is to be treated as *someone's wife.* Without that shield, I felt a slight change in the way I acted or reacted toward men. I was guarded, so as to not come across as flirting—more careful in what I chose to wear, so as not to appear seductive. The difference was subtle, but I was very aware of it for a short period of time.

Three months after John's death, I wrote, "I am hurting worse than any time in the past three months. I had a good cry with Brant and felt better, but I'm heavy with sadness. I go places and do things, but nothing is much fun." A month later, March 11th, I continue, "I say one day I'm better, but I guess I wish I were better. I have days when I think I'm better, then I go back to feeling lost and sad without him. I can feel good, but there is no joy in anything. We shared so many little secrets or special meanings and without him, it all falls flat. Of course, I have the memories, but I miss him constantly. I'm always thinking about what he would be doing and what he would say about this and that. I am trying."

A couple of weeks later, I wrote, "I have been having some really sad and lonely times. In many ways we were one, so when you take away half of something, the other half has to fight a fierce battle to exist until the new parts are in place." Looking back I see that re-generating new parts may be the key to building a life which can be fulfilling. A different life but a meaningful one.

Healing Continues 2004

Life did go on. I visited Mitchell and Madeleine in Monroe. We drove the trailer to Canton, Texas, where there is a huge monthly outdoor arts and craft show. We camped by a large lake, the weather was perfect, and I enjoyed it. Madeleine fixed bacon and eggs one morning, and we ate out on the picnic table by the lake. As we were eating, a large flock of white pelicans swooped down and settled on the water. They stayed there for thirty or forty minutes, providing us with quite a show.

Back in Tallahassee, Suzanne and I got together frequently. I was glad she lived in town. Sometimes we would go to a movie; other times one of us cooked dinner and we ate together. We attended the First Presbyterian Church, so we usually saw each other on Sunday.

I also began asking different women to lunch. I'd never been much on "let's do lunch," but it was one thing I could do to begin to fill the holes in my social life. There were several women friends whom I enjoyed seeing.

I began going to The Economic Club which met at noon for lunch and had a speaker. John had belonged to that club for years, and I took over his membership. Yes, they let women belong; times were changing. I still belong to that and enjoy it.

By the middle of April I wrote, "I've been feeling better the last couple of weeks; just not so sad and tearful. I'm adjusting to the fact that John is gone. I miss him terribly but not so painfully. It was five months on Sunday."

Annie got a Pekinese puppy which she had been lobbying for. She called me to see if it would be all right to name him Poppy. Kids have their ways of expressing their feelings. They brought "Poppy" to see me the next weekend; he was just a handful of black fluff, so cuddly and cute. We walked around Lake Ella, and everyone stopped to admire the puppy. Annie loved it.

Another Decision

I decided it was time to sell our home at 2511 Chamberlin Drive. I hated to part with it; we'd been so happy in it. We'd been married in the house and had spent the twenty-seven years of our marriage in its rooms, which we had changed so much during those years. But it was expensive to keep up and always demanded attention. It was a frame house; wood-rot and insects had always been at war with its structure, and, sometimes I believed they were winning, especially now that I was fighting them alone.

The lawn, the pool, the big wooden house was more than I wanted to manage. I contacted a realtor and put it on the market in May 2004. It might have seemed too soon, but John and I had discussed selling it, and we had agreed I would have to sell it; it was not a hasty decision.

I started thinking about where I wanted to live and looking at places with a realtor. I wanted to stay close in, but there wasn't much to choose from that was within my budget. Or I didn't see anything I liked the first few times I went out.

My hope was that the house would sell quickly, but not many buyers were showing an interest. The big drawback was the fact that it was a two bedroom house.

I went out to look at houses in a new development, a few miles north of Thomasville Road. I looked at one of the models and fell in love with the whole idea of building. I put a deposit on a lot that afternoon. I chose the floor plan I wanted and was busily making some changes with the builder. Bill Furlong discouraged me from building a house, giving me good reasons not to, which I already knew, but was disregarding. I continued meeting with the contractor and kept driving out to the location, imagining living there, rationalizing away all the negatives, especially the location.

I Visit Mitchell & Madeleine 2004

I visited Madeleine, Mitchell and Annie in Durango, Colorado, where they were vacationing. Their trailer was parked in an RV park on the banks of the Animas River, with the Rockies as a back drop. Annie and I went rafting which was fun, but once was enough for me. Annie went rafting as often as someone would pay for it.

Traveling on a couple of tough trails in the mountains, we drove the jeep from Durango to Ouray where we boarded the slow-moving train on a scenic route to Silverton. Each curve offered breathtaking vistas of carved gorges, fast flowing mountain streams, and barren cliffs. The town of Silverton was an adventure into the old West with its saloons, gaudy theaters, and little cafes.

When traveling, I was aware of missing John more than at other times, but I had an enjoyable visit. Mitchell and Madeleine were loving hosts, and the weather was deliciously relaxing. It was great to be with them and Annie for a week.

The Strubbe/Kerr Reunion

I took a break from worrying about where I would live and on Memorial Day weekend, I drove to Ninety-Six, South Carolina, for the first Strubbe/Kerr reunion. It was being held at the Adamson's new lake house, which was gorgeous. This was my first trip driving alone; it was nearly four hundred miles. I enjoyed seeing and visiting with everyone, but I really missed John. Being with his family without him was so different; I had to work at not letting sadness overtake me.

A Townhouse 2004

My weekend away didn't deter my planning for my new house. I continued meeting with the contractor, and the plans were nearly finalized. I still had two weeks in which I could back out of the deal and get my money back. I did have some nagging voices in my head questioning the wisdom of my building a house.

Sunday, June 27th, a townhouse was advertised on a private street not far from Chamberlin Drive. I knew I didn't want a townhouse because of the stairs, but thought it would be fun to look at it. When Teddi, Annie and Suzanne arrived that afternoon to help me celebrate my birthday, we went to see it just for fun.

Five minutes after entering the front door, I knew I wanted to live there. The space was right, the location was perfect, and the neighborhood was inviting. One bedroom was downstairs, so I wouldn't have to use the upstairs if the time came when I couldn't navigate the stairs. Suzanne and Teddi were as enthusiastic as I. "This is the house for you," they chorused. We whispered our remarks because there was a woman with her billfold out talking with the realtor about putting a deposit on it for an out-of-town friend.

I wasted no time; by early evening I had bought myself a townhouse at 1448 Denholm Drive. I had only to make a phone call to get out of the other deal and get my refund for the deposit on the lot. I knew I had made a good decision; sometimes you just know when something is right. Bill would be delighted; he knew I should not be building a house.

I had not asked the appropriate questions that one asks before purchasing a home, but I knew it was what I wanted. I had looked at enough places to know not to let it get away from me. This townhouse was to be my home. Ordinarily, I would not have gone to the trouble of looking at a townhouse. It was another instance when I knew I had been guided in the right direction.

I had quite a bit of work done on the townhouse. I became the general contractor by default. I knew who I wanted to do most of the work and being involved kept me excited about what was happening. And it directed my thoughts toward my future—less time to feel sad about what I had lost.

It looked like the townhouse would be finished by December first, and I was beginning to wish my house would sell. Then on the first Anniversary of John's death, November 11, 2004, a woman came to look at my house the second time. She and her realtor looked more carefully this time, standing out in the driveway talking for an hour afterwards. An hour later the realtor called and offered a contract for the full amount I was asking without any negotiating. The buyer was a female physician from Southern Illinois who had never lived in Florida; she didn't know what she was getting, buying a wood-frame house.

The rest of 2004 went by rapidly. Christmas was not as overshadowed by John's absence as it was the previous year. My family and I celebrated for the last time at the Chamberlin house. There was that touch of nostalgia, but I was looking ahead to what the New Year would bring.

I moved on January 7th, 2005. As I lay in bed in my new home that night, I knew I had made the right decision. The move was not traumatic for me; I had spent so much time fixing up the townhouse that it felt like mine by the time I moved in. I thanked God that night that I had looked at it on that Sunday afternoon, even though I had not intended to buy a townhouse. Life is mysterious.

I enjoyed getting settled in my new home. No more worrying every time it rained hard, no more fussing with the pool. No longer a thousand things that could go wrong; my new home was all brick and had a new roof in addition to all the things I had replaced. I was comfortably settled in a space I liked and felt good about.

I wrote in my journal, "November and December were very hard. I see now how the Anniversary month is so difficult. I'm feeling much better; I have good feelings and happy feelings—more than at any time since John became ill. I like the new life I am building; John would be pleased with my progress."

My Siblings

Five of my six siblings were alive and doing well. Dorothy, an eighty-five year old widow, continued her daily walk each morning. She had moved into an apartment, not far from her big house. Betty, a widow at eighty-three, had to discontinue her morning walks, but enjoyed her life in her lovely old five-bedroom farmhouse. Juanita was healthy and doing well at eighty-one. She and her husband, Haydn, had recently moved into a smaller house in Bloomington, Indiana. Clay, whose leg made it harder and harder for him to get around, at seventy-eight, still enjoyed his garden. He and his wife, Rose, were enthusiastic church members. Glenna, seventy-seven, who had had more than her share of physical problems, was relatively healthy as was her husband, Phil.

London

In the summer of 2005 Annie stayed two weeks with her Dad and Madeleine in Durango. Eight hours a day she volunteered at a stable and loved it. Her payoff was to occasionally lead the customers down the trail on the lead horse. Some of the customers gave her tips. For an eleven-year-old, she did very well. She could throw the heavy saddles over the backs of the largest horses and was eager to do whatever the owner asked of her.

The week following her time with her Dad, I met Annie in Atlanta, and we flew to London to meet her mother, Teddi, who had been teaching there for six weeks. Earlier in the week that we traveled, terrorists had set off bombs in the London Underground, the subway system, killing several people. Even so, I didn't cancel our trip, because I figured London was probably as safe as any big city.

We stayed in the apartment that Teddi had rented. It was quite comfortable and located in a quiet, tree-lined neighborhood. We could walk to Harrods, The Museum of Natural History, and The Science Museum.

On our first day in London, Annie and I walked to the Museum of Natural History, while Teddi took care of some last-minute responsibilities with her students. Annie and I wandered through several rooms, enjoying different displays, especially the very realistic wild animals in their natural habitat. Spotting a bench, I sat down to tie my shoelace. From there we made our way leisurely back toward the entry. As soon as we were downstairs, I realized I didn't have my purse. My passport and my credit cards were in it. We rushed to the elevator to retrace our steps. Annie led the way with me following, praying we'd find it.

I struggled to keep up with Annie; she was intent on covering the route we'd taken earlier. Of course, we didn't see my purse anywhere. Racing down the stairs, we almost ran to the desk where ladies were checking people's bags as they entered the museum. I butted into the line and asked, "Has anyone turned in a purse?"

The female guard asked, "What's your name?"

Great, if they're asking my name, at least one purse must have been turned in. I told her my name as calmly as I could.

She made eye contact with a young man standing nearby. "Follow that man," she ordered.

Annie and I looked at each other, and without saying a word, we followed the young man when he headed for the elevator. As we wound our way through areas Annie and I had not seen before, he didn't say a word. Passing through two sets of heavy, locked doors, we were met by three solemn-looking men in uniforms. My purse was sitting in plain sight on a counter behind them.

The man who was obviously in charge threw questions at me. "What's your name? Where are you from? Don't you know we are on high alert because of the bombings of the last few days?"

When he paused, I meekly said, "Yes, Sir."

Without shifting from his gruffness, he continued, "You presented a huge dilemma for us. We found this purse sitting on a bench. We didn't know whether to open it or to rush it outside; you have given us quite a scare."

With some difficulty, I found my voice enough to tell him how sorry I was—that I realized the position I had put them in. But I was so darned glad to see my purse that they could have kept me the rest of the day, and I wouldn't have complained.

The three men glared at us without a hint of softness. The interrogator handed me the purse and growled, "Be more careful next time, lady."

"Yes, Sir," I answered him softly.

Our guide ushered us back through the locked doors and left; Annie and I took a few steps before we both expelled big sighs and started talking. I could've cried.

Borrowing a small purse with a long strap from Teddi, I put the strap over my head and across my shoulder. For the rest of my stay, I used her purse so I would have no need to set it down. I had learned my lesson.

Cancer Threatens

Soon after returning home, I had my routine mammogram. I got a call to go back to have it repeated which is not too threatening. But then I received a letter saying, "There is moderate suspicion of malignancy." Dr. Judelle arranged for me to see Dr. Snyder for a biopsy. Three days later I got a call asking me to come to Snyder's office which I did that afternoon.

They had good news and bad news. I had Ductal Carcinoma in Situ (DCIS) which is cancer in its earliest stage. It was not good news to find out that I had breast cancer, but to have caught it so early was. Surgery was September 22nd—removal of part of my breast. I recouped quickly. I thought how nice it would have been to have John with me. I missed him, but not with tears.

I was to have a radiation treatment five days a week for six weeks. I met my radiation oncologist, Dr. Bolek, who would be overseeing the radiation regime.

My treatments began on the 29th October at 8:30 AM. I finished the series on December 14th without any serious side effect—just itchy, dark skin. I never lost my energy for which I was grateful. Prognosis: Excellent. Thank you, Lord.

With that behind me, I started to learn how to use the computer. I had heard of a young man named Darrow Fisher whom I contacted and arranged for him to come to my home and work with me for an hour every other Saturday. He was nice and had lots of patience with my slow progress. I needed to learn more than just how to email.

A Visitor in 2008

Philip, Annie's older brother, called to tell me he had been transferred from Valdosta to Tallahassee as manager of the Crystal River restaurant. He wanted to know if he could stay with me for a couple of weeks, while he looked for an apartment. I assured him he'd be more than welcome. He brought a few clothes and started sleeping upstairs the first of March. It was nice having him in the house every night.

After the first week, I told Philip he needn't get an apartment. He was a nice, considerate young man; I enjoyed his staying with me which he did for fourteen months. At that time he was sent back to manage the restaurant in Valdosta—much to his delight. I missed him after he left.

That spring, his brother, Michael, graduated from Valdosta State University with a degree in history. I went to the graduation and the celebration at Teddi's. Philip had gone up the night before to celebrate with Michael and their friends. Philip and Michael had a good relationship, and there was a lot of kidding around with their friends who had been invited. Of course, Annie at age fifteen enjoyed the celebration too, although at her age, she and her brothers operated in different spheres.

Durango, Colorado

Annie went to London as an exchange student that June. She stayed in London as a guest of an exchange student who had stayed with Annie the previous school year. Annie stayed an additional week in London with her mother, who again was teaching a class in London. When she left London, Annie flew to Durango to stay a couple of weeks with her Dad and Madeleine at their newly acquired 'second home,' a three-bedroom house on the outskirts of Durango. A mountain-stream ran through the property with a grove of aspen trees nearby. They soon had a picnic table, comfortable chairs and a fire-ring out in "The Grove". They ate most of their meals, read, napped and entertained there. The temperature was ten degrees cooler in The Grove than it was downtown.

My first visit to their Durango home coincided with Annie's again. One evening Mitchell, Annie and I were out in The Grove playing cards. As usual, we had a fire going in the fire-pit. The wind changed and blew the smoke in my direction. I jumped up to move my chair, caught my foot on it, took a few fast and fancy steps in an effort to regain my balance, and went head first down an incline, stopping only when my head rammed into a tree.

Mitchell and Annie immediately rushed over to me, helping me get up. We staggered up to the level ground, made sure no bones were broken, and slowly made our way to the house. I had a cut over my left eye, a nasty scrape on my left arm, and a badly bruised right thigh. Mitchell and Annie were very solicitous of me. They got me bandaged up, fixed me an ice-pack, and I went to bed. Two days later I flew home looking like I'd fought a dragon and lost. I was sure people thought I had an abusive husband. I didn't really care, I was glad I could walk.

I fell a few more times—once while on my morning walk on Lee Avenue. I caught my foot on a small vine which had grown out into the street. That foot didn't move another inch and my body reacted by falling flat with both arms out in front of me. My face hit the pavement with most of the weight being on my mouth and chin. I raised my head and started spitting blood, thinking I had surely lost a couple of teeth—but not so. I was still lying flat on my stomach when a young man came rushing up

"Are you all right?"

"I think so." He helped me stand up. I kept rubbing my tongue against my front teeth, making sure they were still there.

"Where do you live? May I take you home?"

"My car is parked down at McCord Park; I drive there so I can walk in this neighborhood where I used to live." I began to feel my legs under me again. "I think I can drive," I said.

"Then let me drive you to your car."

I readily agreed to that. I didn't exactly feel like walking the mile back to my car. As soon as I got home, I stood under the shower letting it wash the blood off my face, so I could see how badly my lip was cut and to check if any teeth were loose. I had a sore lip for a couple of weeks, but I lost no teeth.

Annie in High School

Annie was a freshman in high school in the fall of 2006. The first week the social studies class teacher asked if anyone knew what Fannie Mae was.

Annie eagerly raised her hand. "We get Fannie Mae every year at Christmas. My favorite pieces are the light choco..."

"No, the Fannie Mae I'm asking about is not a box of chocolates." He went on to explain what Fannie Mae and Freddie Mac were, and the other students had a great laugh at Annie's expense. Annie felt a little embarrassed, but not overly so. She saw the humor in it also and laughed heartily when telling us about it.

I Visit My Siblings

I went to Illinois and Indiana, visiting my siblings one at a time, staying one night with each of them. Phil picked me up at O'Hare Airport in Chicago, and we drove to their new home. Glenna had decorated it beautifully. Phil seemed to be feeling pretty well; his cancer was in remission. We had a good time shopping, eating and talking. After breakfast the next day, Phil drove me to Dixon for my visit with Clay and Rose.

Clay showed me his orchard and garden—his hobbies. He had undergone surgery on his tongue the year before to remove a malignancy. The doctors told him they thought they got it all—the edges were clear. Rose had undergone eye surgery at the Iowa City Clinic and was doing okay. Their younger son, John, joined us for a game of cards that evening.

Dorothy picked me up at Clay's and drove me to Betty's lovely farm home. A fierce storm blew in that afternoon with hurricane-like winds and driving rain. We were standing on the little side porch where we were protected from the elements, when suddenly two big wagons, which were hooked together, began rolling out of the machine shed, across the farm lot, over the driveway, to stop only when they came to a fence. At the same time a large tree on the other side of the driveway crashed as it fell across the fence and into the corn field. And with that the lights went out.

After the storm blew itself out, Betty's farm manager took us to the farm where Betty and I grew up; it was now one big corn field—no buildings left to tell a stranger that there was once a family of nine living on that hill with all kinds of animals and fowl completing the scene. As I looked at the endless waves of corn, I envisioned the men walking up the hill with pails full of warm milk; kids running over the hill and down by the slough looking for those who had hung a May basket; Mom pacing back-and-forth with Vonnie who had drunk kerosene; Dad sitting on the porch with the dishpan full of popcorn. Things disappear and loved ones die, but memories live on.

Dorothy came to get me at Betty's the next morning. She had moved to a two-bedroom apartment from her lovely big home which she and Roy practically built themselves in 1968. She was the historian and genealogist for both sides of our family—always interesting to talk with her. On our way to dinner that night we saw a large number of windmills busily generating energy—a new phenomenon for the Midwest.

After my visit with Dorothy, she drove me to the Peoria airport, where I rented a car (Toulon had no car rental agency) and drove to my last stop—Juanita and Haydn's. We drove through the scenic part of southern Indiana to Brown County. The next day we drove to French Lick where we had held two of our reunions. I still felt a special tie to Juanita; sometimes, I thought, maybe we really were twins!

They drove me to the Indianapolis airport with my head full of memories. I was glad I had made the trip; I loved my siblings and their spouses—Phil, Haydn and Rose were the three spouses (of the seven) still with us.

Healthcare

In 1970 I had begun riding my bike eight miles each morning before going to work. It was nice on the flat terrain of South Florida, but when I moved to Tallahassee, the hills and lack of bike trails made riding a bike too dangerous, so I began walking. After I met John, we walked together. I soon added three workouts a week at a gym. We continued that regime throughout our lives together, although we had to get up at five to do so and still be at our offices before eight.

We also stuck to a healthy diet. After a few years together we pretty much cut out red meat, but we never gave up fish and chicken. I continue being careful of what I put in my body and work to keep my weight where I want it. It may not add years to my life, but that is not my goal. What I work toward is feeling well and energetic as long as I can, knowing there are many ailments I have no control over. So far I have been fortunate.

Politics In 2008

The New Year of 2008 would be consumed with politics. Hillary Clinton (who would be the first woman candidate) and Barak Obama (the first African-American) fought long and hard for the right to be the Democratic candidate for the presidency. Many were surprised when Obama, an unknown, beat out Clinton, who had been in the political forefront for years. That was just the beginning. John McCain, Obama's opponent, was widely known as a former Viet Nam prisoner of war and a United States Senator. When Obama won the nomination, people who had pulled for Hillary were angry, believing she lost because she was a woman. If Barak Obama had lost, some would have said it was because he was African-American. So goes politics.

I drove to Bonita Springs, Florida, to visit Juanita and Haydn and Glenna and Phil, (at their winter homes) all of whom were Republicans, but we've always been able to talk politics without getting heated up or hostile.

That whole area around Bonita Springs and Naples is quite the resort area—so different from Tallahassee, which revolves around the Capitol and the two Universities.

Abby Potter Dies

Soon after I got home from South Florida, Abby W. called to say her mother, Abby, had died peacefully in her sleep. They were having a service in their little church on the mountain; one would be held in Tallahassee later. Abby would have been ninety in July. She was quite the spunky lady, and I would certainly miss her. She and I had consoled each other after our husbands, Tom and John, died in 2003.

Back to Durango 2008

Annie and I were visiting in Durango at the same time again. We did the usual outdoor things that we all liked—except Annie. At fifteen, she liked being on the river, but didn't care about riding in the mountains—"jeeping." She spent a lot of time that summer down town at a tech café where she could plug in her laptop; there was no Wi-Fi reception at the house.

Mitchell and Madeleine had their new Teepee up when I got there. It had a fire ring in the center; a good fire provided light as well as heat. The temperature dropped into the forties at night; it was nice going to sleep, snuggled in a cozy sleeping bag with the fire dying to red embers. The teepee could sleep eight, but four was nice. Mitchell had it decorated with Indian paraphernalia and many different skins, including fox, beaver and mountain lion. I think Mitchell was either a cowboy or an Indian in a former life. He appeared to be so in tune with the wilderness, and loved driving his jeep on the trails in the mountains. Madeleine shared his interests and loved their Durango home.

Clay

Clay wasn't able to attend our 2008 reunion because cancer had returned on his tongue. He went to the Mayo Clinic and suffered through the chemo and radiation they recommended, all to no avail. They called in hospice mid-June. He died about six weeks later on August 29th. It was hard to lose another sibling. Rose did a heroic job of caring for him—he became unable to talk and had to be fed through a tube. Clay had been a family man; he enjoyed his children, grandchildren, and great-grandchildren, his orchard, garden and flowers.

Our New President 2008

The candidates were working frantically to persuade people to their way of thinking. Obama and McCain had several debates. Sarah Palin,

McCain's running mate, was a big draw wherever she spoke. Joe Biden, Obama's running mate, took a back seat to her.

Adding to the frenzy of the big election year, the country was going through the worst economic crisis since The Big Depression of the 1930s. Foreclosures on homes rose rapidly to unheard of numbers, hundreds of thousands of people lost their jobs, the auto industry was struggling, the banking industry was collapsing, stocks were dropping, and we were fighting two wars. The war in Iraq was in its seventh year; the war in Afghanistan was escalating after having taken second place while we focused on Iraq. To make matters even worse, our country was deeply in debt, with much of it owed to China.

Obama was elected our forty-fourth president. He immediately began naming cabinet members, including Hillary Clinton as Secretary of State. With the war going on in Iraq and Afghanistan and the world-wide economic crisis, he had to get right down to business. He had inherited a mess.

Alex Sent To Iraq

In the spring of 2009, Alex, who had been promoted to the rank of Captain in the National Guard, took leave from his state job to be a full-time employee of the National Guard, helping to ready the troops in the 779th Engineer Battalion for their imminent deployment. They were sent to Mozul, Iraq to be part of the reconstruction effort—rebuilding and repairing. He would be gone for one year.

Phil's Cancer Returns

Phil and Glenna weren't able to come to the reunion. Phil was not up to it; his cancer was back. He was able to go to lunch with some of us who drove over to see him. I surely hated to tell him goodbye, as I knew I wouldn't see him again. He died peacefully on September 28th, 2009, after battling lymphoma for six years. Once more, we all gathered to say goodbye to a beloved member of our family. Glenna and Phil had been married sixty two years. He was a much loved, loving man and a beloved brother-in-law. It was tough having members of our family die.

An Exciting Drive

From the reunion I flew to Durango. Mitchell, Madeleine and I drove to Ouray in their new Toyota FJ which had replaced their Jeep. A downpour caught us on our way home. As we slowly rounded a sharp curve we came to a sudden halt. A heavy flow of water was pouring down a gully, dropping rocks on the road and cascading over the steep drop-off on the other side. Some of the rocks bounced and tumbled over the side, but many were piling up on the road. We could see the cars backed up on the other side of the rockfall. The torrential rain didn't let up. It would be impossible to back up around that narrow winding road. There wasn't room on the passenger's side to get out—we were on the edge of the precipice. No telling how long it would last or how much worse it might get.

After sitting there fearfully for ten minutes watching and speculating what to do, the rain began to ease up. When it was down to a sprinkle, the first car on the other side slowly inched its way through the fallen rocks. We knew if he could make it, we could in the FJ, which could go anywhere a jeep could. Mitchell felt comfortable creeping forward over the rock-littered road. We sighed with relief when we were once more on a road where all we had to worry about was making the curves without meeting a road hog. No more rockslides, please.

Sweet Sixteen

Annie turned sixteen in November, 2009. She had been interested in cars since she was about ten—influenced by her older brothers, no doubt. She had the Driver's Ed course behind her and got her driver's license the week of her birthday. She managed to wait to get a car until her Dad came for Christmas. Madeleine spent the holidays visiting her son, Zach, and his new wife in Hawaii, where Zack was with the Navy.

Between Christmas and the New Year, Mitchell, Suzanne and I went with Annie to pick out her first car—a 2007 Honda Accord with a fabulous navigation system. It was an exciting day for Annie. I wished driving age was seventeen or eighteen, but I didn't have much to do with it. She heard from each of us and her Mom about the dangers of driving and seemed to pay attention.

Later that month, when I visited Mitchell and Madeleine in Monroe, Mitchell gave me a tour of his clinic, named "BMAD" for Behavioral Medical Addictive Disorders. He treats his Vets there also.

Family in 2010

I flew to Illinois for the party for Dorothy's ninetieth birthday, June 5, 2010. She really was surprised when Juanita, Haydn, and I arrived. She didn't know we were coming. The gathering substituted for our family reunion that year. Dorothy's son, Don, and his wife, Bonnie, entertained over twenty guests that evening in their Toulon home, located near Dorothy's. Her daughter, Alexis, helped plan and pull off the surprise.

Dorothy, ninety, Juanita, eighty-six, Kate, eighty-five, Glenna, eighty-two, Hadyn, my brother-in-law, eighty-six, and Rose, my sister-in-law, seventy-nine, are all in relatively good health. Betty, eighty-nine, is battling several health problems. My youngest sister, Vonnie, and my only brother, Clay, are deceased.

2011

As a new decade begins, I am more content than I thought was possible when John died. I will always love him; I miss him and think of him many times every day. However, with the help of God and the love that comes to me from family and friends, there is no longer pain in those memories. I feel extremely fortunate to have had twenty-seven years with him.

I have a good life. I have my family and John's family, all of whom I love and know they love me. I have many friends with whom I socialize; my church and church family; my friends in the writing groups to which I belong, and friends whom I've known a long time. I take at least one six-week course each semester at Olli—the Osher Livelong Learning Institute at FSU.

Life is peppered with sadness, grief, and difficulties which seem to be unbearable at times. But we hang on somehow. Through our trials, we grow and gain empathy for and understanding of others who are lost in one of those valleys. Our souls reveal the essence of our life experiences.

2004 New Year's Eve at Georgio's – Suzanne,
Annie, Mitchell, Madeleine and Kate

2005 Annie working with horses

2005 Kate, Mitchell, Annie and Suzanne

2006 Philip, Annie, Michael and Teddi

2006 Kate and Juanita

2006 Schelley, Ian and Paul

2007 Alex, Rae, Emma and Sarah

2008 Annie

2008 Mitchell and Madeleine

2009 Alex in uniform the day before he leaves for Iraq

2010 Emma, Rae, Sarah and Alex Kerr

2010 Ian, Paul and Schelley

Weathering the storms